COLLECTED POEMS

COLLECTED POEMS

ROBERT CONQUEST

EDITED BY

ELIZABETH CONQUEST

WAYWISER

First published in 2020 by

THE WAYWISER PRESS

Christmas Cottage, Church Enstone, Chipping Norton, Oxfordshire, OX7 4NN, UK
P. O. Box 6205, Baltimore, MD 21206, USA

https://waywiser-press.com

EDITOR-IN-CHIEF
Philip Hoy

SENIOR AMERICAN EDITOR
Joseph Harrison

ASSOCIATE EDITORS
Eric McHenry | Dora Malech | V. Penelope Pelizzon | Clive Watkins
Greg Williamson | Matthew Yorke

9 7 5 3 1 2 4 6 8

A CIP catalogue record for this book is available from the British Library

ISBN 978-1-904130-96-3

Printed and bound by
T. J. Books Limited, Padstow, Cornwall, PL28 8RW

for Liddie

CONTENTS

from BETWEEN MARS AND VENUS [1962]

from ARIAS FROM A LOVE OPERA [1969]

COMING ACROSS [1978]

from THE ABOMINATION OF MOAB [1979]

from FORAYS [1979]

from NEW AND COLLECTED POEMS [1988]

from PENULTIMATA [2009]

GETTING ON [2010]

from BLOKELORE & BLOKESONGS [2012]

from REASONABLE RHYMES BY TED PAUKER

LIMERICKS

POEMS PUBLISHED ONLY IN JOURNALS

APPENDIX I: JUVENILIA

APPENDIX II: *from* OXFORD NOTEBOOKS [1937–1939]

APPENDIX III: *from* WAR NOTEBOOKS [1940–1945]

APPENDIX IV: *from* THE DEATH OF DIMITROV

APPENDIX V: MISCELLANEOUS UNPUBLISHED POEMS

ACKNOWLEDGEMENTS

Some of these poems first appeared in the following periodicals and anthologies: *A Garden of Erses* (courtesy of Orchises Press); *The American Spectator*; *The Beloit Poetry Journal*; *The Book of the PEN*; *Botteghe Oscure*; *The Dragons of Expectation*; *Encounter*; *First Things*; *The Formalist*; *The Guardian*; *The Guinness Book of Poetry*; *Hellas*; *The Liberal*; *Light Quarterly*; *Listen*; *The Listener*; *London Magazine*; *The Los Angeles Times*; *Moments of Truth*; *The New Criterion*; *The New Humanist*; *The New Oxford Book of English Light Verse*; *New Poems 1952, 1953, 1954, 1956, 1957, 1958*; *The New Statesman and Nation*; *The New Statesman*; *The Observer*; *Outposts*; *The Oxford Book of Comic Verse*; *P. N. Review*; *The Penguin Book of Limericks*; *The Poem of the Month Club*; *Poems of the 1950s*; *Poems 1951*; *Poetry Northwest*; *Poetry Now*; *The Poetry Society Christmas Supplement*; *The Spectator*; *Standpoint*; *Time and Tide*; *The Times Literary Supplement*; *Tribune*; *Twentieth Century Verse*; *The Vanderbilt Poetry Review*; *Wave*; and *World Review*.

Maurice Langlois, Portrait of Robert Conquest, 1936.
Ink on paper.
© Estate of Robert Conquest.

EDITOR'S NOTE

Why do some creative people continue to produce, while others retire from the field? Part of the reason is simply that people age at different rates. Kingsley Amis, complaining to Philip Larkin of getting old, wrote: "Bob just goes on and on, as if nothing has happened." And so he did, walking a mile at light infantry pace until his eighty-ninth year, dying at age ninety-eight in the midst of editing his thirty-fourth book, while also writing a poem. At the same time, with a view towards publishing a final *Collected Poems*, Robert Conquest was also going through earlier collections of his verse, correcting misprints, and in some cases making minor alterations. The poems from those earlier collections appear here as he intended.

It should be noted that – as was his practice – the poems themselves do not always appear in their order of original periodical publication, and even that was not necessarily the order of their composition. For example, the poem "For the Death of a Poet" – though written in 1944, and in 1945 awarded the PEN Brazil prize for the best long poem of the Second World War – was not published until 1950 (in *The Book of the PEN*). In the collections, there are a number which appeared in various periodicals but for various reasons were postponed from book to book, so that each section contains earlier, sometimes much earlier, work. Many of the limericks included here were published over the years in various anthologies and periodicals, usually under two of Conquest's pseudonyms: Victor Gray or Ted Pauker.

From a young age, Conquest wrote poetry. In 1931, as part of the Common Entrance exam that won him both a scholarship at Charterhouse and a place at Winchester, he wrote "Perseus" – 34 lines of heroic couplets in which Polydectes, Hermes, Pallas Athena and Andromeda make appearances. At Winchester, and at Oxford, he filled notebooks with verse, much of it surrealist. While still an undergraduate, two of these appeared in 1938, in Julian Symons' magazine *Twentieth Century Verse*. The first of these, a surrealist poem entitled merely "Sonnet" (in the No 10 issue, May 1938, cover design by Wyndham Lewis), resurfaced later in *The Penguin Book of Surrealist Verse*, but was not included in the first four volumes of poetry Conquest published. Retitled "High", fifty years later he added it to his *New and Collected Poems* (1988). The second – "The Agents", also a sonnet – appeared in the No. 14 issue, December 1938; an improved version, retitled "Dictator", appears in his third volume of poetry, *Arias from a Love Opera* (1969).

He filled more notebooks during the war – battered but still legible records of his early work. In 1945, while serving in Bulgaria, Conquest received a letter from Julian Symons suggesting he enter a competition sponsored by PEN for the Brazil Prize, to be awarded to the best long poem by a British author about the war. He sent – in four sections on Service airmail letters – "For the Death of a Poet, *for D. A., killed in Italy, December 1943*". The judges – Richard Church, C. Day Lewis, and Herbert Read – were unanimous in selecting this poem from the 250 entries submitted. (Another, "In the Marshes", won a Festival of Britain prize.) Years later he wrote

> The war's effect on my own writing (in intention at least) was to make me seek clarity and honesty untainted by the symbolism and pretentiousness that marred the poetry I had written as an undergraduate. It also – in the Mediterranean Theatre, though this would not probably be so true to the Western Front – made one more sensitive and responsive to the qualities of sky and landscape, of the phenomenal world, in contrast both to the ruined cities and desolated farmlands and to one's own possible impending extinction.

Some of the poems in these notebooks appeared in Conquest's first collection, originally titled *The Colour of Doubt*, but published by Macmillan in 1955 as *Poems*. But not all. In the unpublished poems one glimpses the turbulence – personal and political – of those years. Much later he observed that the poems in the notebooks seemed to form something of a record in verse of the decade 1940 – 1950. Though not in any direct sense autobiographical, he recognised a certain personal development running through the series:

> In a way I find this rather surprising. I would be the last person to look for any signs of the *Zeitgeist* in my own poetry, which has, indeed, been largely lyrical. Moreover, it is true, and I think it is more than personally significant, that the 'sequence', even though still in a social context, ends with nothing more than a simple and tentative attitude to individual experience. Fear of death, most public and most private of all feelings, certainly appears, for at that time many of us fully expected to run a serious risk of dying after discomfort and pain. Some did, of whom (apart from Keith Douglas) Drummond Allison was the best of the English poets. He was not a close friend:

indeed, I do not see how one could write a poem of that sort about a close friend's death.

In 1946 Conquest was demobilised, flying to Bari, then boarding a troop train to London, via Milan, through France. In Paris, he learned that a close friend, Maurice Langlois, had been working with one of the underground groups, taken by the Gestapo, and executed. He would dedicate his first collection of poems to Maurice, but made no attempt to write of his death as he had done when Allison was killed. In a section of *Poems* titled "War and After", the published verses are more general.

Perhaps it is not surprising that Conquest's serious verse took the lyrical form. Anna Akhmatova wrote "Lyric verse is the best armour, the best cover. You don't give yourself away" – and like her, he was discreet about events in his personal life, and restrained in expression. At the end of the war he had written to his mother "All I really want to do is go somewhere alone and write." Instead, with a family to support, he joined the Foreign Office, and over the next ten years was posted to Bulgaria (where he witnessed the brutal Stalinist takeover), to the United Nations, and then to the Information Research Department.

Throughout his time at the Foreign Office, Conquest continued to write – and publish – poetry. Indeed, he first came to public attention as a poet. The first reference to him in the USSR was in the *Large Soviet Encyclopaedia Yearbook* for 1957, there described as a poet and anthologist – a reference to *New Lines,* an anthology Macmillan had asked him to put together. Published in 1956, it was described in *The Cambridge Introduction to British Poetry, 1945–2010* as "the pivotal anthology of midcentury poetry" which "had an outsized influence on the course of British poetry in the latter half of the twentieth century and helped shape a discourse and set of arguments around English poetry that linger today". In the Introduction, Conquest made the case for poetry "written by and for the whole man, intellect, emotions, senses and all … empirical in its attitude to all that comes". Fifty years later, describing the poets in the anthology (Kingsley Amis, Donald Davie, D. J. Enright, Thom Gunn, John Holloway, Elizabeth Jennings, Philip Larkin, John Wain, and himself), he wrote "We would have agreed with no less a product of classicism than Gibbon himself, who spoke of the alternative aims of poetry being to 'satisfy, or silence, our reason'. This seems a frightfully good account of what the poet should do." Certainly his own poems fit that description, as we find in the last lines of "Galatea", where the sculptor regards his creation with "The whole intent of art – /*With passion and reserve.*"

In all, Conquest published nine volumes of poetry, though his works of history tended to overshadow this achievement. The last two – *Blokelore and Blokesongs* and *A Garden of Erses* – showcase his talent for light verse, particularly the limerick form. Philip Larkin inscribed a copy of *High Windows* "For Bob – *il miglior fabbro* (or whatever it was) – at least over 5 lines, Philip". Some years later, reciting "Seven Ages", Conquest's reworking of Jacques's soliloquy in Shakespeare's *As You Like It*, Larkin declared "He is a genius." Others were less appreciative. Clive James tells of the late Karl Miller "expressing acidly sardonic moral disapproval of how Bob wasted his poetic talent on these little jokes", and James himself has often expressed regret that there were not more of the "fastidiously chiselled poems which proved his point that cool reason was not necessarily lyricism's enemy". I share that view, but remember the opening remarks of my husband's 1997 address to the American Academy of Arts and Letters, when he said that of all the various awards for histories and serious verse he'd received over the years, he was "particularly touched and delighted to receive the Michael Braude Award for Light Verse – which honours those who are often thought of as skirmishers and sharpshooters rather than solid citizens of the world of arts and letters".

David Yezzi wrote that Conquest's "wry and devastating 'Progress'" [*There was a great Marxist named Lenin ...*] was "perhaps the most brilliant limerick of the twentieth-century", making the point that "humor can also be fraught with emotion: like poetry, it accesses our most difficult feelings, even as it orders them and elucidates them". Conquest would have agreed: in the last chapter of his memoir, *Two Muses*, he writes of his own poetry as "an effort to impose artistic order on barely explored borderline regions of feeling". His working habit was to write two or three books at once, penning the odd article or essay or poem at the same time. He thought it made a change in one's day, and perhaps kept any of the lines from going stale. Noting that light verse almost always requires not only concentrated clarity, but regular form selected soon after the original concept comes to mind, he found wrestling with the material in that context a pleasure. Sometimes he abandoned a project for years, until a phrase adequate to the theme came up to give life and surprise to the old form.

I am deeply grateful to Philip Hoy, R. S. Gwynn, and Alan Jenkins for advice and encouragement while assembling this collection. In addition to those poems published during my husband's lifetime, I have added some – though by no means all – of the unpublished ones found among his papers. When choosing from this vast trove of manuscripts and poetry notebooks, I followed Philip Hoy's suggestion, when he commissioned this work, that the collection contain "all that there is reason to believe Robert Conquest would have liked to see preserved". So this is not a "complete" poems, containing every scrap of verse that can be attributed to the poet, but instead a comprehensive edition of his work, compiled in the belief that it contains those poems which – had he lived to supervise the final version – my husband would have chosen to represent his poetic achievement.

Elizabeth Conquest
Stanford, 2019

[1944–1947]

FOR THE DEATH OF A POET

for Drummon Allison, Killed in Italy, December 1943

I

I sit alone in the impersonal sunlight;
Drenched in its pale flame, beside the white waters,
I receive the intense perfection of the heavens,
Complete, serene.

Feeling purely nature's absolute moment,
Passionless melody of revelation
Under a blue and infinitely transparent sky
And wisps of cirrus.

The magnolias shining like white wax, and the dark poplars,
In the sleek meadows the little river gleaming,
And the landscape immaculate and motionless
In the blue heat.

But in this pastoral enchanted air
Sweet with the liquid glitter of Debussy,
Out of a deluge of light your voice speaks to me
Not as for months

Vague and obscurely terrible, in the background,
A note of sadness under all my feeling,
A despairing criticism of every action,
A spoken song,

But clearly stating its case, unanswerably
Putting its claim against the loud avengers
And asking me insistently for at any rate
Some sort of answer.

But how shall I answer? I am like you,
I have only a voice and the universal zeals
And severities continue to state loudly
That all is well.

Even the landscape has no help to offer.
A man dies and the river flows softly on.
There is no sign of recognition from the calm
And marvellous sky.

Yes, this innocent and sensuous air lies helpless
Above the silky waters. And perhaps your only hope is truly
With me, in all my weakness, and with my tongue that speaks
This ephemeral poem.

II

The afternoon fades subtly across the pine trees
And under a soft and elegiac breeze
The approaching dusk lays down its glowing shadows,

And I think of you there, under the sharp peaks,
In a narrow grave surmounted by a wooden cross,
Emblematic of a faith you did not hold.

I do not deny that on the long view it was worth it,
As one of millions your death paid its expenses
A half-share in a thirty-yard advance.

Nor can I ask a special treatment for the singer
Who sees the sun's light split through a heart's spectrum
And holds love in his hand like a scalding jewel.

– Yet why was it you and not some self-important fool?
Why not, for instance, that petty little major
Who in the long run sent you to your death

And now in ease and comfort in America?
– But how I feel abominably in my heart
Arise the images of disgust and contempt!

– I must put them away. Instead let me hear your poems,
Your young, incomplete, and yet irreplaceable voice
Talking of Doughty or the brass horse. Yes, for years

A few dozen of us will speak and remember
The lines which had to be written, which no one else wrote,
Not overwhelming, not supreme, but unique, a life:

"The dead inside my head are dying of cold"
"Burning in the sky of time like a flare made of fear"
"O strengthen me to number now my heart's Lavals"

Occasionally such words will fall from our speaking brains
To illuminate a spirit's moment or a tongue of love
And reconcile the flesh to its enchanting bells.

– But still, through this golden air, under the clouds'
Mirror of creamy smoke, I ask a reason why you died,
And must the heart's witnesses all stammer and fall silent?

I listen to the public voice and try to believe it.
I repeat the usual litanies of explanation.
"He died in a good cause", "We sacrifice our best",

"He lives in our memory". All this is not untrue
But its irrelevance shakes me like a fever;
No, they cannot help me, I cannot reconcile

The public need against the private loss,
The just war and the individual's unjust
Death. Cannot admit in fair exchange

The large-scale triumph for the lone disaster,
Or heavens of the future for the present pain.
This is an absolute and total loss

Which no future can ever possibly repay.
– I am alone here. The lake shines softly,
Becomes a mirror of mercury, bright and wet.

Down the valley a mist rises, forms like flesh
On the skeleton trees. Upon the towering clouds
The brown sunset carves its colour. And I am alone.

III

Now the world deepens and the dark grows richer;
A red and mournful splendour fills the eye;
A sharp sweetness informs the whole of nature,
Holds in a sad, dissolving bliss
Its glories and its agonies.
A golden darkness bleeds across the sky.

Did death perhaps take you with a stunning wonder,
Strange exaltations seize your bursting heart?
Your face transfigured with passion and splendour
Fade through the absolutely black
Out of the flames of the attack
As the universal harmonies blew apart?

As on that horrible abyss you trod
Did there walk on across your sea of slaughter
A crucified and all-atoning god,
The aura blazing round its head
Bright as these clouds, as now they spread
Their ample twilight down the crescent water?

Did some strange call possess you? Really summon
Heart out of blood-soaked body into pain?
Death call to you like a woman,
Emerging from that haze of rape
Blood in the air, a liquid shape
Shining in moonlight over all that plain?

– But I am dazed now by your lost blood's brilliance,
Cannot interpret the flames' halo round your head
Nor see the beauty through that blinding violence
Till clearly, as these splendours die,
There rises through the sad night sky
The awareness of the insulated dead.

IV

Out, high, far out over the night horizon
A bomber's drone recedes into the writhing clouds
And pulls me out of an abyss of sleep. I have been dreaming,

And even now the night still simmers like the nightmare:
The ground sweats, and the sky is thick; and a raw wind
Rips the edges off all sound and vision, just as when

Below a white air huddled in the dark
The dream drew another eyelid over the sky
And opened a window on a world of ghosts,

Where under a black light I saw your image wander
Into horrible scenes and through disrupted landscapes,
Prey to the hairless monster in the ruined abbey,

Or bleeding to death in a subterranean room
Surrounded by impassive watching faces,
Or endlessly falling down a flame's abyss... .

I cannot believe you met a death of passion,
That your ironic individual heart
Could blaze to such a simplifying love;

Surely you felt only terror and fatigue
Caught in the machinery and champed to a bloody pulp
In the hostile universe's iron mouth,

As the fate that here constructs this violent night
Gave you the message that it yet propounds:
Rupture of flesh and iron, stone and spirit.

And your glorified, transfigured face was only
A bronze mask flung upon you by the sunset:
Really there is only the parching sweat of fear;

The furred tongue and the headache; the cold of early morning
Cracking in the knee-joints; the bowels tight with apprehension,
And only the will's carapace around the shrinking flesh.

For now the dream can be reassembled:
The assassin shadow moving down its corridors
Be submitted to a close interrogation,

And it says, not pity or regret, but fear. Not only
For you, but for myself. It might have been me,
The dream states, and may be yet: under some slashing barrage

This body and this self may yet be destroyed
In a moment of terror and weakness drop down those cliffs,
Bleed in that room, be crushed in those cold jaws.

– Around me now the sleeping people lie
Inside the glass walls of their thousand nightmares.
An odour of cold corruption from the soil

Hangs in the air. The sky clots into vapour;
Occasionally shudders with light, splashing phosphorus –
Sudden poisonous flames. The trees shake gently

To distant guns. And a black cold air is pouring
Endlessly from the abyss through which for ever
The outlaw planet pants for sanctuary.

And against the universe I can only put love;
Against the constellations of despair can only
Give you my hand, and sooner or later die
                                        – Or am I wrong?

        V

Midnight: the sky has cleared and the wind ceased.
Behind the motionless poplars now the stars
Shine clear-cut in a very distant sky.
And this meticulous starlight, without mist or eyelid,
Is the only framework for the frozen darkness, its clear
Infrangible bars.

An absolutely naked night whose alien beauty
Contains no element that says "Rejoice",
But in the perfect crystal of its sky reveals
– Breaking those engines of the lute and lyre
That claim to speak for us – the quiet image
Of your real voice:

"The world is as it is. There is no helpful answer,
No saving parable or spell that can be told
In blinding rhetorics of star and rainbow.
And the poetry must adorn its indecision
And never can articulate as clearly
As frost or gold.

Out of its decorated and religious dreams
Blaze no despairs or revelations for us both.
Our only hope must be the truly human
Unclearly visible through poetry's mist and dazzle
But shining so brilliantly beneath the inhuman stars:
No angel; no hero; but truth.

A cool flame streaming from the brain and body
In which the heart is liberated and possessed;
Seen as a stubborn muscle working inside a star,
And more than that: felt as a hand,
A fist in the flames or a feather of five fingers
Upon the ripening breast.

Yes, I accept death. I have only the usual regrets.
The individual lives by luck alone.
– But now I must return, under the Italian pines
To stand forever, while in that crouching sky
There hangs enormously above my fatal valley
The blue moon."

And now you have gone: passed through a spirit's violence
Back to the everlasting tryst from which you came,
And only the night's outlandish excellence remains.
I stare up through its brilliance and its distances
While in my charred brain your clear directed voice
Formulates flame.

The river flows across the silence.

1944

DAWN NEAR BARI

Extinguishing the cyclone lamp
I watch by the sea's edge the night collapsing.
The moon, a mirror of ash, has set and then
    A last Perseid flaws
This glass sky as it blurs with light and damp.

But quickly now from sea and field
The mist melts. The grass is splashing white
Under an early breeze. The dust and metal
    On the airfield's runway shines
Greyly beyond the stream. The full world is revealed.

And the river bubbles sharply by
The bridge where it enters the warm and bluer sea,
And on it a swan drifts, the first of ten
    Shot for food last winter,
But still a cool curved whiteness, foreign beauty.

But I can only show problems whirling
Like the dust spun beyond that Venom's take-off,
Cannot even say if they are soluble,
    And know, too, that some future may bring
Complete retraction of my present feeling:

And yet as I turn and see
The ochre glow of the Byzantine fort
And the sea which a quick wind chops and freshens now
    – Ordinary images – I hope I must
Seek knowledge, love, and with them poetry.

IN THE MARSHES

for Ivan Ranchev

Retrospect,
The sunlight filters
Through ten worse years, its categories cooling.
What cannot be reduced to order now
Is irresoluble life. Let rage or reason take it –

By a willow, on a narrow bank of moss
And overlooking an almost motionless creek –
The grey-green plain flecked with water
Stretches to a horizonless fading in the distance,
A few mosquitoes whine and a fish leaps –

Ilya is not really in all this, it is
Only a background to a twisting brain,
A symbol of despair like any other landscape.
He is a student. The city and the University
Are far away. The traffic down the liberation Avenue
And by the National Theatre seems impossible.
The blanketing air contrives to soothe him a little
As he thinks of Stoyanka, lost to him
Probably for ever; partly his own fault.
He reads the French poet he is trying to translate
But the translation fades into his brain
Or moves impossibly above the non-poetic landscape
And disappears.
                                This is the best season
In the Marshes.
                                In the village the wooden huts
Look almost white under a clear sun,
And the faint haze is slightly luminous around it.
Down in the canal a barge is filled with leather,
The product of the little tannery. The sun is falling.
A flash like a rainbow comes from the oil-tinged mere
In which the abandoned railway breaks and ends;
Its embankment stretches away eastwards; it sags in places
And has been entirely washed away in others,
And in one of these the derelict locomotive
Stands like a frozen mammoth in a Yakutsk glacier.
                                Nevertheless, life is lived here.
In a small but handsome house beyond the village
Lives Professor Mantev, former Minister of Trade
And now in exile. The daughter of Tomasin
The dram-shop owner dreams of love. And in a hut
By the canal Pirov the lock-keeper
Holds the secret meetings of the party branch.
There is no gendarme nearer than Shtip, five miles away;
But the village has suffered several times.
In 1925, in the Civil War

A platoon of legionaries burnt down half the houses
And killed three men. (It was then that the engine
Was sabotaged). In '39 for seven weeks
The inn was occupied by a punitive committee
With several inhabitants beaten up.
                              (And who can see
Or would believe that barren future which
Expropriating their own violences
Will put these enemies together
Under the coldest terror of all?)
                              Ilya returns;
It is not only Stoyanka and Laforgue, but
Everything as well. Every world-view seems
To present him with horrifying contradictions
Or baffle his conscience with inhuman clarities:
He feels pitiable, yet better than last week
When he either drank himself senseless every day
Or meditated suicide.

    II

Professor Mantev walks slowly every morning
Along the corduroy road and then by a pathway
Into a little copse on an island of high ground
And back in time for lunch. He is doing very little,
Occasionally annotating or correcting
A chapter in his book on Nogay place-names.
He reads the papers and is sometimes angry
At the government's clear treachery and meanness, but
He seldom really thinks of returning. He has lost ambition.
Perhaps he is getting old.
                              Two days ago
There was an accident in the lock, a man fell
Between a barge and the lock-side, was crushed to death,
Brown blood floating on the scummy water.
This happens occasionally.
                              Mantev was not really
Affected by it. In theory he is a humanist,
But in the marshes a curious lethargy of feeling
Has taken him. He looks at the landscape,
Affected rather oddly, feeling its horizons
As flat, receding agencies of life.

And the recession draws him on into a spirit's mere.

III

Maria Tomasinova sits in her father's inn,
On a wooden stool in front of the enormous stove
Which will not be lit till late October.
She thinks of Ilya and thinks it love.
And perhaps it is, or will be. In her heart
At any rate it moves more piercingly
Than many greater passions.
                              In this country
The primary education is extremely good,
And the peasants are politically informed
And read the national poets.
                              But still,
Ilya has the glamour of a higher culture
For a girl who has been through progymnasium. He is not
Particularly handsome, but has a distant look
And fading violence in his eyes and brow.
She is not thinking of the sexual act,
Which is uncommon in the countryside
Among the unmarried. But her body moves
In a fresher and more pleasing way.
                              The sun
Strikes through the open door and makes the dust
Into a fog of light. She sighs;
And a light breeze ruffles the water of the marshes
And bends the high grass on the little islands
On which are browsing the small local cattle;
Pirov is oiling the lock-machinery and whistling.
And far down the dusty road some carts are toiling
Towards Zopol, with fish.

IV

The Marshes have their own allure. The yielding air,
The cowmen's horns, the fish flashing,
And all the smoothness of the heavy summer
To some are more appealing than the snowbound peaks
Or the rolling garden country of the Central Province.
A grebe cries.

41

                              Yes, we all know
That history holds the Marshes in its iron grip
Like every other region, that next year will see
The alliance with Germany and the small beginnings
Of the partisan movement: in all the area
A few groups of half a dozen men
Occasionally shooting up a gendarmes' post
Or cutting the telegraph wires; and a rule of torture
Set up against them. Pirov beaten to death
In the reception cell at Zopol jail;
Ilya a conscript, invalided out
With an incurable leg; Maria surviving;
The short October fighting in the Marshes,
A threshing blindness of noise and lightning,
A smell of cordite mixing with the swamp smell,
And spreading areas of black upon the water;
And then the coup d'état: everything different;
Professor Mantev recalled to the capital
To take part in the government of the National Front,
And yet a more bitter cycle of betrayals.
And gradually all fading into their other lives,
With these Marshes and this summer forgotten.

– None of these threads work out.
We cannot pursue them down the twisting future
Nor form a close-knit tragic destiny,
Or even some fulfilment for the promised local lyrics
Of Ilya or Maria. No, it all dissolves.

Yet
Although this area has no especial beauty
And the season is pleasant but not unusual,
It is unique. These moments and these people
Meet in an absolutely new and unforgettable
Fusion. For this time and place
Like any other, every life must bear
Always its vague regrets, and sometimes piercingly
Pangs of nostalgia
For what can never be repeated in them.

from

POEMS
[1955]

In memory of Maurice Langlois, poet,

died in the hands of the secret police

of the occupying power

NANTUCKET

It lay in the mist or the wind.

Perhaps Karlsefni saw it to starboard
On the voyage to Hop from Straumfjord.

Fisherman, farmers and theologians
Settled the swept bay and the crescent bluffs.

And then its attention was filled with whales.
A blunt, chipped sickle: it reaped the sea.
Oh, that was an astonishing empire!
All the oceans gave up to its hunters
Dangerous and profitable monsters.
Folgers and Husseys, Starbucks and Coffins,
Branded the salt wrath with their keels and spears.

Melville chose them, the boldest men on earth,
To be his champions on the demon seas
Of his heart. Even they succumbed.
Ahab died. The waters washed
The ruined survivor to another coast.

The whaling went elsewhere, to techniques and guns.
And the island lies in its parish, weather and past.

GUIDED MISSILES EXPERIMENTAL RANGE

Soft sounds and odours brim up through the night
A wealth below the level of the eye,
Out of a black, an almost violet sky
Abundance flowers into points of light.

Till from the south-west, as their low scream mars
And halts this warm hypnosis of the dark,
Three black automata cut swift and stark,
Shaped clearly by the backward flow of stars.

Stronger than lives, by empty purpose blinded,
The only thought their circuits can endure is
The target-hunting rigour of their flight;

And by that loveless haste I am reminded
Of Aeschylus' description of the Furies:
"O barren daughters of the fruitful night."

STENDHAL'S CONSULATE

He already knows everything that needs to be known.
He has examined his life: his gifts have been shown.
    Immensely capable, he looks from his niche
        Wishing he were reasonably rich.

Reverencing art and love only, still his critique
Does not exempt their instruments or their technique.
    And even in this hot, boring town
        He can still write life down,

Demonstrating what, he feels, must already be plain
To the intelligent and even the sensitive: that life can contain
    A hardness society's verminous power
        May savage but cannot devour.

With evasion and skill he is not wholly separate from
Giulia Rinieri, the music of Mozart, or Rome.
    And with an occasional testing glance
        He continues to watch for his chance.

And his calm gaze penetrates poets' and nations' rage
Expecting us too to be, even in this hot age,
    Fairly resigned to our portions of
        That alloy of failure and love.

BACKGROUND MUSIC

Summer in Copenhagen; light on green spires.
Once a philosopher walked beneath these lindens
Thinking: "Man through imagination enters
The real; ideas and women are its lures."

– The life-bound in the sexual act set free
Or in a woman's ambience, split their instants
To quanta from the edge of Time's existence,
And enter the concept of eternity.

Not only that: it gives the landscape form,
And is the immanence of every art.
–Yet though in this green day the idea is yours

It stammers in me to expound in verse
A philosophy deriving from the calm
As you move into the centre of my heart.

CATULLUS AT SIRMIO (56 B.C.)

At Sirmio, peninsula and island,
It's winter now. The willows are like iron;
A little snow lies in the furrows; and mist hides
The far part of the lake's grey shield:
– Not my sort of weather. Light
Comes through the low and heavy sky
With the unequal glare and blur of ice.
Some poet could get beauty out of it, perhaps:
The vaguely outlined mountains, even this blasted wind
Whipping the water.
                            Bring me some hot wine.
This sort of weather's like Caesar,
Single-mindedness with a few cold contrary gusts
– Perversions. I've written about that. He says
I've given him ill-fame for ever. But
He'll get power (if that wet Pompey doesn't)
And then he'll get poets. Still, it's satisfactory
That he minds my cuts: *I* wouldn't. It's the relics
Of shame before the civilized. It'll pass.

Beauty indeed – give me the guts of it – passion;
And pride if you will. Sweetness I've sought,
The lyrics of simple guiltless lust.
But it was always nonsense. I found the poem
And hid the truth in it – which was fair enough.
Look at Clodia: breath-taking breasts;

A green sweat of pleasure; and my heart whipped
By her bitchiness like this lake by wind – there's beauty!
– But there are worse things: to be frozen
Into the deep black ice of Caesar's epoch.
Oh, they'll fix it. The people want peace and quiet.
They'll back the thug up to dictator;
If they must have such leaders, let them rot.
Poets will write about victories and buildings,
Tack bits of beauty on to the rulers' conscience
Or do exercises to order about their hearts.

                    It's a bit warmer.
Noon loosens the water; the stream flows more freely;
The trees unstiffen; the leaves' tongues move and speak.
Beauty, I was saying. Well, what have I got?
I'll die young and with nothing to show for it
But a few verses and a few brilliant nights
And endless irritation.
– Yet one can't calculate. Timidity and trade
Aren't for Valerians. And I couldn't live in
The ages of disgust ahead. The great make me sick.
Women are whores. And poems? – it's not as a poet I'm proud.
Still, there may be others of me later. Damn posterity;
Let *them* read my stuff, if Caesar's boys don't burn it.
In their minds let my pride revel; and my revenge.

A GIRL IN THE SNOW

for Tatiana Mihailova

Autumn's attrition. Then this world laid waste
Under a low white sky, diffusing glare
On blurs of snow as motionless and bare
As the dead epoch where our luck is placed.

Till from the imprecise close distance flies,
Winged on your skis and stillness-breaking nerve
Colour, towards me down this vital curve,
Blue suit, bronze hair and honey-coloured eyes.

Under this hollow cloud, a sky of rime,
The eyes' one focus in an empty mirror
You come towards my arms until I hold

Close to my heart, beyond all fear and error,
A clear-cut warmth in this vague waste of cold:
A road of meaning through the shapeless time.

LAKE SUCCESS

Fall in Long Island:
Deep in the dying fires of beech and sumac
Under a motionless air holding vapour
Invisible but enough to filter the sun
From a rage of light to a source of clarity,
In these buildings there is talk of peace.

In the Security Council and the six Committees,
In the air-conditioned ambience and too-ideal lighting,
A notoriously maladministered state is smug about mandates,
The sponsor of an aggressor utters pacific phrases,
A state ruled by a foreign marshal condemns colonial oppression,
A middle-easterner makes a statesmanlike speech in very elegant French.

These little men, vain and silly, tough and intelligent, cunning and mean,
Good and patient, selfish and loud, cultured and weak,
Are here distinguished by a different standard of value:
One represents twenty-five thousand tanks,
One speaks with the voice of a whole potential continent,
One has successfully resisted the will of a powerful neighbour,
One of the most impressive is merely an empty voice.

Miles away to the west, high in the air which is
A pale single fluid, the summits of great buildings
Glitter like masked and very distant snow;
In the foreground, outside the vacant lawns,
Amazingly vivid leaves are slowly falling;
And in here, in a sense at the heart of the human world,

These tangibles are merely memory,
And paper and words are immediately real. And yet,

In this web of power and propaganda, sufficient
Devotion and intelligence are assembled
To ensure at least a painstaking effort to see
That the chances of peace may not (and that bombs may not)
Fall in Long Island.

TO A GIRL WHO DREAMT ABOUT A POEM

Softly, beneath a scarcely trembling starlight,
A blue sleep rises and engulfs her bed.
That sweet intelligence, transfigured only,
Distils its music in the pillowed head.

The soft night air, through pastures of a legend,
Lets her unmoving body drift along
A tide of flutes. That clear imagination
Sways like a dancer to the unheard song.

But formal resonances of those lines
Arguing aspects of a view of art
Take up the ground-bass, their crude rhythms softened
To beat in concord with that sleeping heart.

And I ask her to believe no sort of praises
Could raise them further in the poet's esteem
Than if I honestly could think those verses
Deserved admittance to the gracious dream.

THE LANDING IN DEUCALION*

Screened by the next few decades from our vision
Their image, none the less, is fairly clear,
Emerging from the air-lock into light
Sharp, unfamiliar in its composition,
From cold stars and a small blue flaming sun
As glints of racing Phobos disappear.

Leaving the rocket pointing at that sky
Their steps and sight turn to the chosen spot
Through this thin air through which the thin winds keen;

The valves hiss in their helmets as they cross
The crumbling sand towards the belt of green
Where long-sought strangeness will reveal – what?

And why this subject should be set to verse
Is only partly in what fuels their hearts
More powerful than those great atomic drives
(Resembling as it does the thrust of poetry
The full momentum of the poets' whole lives) –
Its consummation is yet more like art's:

For as they reach that unknown vegetation
Their thirst is given satisfaction greater
Than ever found but when great arts result;
Not just new detail or a changed equation
But freshly flaming into all the senses
And from the full field of the whole gestalt.
And so I sing them now, as others later.

* *Deucalionis Regio, the area to the south of the Sinus Sabaeus, on Mars.*

A WOMAN POET

The superficial graces go,
And yet such grace remains
About that bare iambic flow
Although the syntax strains
To a tense symmetry, and so
Remotely entertains
        The thundering percussion

Out of the distant heartbeat caught
And never turned away,
Though hidden in a careful thought
No image would delay,
If any image could support
A femininity
        Made flame to purge its vision:

Which saw that fair correcting hand
Resolve the faults of love

In a sweet calculus that spanned
The diapason of
All that a mind could understand
Or mindless music move
     Of passion and compassion.

NEAR JAKOBSELV

for John Blakeway

Dwarf willow, bilberry, bogcotton; a land of lakes,
And to the north a flat transparent ocean
That stretches to the ice-cap. For those millions
Of frozen tons are always somewhere there,
Though out of sight now and far at the back of the mind
In the long hot day and the green efflorescence.

The insects pipe and drone. The arctic sky,
A very pale blue, completely bare of cloud,
Lays down its haunting midnight on the tundra.
There is no human trace for hours behind us,
And now we lie and sleep, or watch the new

Arctic world that rises like a mayfly
Out of each melting winter and never grows old,
But dies. Nothing here
Is in connexion with the central planet,
With the long histories and the human vision.

Its images are not ours. This speed and brightness
Are innocent of purpose. And in that huge returning
Winter that waits in the north there is no moral
– The ice bears no relation to the anger.
I lie and listen

To the desolating cry of an eagle.
                     Perhaps
This very newness and this isolation
May strike some hidden tremor in the heart
And make its rock gush water.

My companion
Sleeps, scarcely breathing, on the blue-green lichen.
And a faint unchanging radiance plays on us
Out of the whole young landscape, as I lie and watch for hours
The motionless lake and the grebe diving.

THE ROKEBY VENUS

Life pours out images, the accidental
At once deleted when the purging mind
Detects their resonance as inessential:
Yet these may leave some fruitful trace behind.

Thus on this painted mirror is projected
The shield that rendered safe the Gorgon's head.
A travesty. – Yet even as reflected
The young face seems to strike us, if not dead,

At least into an instantaneous winter
Which life and reason can do nothing with,
Freezing the watcher and the painting into
A single immobility of myth.

But underneath the pigments' changeless weather
The artist only wanted to devise
A posture that could show him, all together,
Face, shoulders, waist, delectable smooth thighs.

So with the faulty image as a start
We come at length to analyse and name
The luminous darkness in the depths of art:
The timelessness that holds us is the same

As that of the transcendent sexual glance
And art grows brilliant in the light it sheds,
Direct or not, on the inhabitants
Of our imagination and our beds.

ANTHÉOR

A heavy light hangs in these silent airs.
Out to the west the failing day prepares
A sultry splendour. Lying on the cliff
I watch the little bay below, the beach,
Red rocks, the slow vibrations of the sea,
Gazing deep into it all as if
     I could find beneath it a truth
     And be free.

What can a poem do with a landscape? What
Extract that pure philosophies cannot?
Express the universe in terms of parts
Chosen to illustrate all time and space,
Deducing then beyond those images
The general essence of all human hearts
     And the most transitory look
     On a face?

The emblems are too crude. The poetry sees
A giant static set-piece where the trees'
Variety shows a single streak of green,
Or overcharged intense cosmographies
Where the light becomes too fluid, spills and soaks,
Washing away the landscape's flickering screen,
     And the hot stars crackle
     In a sky of ice.

Even the parts escape the dying words.
How can they seize precisely on that bird's
White spiral past the bastion of red rock?
Even the redness is too subtle for
The inexact impressions of a phrase
That draws strength only from the hard-won stock
     Of image flowering from
     Our speech's core.

But word and image, the whole outer song
Can only live as surface to the strong
Thrust of the poet's whole self and language into
Perfection of his knowledge and his life,

Which unintentioned still selects the detail
From sense and vision which may help it win to
    Its own interpretation of
    That hieroglyph.

And yet each day provides its contribution
Of vision to constructing that solution.
And working, upon these red cliffs today,
To let the static and the moving reach
Their place inside one complex of relations,
I find a tentative image in the bay:
    It is the waves of the sea
    On its beach.

POEM FOR JULIAN SYMONS

A not uncommon image nags the verse
(Burke made it grace from dead religions' clash)
– Lacrima Christi from Vesuvius:
Wine out of ash.

Till the excitement of a myth proclaims
Their opposition as the emblem of
Something like the calm of Keats's poems
And the rage of his love.

But I remember, as the image gropes,
That any thirst might relish even more
A vintage pressed out of such gentle slopes
As the Côte d'Or.

For, like all images, this ash-born wine
Is no reliable or fruitful start
For anyone attempting to define
The problems of art.

THE DEATH OF HART CRANE

At first his own effortless high tension
Could match and move the edged electric city,

While under the great bridge sloped the waves,
Flat, tamed, shimmering with oil,
Vestigial to the dying endless sea.

O Queens, keep off the killing wind.
O Bronx, bring close the seasons and the soil.
O Brooklyn and Richmond, let the sea come through.
And O Manhattan, Manhattan, root and live.

For years the raving city fattened on
Protein of his, as of a million hearts,
But the silent hunger of the sea went on.

Yet if Manhattan by an effort of will
Slowed down for thirty seconds for a prayer
It would no longer be the mindless city
Which, irritating, hurting, driving him to die,
Was none the less his only home.

Blinded at least by neon dawn
He sought the sea with different images,
All the lost galleons and the gazing seals.

But between the Bacardi ports he found that though
The city had too much and meaningless action
The sea had too much death.

SIGNIFICANT FORM

Underneath a rose hemisphere
Or by a river of instrumental stars
We search inside the dawn's and dark's strangeness,
And to our bodies' touch comes clear
That under its tangible bars
Still simmer all the essences and dangers.

Until in a grave resolution
It speaks the whole air's fluency and sex,
A snow of gold down from the rainless cirrus:
And we see in clear and passionate fusion

The purity of image love selects
Out of the glass-green sea and the sky's mirrors.

A PAINTING BY PAUL KLEE

O like the shadows now in Plato's cave
The flower throws its outline on the canvas screen
In a grey landscape where each stone
Is as receptive as an eye,
The meticulous petals lying flat and still.

And the sky is calm; the moon resembles
A glass cave hollowed from the neutral night,
And holds through an agony of silence,
Hearing invisible dust falling,
This bitter fragile lightning and pool of stars.

I see him outline love like an abstract
As with a surgeon's delicacy now
He lays upon the canvas membrane
With a very narrow brush

The coldest colour of the heart.

DÉDÉE D'ANVERS

Around the iron bed the camera moves
Or follows where, across the fog-wet stone
She and her life, like one automaton,
Run to exhaustion down the usual grooves.

Quick with desire to glimpse the unobsessed,
It switches restlessly from view to view,
Pauses an instant on a seeming clue;
Rejects it; and resumes its nervous quest.

Till in that trajectory of fear and boredom,
Letting the iron twilight slip and slough,
Life burns through briefly to its inch of freedom

And in the flicker of a lens or eye
Forms to one microcosm of all love
A woman's body and her fantasy.

A LEVEL OF ABSTRACTION

Summer, stream and stillness:
A solstice of the heart
Where she calls to its fullness
That endless search, that art.

The clear sweet known stream
Could not abstract to absolute
Crystal: he broke from that dream
A heart made desolate
In preparation for
Extremes of fruitfulness.

Briefly a kingfisher
Slashes the motionless
Vision of soft grey water
Where grey-green willows bend,
With violent speed and colour.

And yet is congruent
To deep blue clarities
Of a delighting mind
As he looks deep into eyes
Through which strong virtues bind
The reciprocal beauties
Of her heart and face.

The apparatus of paradise
Is here, is made their own.
Roses and dragonflies
Glow on water or lawn;
The gold leaf does not move;
The soft air has not stirred;
She stands, the form of love.

Love is a general word.

THE CLASSICAL POETS

Herbert and Vaughan had been able to note in the study
Occasional brilliance that shook through the depths of a soul,
And, later, romantics readily slashed into poetry
The mountain-top flares from hearts made of tinder or coal.

It was different for these: they could energize only by angers
Their clear illustrations of aspects of truth which were well
Understood. Tears would burn through the crystal: to sing about Orpheus
Nor question his motives, who had descended to Hell.

They accepted. They valued the lake at its glittering surface;
Yet their hearts were too deep. Though they ordered all doubt to disperse
They were poets, and they could not be wholly exempt from its urges
To open the weirs on their taut or magnificent verse.

With descriptions of reason or nymphs or military glory
They corrected the impulse. And, for the whole of their lives,
Like the mermaid on land in the Hans Andersen story,
Pretending to notice nothing, they walked upon knives.

READING POETRY AFTER A QUARREL

Now the brain's tightnesses unclench
    Into the timeless forms
Where the golden leaf and the snow-bud
Hang from the always-springtime branch.

And that translucence of the best
    Even among its storms
Rebuilds the great impervious dream
On which the world's foundations rest.

EPISTEMOLOGY OF POETRY

Across the long-curved bight or bay
The waves move clear beneath the day
And, rolling in obliquely, each
Unwinds its white torque up the beach.

Beneath the full semantic sun
The twisting currents race and run.
Words and evaluations start.
And yet the verse should play its part.

Below a certain threshold light
Is insufficient to excite
Those mechanisms which the eye
Constructs its daytime objects by:

A different system wakes behind
The dark, wide pupils till the mind
Accepts an image of this sea
As clear, but in an altered key.

Now darkness falls. And poems attempt
Light reconciling done and dreamt.
I do not find it in the rash
Disruption of the lightning flash.

Those vivid rigours stun the verse
And neural structure still prefers
The moon beneath whose moderate light
The great seas glitter in the bight.

MATING SEASON

Now love and summer hold.
Birds sleep. A distant bell
Informs the fading air
Out of this evening gold.
Yet still the midday's glare
Aches in the failing well.

And now a sunset wind
Shakes sweetness from the trees
And off the stream's surface;
But blows back in the mind
How the best season suffers
The air's worst agonies.

In March our birds unwinter
Against creative sleets,
But have less strength when this
Close outspoken thunder
Utters its energies
Into the withering heats.

– An image comes that shocks,
So hostile to our love
The purpose it fulfils:
Across the parching rocks
A scorpion stalks and kills
The soft exhausted dove.

HUMANITIES

Hypnotized and told they're seeing red
When really looking at a yellow wall
The children speak of orange seen instead:
Split to such rainbow through that verbal lens
It takes a whole heart's effort to see all
The human plenum as a single ens.

The word on the objective breath must be
A wind to winnow the emotive out;
Music can generalize the inner sea
In dark harmonics of the blinded heart;
But, hot with certainty and keen with doubt,
Verse sweats out heartfelt knowledge, clear-eyed art.

Is it, when paper roses make you sneeze,
A mental or a physical event?
The word can freeze us to such categories,
Yet verse can warm the mirrors of the word
And through their loose distortions represent
The scene, the heart, the life, as they occurred.

– In a dream's blueness or a sunset's bronze
Poets seek the images of love and wonder,
But absolutes of music, gold or swans
Are only froth unless they go to swell

That harmony of science pealing under
The poem's waters like a sunken bell.

ANOTHER KLEE

Sliced to a section for the microscope
And stained to fit the habits of the eye,
Which must deduce this sun upon its sky
Circumference to disc and disc to globe,

The shock of art has stopped the moving parts:
The shadow-fish, caught in its needled fins,
Drifts through a sea of unperspectived lines
That cannot be distinguished from its charts.

That cool expanse of unapparent water
Dissolves the stains left by creative violence
And lies untensed along the canvas wove,

But six short lines are locked upon its silence
Seeming an unknown written character
To express what this strange culture means by "love".

"HEAD OF A FAUN" BY SALVATOR ROSA

With brilliant eyes and quick brown face out-thrust
Against the varnish glaze that holds him far
He leans one moment from the world of legend,
A reassuring and unhurried glimpse
        Pausing between two nymphs
        And unselfconscious lust.
Friendly, uncondescending, self-sufficient
But never breaking into the depths of the heart
He comes to intelligence and gives his message:
"We met once in a brothel or a bar".
Well, we meet again in what is, after all, art.

A PROBLEM

Liguria tingles with peculiar light.
The sea and sky exchange their various blues.
The asphodel that even goats refuse
    Glows dryly on each rocky height,
Whose foothills' wooded convolutions rise
      Through a heavy, luminous air. And here
      Man might, as well as anywhere,
Combine his landscapes and philosophies.

There Sestri, crammed into its littoral shelf,
Seems motionless with distance; motionless
Green flames pour up, the pines and cypresses
    Beyond the stream. The stream itself
Ripples and ripens to a falling sun
      Whose light makes metal at this hour
      Its golden froth of leaf and flower.
A dragonfly is basking on a stone.

Foam spurts between the pebbles; currents swirl;
It slides, a shining film, over rock
Smooth as itself, or into pools of dark.
    Where wood and sea and sky and hill
Give static broad simplicities, its course
      At once more complex and more simple
      Appears to thought as an example,
Like the complex, simple movement of great verse.

Gaze in that liquid crystal; let it run,
Some simple, fluent structure of the all,
No many-corridored dark Escorial,
    But, poem or stream, a Parthenon:
The clear completeness of a gnomic rhyme;
      Or, off the beat of pure despair
      But purer to the subtle ear,
The assonance of eternity with time.

How would it come? This war gave nothing. If
No abstract thought can generate its laws
Unless some special impulse cracks or thaws
    The present icefields of belief:

– Perhaps from the strange new telepathic data,
    Or when the first craft, fairly soon,
    Its rockets flaring, eases down
To total strangeness under Deimos' glitter.

Till then, or till forever, those who've sought
Philosophies like verse, evoking verse,
Must take, as I beneath these junipers,
    Empiric rules of joy and thought,
And be content to break the idiot calm;
    While many poems that dare not guide
    Yet bring the violent world inside
Some girl's ephemeral happiness and charm.

POSILLIPO: 1944

Mingling the sea and the dawn
He stood inside his happy senses
In the green-and-white light and the summer air
Under two pines on the rocky shore
By the sea's blue lawn.

O Tritons and nymphs of the sea,
Come to him from the blue and fresh
Mind of that Sicilian poet and sing
Of a clear delight under the wave's wing
For the unhappy and free.

But let him return
To the hollows of the day
With the sensual lyric still in his veins,
To the arenas where in brilliant hearts and brains
The lives burn, burn.

LOVE AND WAR

In the iron gardens the lilac high explosive …
There is always error rhyming in my veins,
The perfect colour of the echo stains
The images that try to stay impassive.

For the mouth must sing. It cannot sing about
Nothing, or about the War, not only
That the brilliance of the echo makes it lonely
But that it needs more pleasure and more doubt.

So it sings, as usual, about a person
Round whom the echoes and the fighting swarm
Into a new and inconsistent version
Of things so often sung before.

– The heart tries never to deceive the poem,
But it changes, as her image changes, into War.

POEM IN 1944

No, I cannot write the poem of war,
Neither the colossal dying nor the local scene,
A platoon asleep and dreaming of girls' warmth
Or by the petrol-cooker scraping out a laughter.
– Only the images that are not even nightmare:
A globe encrusted with a skin of seaweed,
Or razors at the roots. The heart is no man's prism
To cast a frozen shadow down the streaming future;
At most a cold slipstream of empty sorrow,
The grapes and melody of a dreamed love
Or a vague roar of courage.
                  No, I am not
The meeting point of event and vision, where the poem
Bursts into flame, and the heart's engine
Takes on the load of these broken years and lifts it.
I am not even the tongue and the hand that write
The dissolving sweetness of a personal view
Like those who now in greater luck and liberty
Are professionally pitiful or heroic... .

Into what eye to imagine the vista pouring
Its violent treasures? For I must believe
That somewhere the poet is working who can handle
The flung world and his own heart. To him I say
The little I can. I offer him the debris
Of five years' undirected storm in self and Europe,

And my love. Let him take it for what it's worth
In this poem scarcely made and already forgotten.

CASERTA

Water on bronze postures, a trickle of light
Suggests the slipping arm to the held sight;
The statues in the fountains are almost moving,
Fauns ready to fall into the groove of loving.

It is a moment, a view from the top of a war.
He became a faun the moment he saw
The nymph immobile in the metal grove.
Her delicate shoulder carries a living dove.

O the slim bronze body can never be woken.
The dove flies. But its myth is not quite broken;
Though behind it the war is as real as ever,
Is it to be a phoenix to the lover?

Caught by quick fire in the sharp air's mesh
Can the grace remain in its raw roasting flesh
As in its flight beak, entrail and plume
Historic flames consume?

A MINOR FRONT

The bridge attributed to Belisarius
Is blown, and we cross the stream on foot
Towards the little town.
                              Absolute power
Has receded like a tide from the Thracian hills
And the people reappear, a streaming rock
Surrounded by dead monsters.
                              Across the Struma
The German outposts can be seen, and their patrols
Still cross the river almost unopposed.
For the retreat was caused by pressure elsewhere
And here no force of partisans can yet
Resist them. Half a dozen towns

Still lie in a no-man's-land which small patrols
Alone can enter.
                    The clouds appear
Fully created in the Aegean sky
And ahead of us the stony and half-empty
Struma glistens.
                    Among the buildings
(Not too badly wrecked) people are moving.
An old man, carrying a wooden bucket
Full of goat's milk, staggers to his neighbour's.
– The quick withdrawal of that violent empire
Has left a vacuum of rule. Government is dead;
And after the executions by patrols the tired survivors
Learn, for a few days, to work together, to live.
The best are in the mountains with the partisans
Or rotting in Salonika jail. The worst come out
To loot or denounce. And among the others only,
Mediocre and stupid, in small and selfish cities,
Half-suffocated by starvation and disease,
The free life of the holiday camp arises.
Very dimly through a host of more immediate noises
They faintly hear the music of the stateless future
Like a distant waterfall.
                    But there is too much.
Too much confusion! Too much metal!
They have gazed too long into a mirror of Europe
And seen the Minotaur reflections gnash their teeth,
And they cannot keep their eyes on the green star
Nor listen to the bells.
                    The sky glitters, burning coldly.
The moment is losing its illumination;
The world of politics and rifles reappears;
In Seres, Drama, Sidhirokastron, life will revert
To the visionless present.
                    We lower our field-glasses,
And walk back to the far end of the village,
And pull out our rations and begin to eat,
As by the failing light we try to interpret
The gilt inscription on the public monument
In front of which, their hands still tied behind them,
The bodies of two gendarmes lie in the street.

ARION

Death and the sea transcended verbal shape.

He gazed at the olive-green unsmooth water, a salt pyre.
To die was more dreadful in his strong imagination,
But through its exalted centre he foresaw an escape.

Oh, the sailors realised the solemnity of the occasion:
Dressed in his ritual clothing, holding the lyre,
He sang an appropriate poem, and when it was done he
Came to the business of the day, was flung in the sea.

No one knows quite what his words were. Fragments of song
Picked up later from sailors in harbourside taverns
Do not sound authentic. And other singers, unfree
For lack of faith or intellectual strength or money,
Have since invented the dolphin for which they all long.

But perhaps as he unhooked his golden collar, ready,
A dolphin on its natural ways, or tempest-driven,
Really appeared and then vanished into the waves
Leaving for a moment an extra streak of foam
To be scattered at once by the splash of his plunging body.

And sailors, and after them poets, made the best of the story
And for ever distorted and fixed the inadequate data
But the truth is: even his corpse was not swept ashore. He,
After a brief agony, sank into calmer water
And with the manuscripts of his best and latest poems
Was rolled by the groundswell through its deepest caves.

ON THE DANUBE

I

The convicts working on the frontier forts
Have been marched back. The palpable cool air
Of evening lies round me now. A single peasant
Passes unsteadily, reeking of plum brandy,
And then I am alone.

                    The day pauses. The great river
Slides softly by towards the delta and the sea;
And now the sun strikes from an unaccustomed angle
And the light changes:
                    always at this hour
And in such scenery I wait for revelation,
Under a sky as pale as mother-of-pearl.
It is not that this pure moment can admit
A supernatural vision to the unclear heart,
But it hides the worn planet with its freshness;
The light is no more absolute, but only
Closer to some untried colour of the air,
And there flickers round the horizons of my heart
The brilliance that precedes a greater brilliance.

        II

The winds of Europe and of tragedy
Are filling the sails of poetry here and everywhere.
And I wonder now in what tall uncaused singer
This rich and bitter land warms out.
                        Last night
In a little inn beside the landing stage
A young man was writing verses at a table
And eating sturgeon stuffed with aubergines.
And perhaps he was the poet for whom the Balkans wait,
Though this is hardly likely.
                        The day before
I saw him reading Marx on a bench beside the river,
The witty laboured blueprints for perfect anarchy,
Now legal in this country. (The social sky
Holds only now his dialectic for its sun,
But I find a shade by the poetic tree
Under a moon of love.)
                        Night has fallen,
A young heron rises awkwardly into the air
Under the vague starlight, heading west.
The river ripples as some big fish dives.
And I walk back to the inn.
                        The moon is rising.

III

I stumble over a machine-gun tripod
Half-buried in the sand. It is now almost eight months
Since the S.S. Regiment "Turkestan"
Was brought to battle here, surrounded and destroyed,
And a cold complexity of violence still
Lies heavy on this broken continent,
Which these bronze waters and this natural night
Can never answer.
                                    Yet here I am alone and far
From the brilliance of the fighting ideologies,
And I think of a girl in a small provincial town
Looking through a spring rain and imagining love.

LAMENT FOR A LANDING CRAFT

Four fathoms under the green
Water, canted between
Two rocks, half on its side
Under the lowest low tide

The flat hull now dimly seen
Bore an armoured machine
Towards the golden wide
Beach, but the forts replied,

Till the swell and the fury were clean
Gone, and it entered a scene
Of soundless shimmer and glide
Heavy with myth. Time died.

And the years' and the waters' sheen
Smoothed out this image, serene
Enough, perhaps, to provide
For eternity's moods, and to guide.

Men escaped, or have been
Made smooth bone by the keen
Teeth. And the weeds hide
Skull, keel, plan, pride.

SUNSET UNDER VITOSHA

for Tatiana Mihailova

The song tries often to give the true relation
Between the human figure and the face of nature,
To find in the one the other's hidden features.
– It sometimes seems to find an explanation.

But now in the sea-green air and the soft light
It leaves aside your beauty and your kindness,
Its strangeness strikes down through habitual blindness,
Its unknown colours waken and excite.

A sudden absolute silence from the birds,
The sycamore become an orange fire
And every shadow turned to depths of blue:

How can this strangeness shape the whole desire
Into that other beauty which is you?
What does it mean? Where are its words?

LAMARTINE AT PHILIPPOPOLIS

Dawn, pale and hot, came through the Turkish blind.
He opened it and stood and looked at Thrace,
The plain and town conveying to his mind
Such truth as he could draw from fact and place.

Caught like clear water by a curving range
– The blurred rose of Rhodope to the south –
Its very clarity grown strong and strange
The early air came sweetly to his mouth.

Clear light diffused by the outcropping rock
Above the straight Maritza's ochre flow
Entered his heart. And did it there unlock
The politics of fifteen years, and show

The blue and breaking wave on which he soared;
His songs' clear motives wreck the ancient curse;

When history gathered to a single chord
And all the rostra spoke heroic verse?

Or could he in the inn's reviving stink,
The haggling envies rising from the street,
Suspect his gold conceptions' broken link,
The tyrant's pension and the poem's defeat?

PLISKA

History again, but different: the ancient capital
From which Bulgaria draws its age and fullness;
    The early Khans from here
    Struck their forgotten empire
    Across the Balkan map,
And Krum drank from Nicephorus' gilded skull.

And though a barren nationalism may rant and raise
The giant stones as engines of aggressive war,
    These tombs and temples give
    A real pride and life
    And a felt depth
Beyond the lost five hundred years of Beys.

Their weight can hold that wildness to a fair control
At single points like this, or where, ten miles away,
    History roars from the rocks at Madara
    Where Krum puts a spear through the lion's shoulder
    In a fanfare of inscriptions,
And an ancient honest people become a living whole.

AEGEAN

    Sea and evening: in the sky
    Colours of honey, ice and lime.
      I lie in the coastal grove
Of ilexes and cork-trees on the dry
And aromatic ground, relaxed into
My brain and body, not concerned with love.

Though with you I have often seen
Occasional objects, branches and stones,
Glowing with love in your eyes,
Now a more physically haunting dream
Grasps me in this seascape as the summer
Lightning drones around these evening skies.

Till I am saturated with
The impersonal magic which long ago
From women loosed dryads to roam
Through groves like these.
— In such a sexual myth
You were the first and only one to show me
The relation between a woman and a poem.

MESSEMVRIA AT NOON

Here is the little building-crowded island
Joined by a narrow causeway to the land:
Rich brick-reds, and pale browns and whites.

For more than two millennia in this narrow space,
Since the Megarans laid the first foundations.
Houses and churches have been always rising
And falling, like seasonal plants.
In the little square
Labourers are digging out the cellars
For some new building. They cut through human strata,
Layers of carved stone and brick, of arch and pillar,
And ghost-talk breaks out from inscriptions
Gagged for centuries. History speaks
With a stone tongue, and also in the gestures
Of fishermen in the little inn repeating
Their ancestors' attitudes and even words.

Back on the mainland now we turn
Where the wind hisses through the sawgrass,
Among scattered light-blue flowers, high up
Among the pale green vegetation of the dunes
And the pale sand, and under a pale blue sky;
An empty grassland stretches towards the hills,

And far into the distance goes
The long white curve of empty beach
                                And the town
Shines, a concentrate of human living
Set in a desert of natural beauty here.

The heat-haze crystallizes to a prism
Through which we see it clearly, caught in a pale gold
Except for a darkness by the northern cliff
Where the curve of a Byzantine church cupola
Gives from the shadow a single striking light
                                And turning left we see
Far down the bay and visible for miles
The blinding white of a gull.

BY RAIL THROUGH ISTRIA

    Limestone and pine: a dry country.
The train curves downhill through the early light
   Towards another day and sea
   That put before the sensitized sight
Complexity that hints of symmetry,
Fit background for the hard thoughts' resolution.
A trace of haze softens the sky's blueness
And this clarity and freshness once again
Present the problem in its old quick newness:
The usual attempt to make perfection plain,
To reduce the world to reason and to poetry;
   To let the landscape's chthonic impulse
   Flow like a stream to bear the symbols
Through a poem as strictly driven as this train.

   But the poems are waterlogged and lift
Too slowly to the swell of the idea.
   Today I can only begin to clear
   The ground, to note the general drift
Of a poem's necessity. It is not enough
To find a mood to ride the thrust of love,
Nor should the detail of this rock and tree
Fade in a single brilliant light, be lost
In imprecisions of immensity,

Nor golden images proliferate
Except as phosphorescence forming on
    A sea of close secretive strength.
    And by such strictness perhaps at length
I could merge joy with precision; and create.

    And now we run by the sea,
A streak of blue and shimmer on the shore
    Above which whitish sea-birds soar
    – Specks to an unresolving eye.
And what, for example, is the strict relation
Between the sea which in the last verse figured
As abstract image in a thought's defence,
And this emotive single clear impression
On the visual nerve; or with the real liquid
Full of weeds and plankton where the fish
Are dumb and the myth-illustrating dolphins
    Grunt, they say, like pigs? Does some
    Answer pend, or would the poem
Just turn to logic or to gibberish?

    And now in Monfalcone station
A dark girl, motionless, distracts the heart
From that: its light remembers concentration,
Till single objects fluoresce exact
Radiance to illuminate and illustrate
    The philosophic whole. To sing
    Might flower out of anything:
I learn to seek the fruitful thing or act.

IN THE RHODOPE

The poem tries to speak of the heart
And to relate it to the natural plectrum
Which plucks so clear a note out of its sunlight,
To make its vague, neglected virtues flare
From the ocean and air.

But how does the poem come?
Its voices bubbling from a pool of darkness
To a deliberate fruit of grapes and peaches?

Or striking a horror and a melody at night
Down corridors of dead light?

And how does it distort?
Like the pearl-diver's hand trembling under water
Towards his stone of food and beauty? Or
Absolute mirage into a lonely eye
Out of the swan sky?

– Let me write one more poem,
About this lake at night, black with a golden ice,
Or some green transparent atmosphere at daybreak
Made beautiful by that strange illumination
That poets are always working to bring out

– *The colour of doubt.*

from

BETWEEN MARS AND VENUS

[1962]

for my mother

ART AND LOVE

In a corner of the exhibition
He sees two pictures by his wife,
A portrait and a still life;
Cyclamen bursts red from the pot
In a green material of leaf;
And (hoping no one thinks this oaf
In ochre planes is him), he's caught
In affection and recognition.

But it is not anything in
Painting (or in poetry either)
Would keep them together.
– Not in a supposed completeness
Through the grand fusions of art
The deeper life is shared,
But by some fantasy of sweetness
And the honey smell of her skin.

FOR THE 1956 OPPOSITION OF MARS

Red on the south horizon, brighter than
For fifteen years, the little planet glows,
And brightest yet its kindled themes impose
        On the imaginings of man.
War's omen once. Then source of fate's firm rays,
        Or, punched through the precarious sky,
        A hole on hell. And then a dry
Quantum of knowledge merely, cold in space.

Only in names from legend, history, dream,
The heart showed on its map the regions drawn:
The Horn of Ammon and the Bay of Dawn.
        Now, fantasy and knowledge gleam
One red; and by the next close opposition
        Observers in the exosphere
        Should see it many times as clear,
And by the next one yet, match touch with vision,

Grasping whatever starts beneath those noons'
Blue-black intensities of sky; on sand
Blood-orange where the blue-green lowlands end;
     In thin air; under two small moons;
As spring's green flux pours down from where the pole is;
     Till yellow clouds fade, while blue, higher,
     Catch the set sun with faintest fire
Over Arcadia or the Lacus Solis.

Pure joy of knowledge rides as high as art.
The whole heart cannot keep alive on either.
Wills as of Drake and Shakespeare strike together;
     Cultures turn rotten when they part.
True frontiers march with those in the mind's eye:
     – The white sound rising now to fury
     In efflux from the hot venturi
As Earth's close down, gives us the endless sky.

LAKE IN VERMONT

After sunset, under the spread gleam
And over turtle, bass and crawfish,
The surface now is slate, yes,
But also perspex, polythene:
A disorientating light
Spills out from that thick glaze,
Concussively serene.

But as we turn, behind us
There is a holding of darkness;
In the warm glooms of the pinewood
Already fireflies rouse
Silent points, small puffs of light,
Over the aromatic fallings,
Under the night-green boughs.

These are themselves, not images.
Yet such is the drift of life
That I cannot help seeing, saying
Other sparks now that ignite
In the warm glooms of my body;

In the smooth grey of her eyes
Another indescribable light.

PYTHEAS

Heat falls away like water from the headland.
Evening enters Marseilles. And a ghost
Starts up before us from its rocky bed and,
Quite justifiably, begins to boast:

"Outsailing, close-hauled to a Pillar's lee,
The swift black Punic galleys on patrol,
I felt her lift to a more living sea,
Her prow swing to the calculated Pole.

Cantion, Orcas – to fresh lands we steered.
Thulé was green beneath a circling sun.
Salt of a new sea glittered in my beard,
And still I turned her northward, let her run.

Till a thick silence, robbed of seas and skies,
Mixed to a single element of murk
The wet grey fog, the pulsing mush of ice.
– All this I mentioned in my published work.

Polybius, Strabo, scholars by the score
Praised my abstractions and astronomy,
But since it clashed with academic lore
They called all my experience a lie."

The beachside's dry luxuriance – cactus, coral –
Glimmers and he is gone. We sympathize,
Who see our literary students quarrel
With verse that ventures to survive the ice.

Love rots beneath that calm cerebral mere;
Calling unknowable what is just unknown
They shrink the Ocean to a pure idea
And speak of Thulé as a frozen stone.

81

GALATEA

What wind can cool the mirror
That weaves unending fire?

Such labour and desire
Assemble from his life
Out of a mass of error
Verities that revive
In brief emotive gestures
Or hints of a physique,
Intent into the texture
And smoothness of the stone.
One night the work's complete.

The chisel drops. A candle
Assists the waning moon
To supernaturalize
The surfaces of art.
He can no longer handle
The pressures of a heart
Whose blind mythologies
Insatiably summon
Through to this further truth:
True, though transcendent, woman.

She stirs. And love runs free.
Yet, as a supple light
Moves on the moving curve
Of warm and stone-smooth thigh,
He still regards her with
The whole intent of art –

With passion and reserve.

LOCALITY

Desert: to hundreds of suns
Acrid and sinister
In this bedraggled cadence
The empty hectares glow.

It filters the hoarse terrain
To kinaesthetic images.
And the lifeless strikes its blow
Again and again and again.

Sea scuffles its freight of corpses
Rowelled over blunt rocks,
And jetsam thumps the oil-drums
By the edge of the pebbles and piers.
Through curtains bulging tight
With glut of a queasy moon
It plucks at latent ears
Night after night after night.

Embedded in the city
As the last arcs sputter
And the sky is black and blank,
Only abstraction can face
The purged unsensuous flavour,
And venom and sloth ride high
Through an imageless, timeless place
For ever and ever and ever.

IF YOU MUST

Shut your eyes.

The great tides of the dark
Tug at your heart. Storm dies
As insensible currents sweep
Your elaborate senses back
Into the timeless deep.

And that is good. But when
The long waves cast you up
What reaches for the pen?
A firm and honest hand?
Or is the inordinate grip
Trembling still, half-stunned?

Do you label it with
Symbols thawed from the cold

Storage of a myth?
Or even, killed and caught,
Cram it through some old
Slicer of structured thought?

Does the loud dithyramb
Or high dramatic pose
Overexpose the dumb
Moment of furthest night
When the great tide rose
And darkness subsumed light?

Or can you set down clear
That sole experience
Strictly received, as near
As light can realize
To what flowed only once
When you shut your eyes?

EXCERPT FROM A REPORT TO
THE GALACTIC COUNCIL

… on the third planet too, life is found.

LXI

(These sections are presented in this form under the regulation
Which requires a local language and an attempt at least
To employ its fullest method: so that the Council's evaluation
Of the species may be in accord with the nature of the beast.)

The race is one of those which use (in this case orally) discrete
Invariant symbols, recombination of whose elements
Can in no sort of circumstances be complete
Or even sound as descriptions of real events.

The "poem" (at which this, in the biped dialect "English", is an attempt)
Is an integration of symbols which may be defined
As a semantic composition fusing what is thought and dreamt,
And working in senses and thalamus as well as what is called mind.

Moreover it liberates their symbolism from over-definition.
In that unwonted flexibility is released by the act
Of no longer holding the symbols' split for rigid fission
Nor the symbol itself as object, but as artefact.

Observation of real events includes the observer, "heart" and all;
(The common measurable features are obtained by omitting this part.)
But there is also a common aspect in the emotional
Shared by other members of the species: this is conveyed by "art".

The poem combines all these, so that the whole scene
Can penetrate the biped's organism at every level.
With the aid of the empathy conditioner and the translation machine
We believe that the Council will find the method intelligible.

A further note on this race is that, like those of Deneb III
Its reproductive method is the sexual, which has led
(Relevant at this point) to ability to conceive otherness, mystery,
Illumining life, thought, and especially poem, from the bed.

Before the body of the report it would be well to enter the caveat
That "verse" is better than the race's thought as a whole.
In general practice they reify abstractions; at
The price of wars, etc., fail to keep symbols under control.

LXII

We can now proceed to the detailed evidence: An O.P.
Was established on the nearby satellite, from which
Descent was effected to the surface, in spite of the higher g;
Normal secrecy precautions worked without a hitch.

Accompanying records show ...

GREAT LAKES

As ever, the visual affect
Streams fresh from a new water,
A fresh light, different spectra
– In fact, from a negation.

Negation of sensuous habit
Extrapolating the blue
Sweep into arms of ocean,
Inventing the tart salt

Not only into the concept
But upon the actual air:
A saline tang or iodic
Effluvium of absent seaweed

Rise for a moment, ghosts,
As stiffened reflexes firing
In flashes of an old musketry
Dazzle the sensuous field.

Such shatterings build up the reason
That a new light more enlightens,
A new love more liberates,
But frees, illuminates what

But the riches of the already,
Stacked in sluggish columns:
The dusty, sleeping palace
Magnificent and wakeable

Which when the prince enters
Can no longer bear to be dead
But dancing, spins and glitters
Like these waves under my eye,

Bringing all to excitement
Like this water cooler than air,
A slight shock fresh to the wrist
As I dangle my arm from the jetty.

None of which must blur the intrinsic:
The green wave laps the beach,
The sharp air parts the persimmon.
They move or gleam in my life.

KARNOBAT

The black stump of a hill
Hangs over the dusty town.
And we sit in front of the inn
In the even morning light
Hearing the pattern of problems
Which everywhere nearly outpaces
The second wind of the will
Speak from these buildings, languages and faces.

In the golden face of this woman
Repeating the violence and pride
Of forgotten Avars or Huns;
In the earthy face of a tinker
From the Omayyad hosts' disaster;
And, as he jigs in the street,
In that errand-boy's Roman
Brow and his straight Varangian hair like wheat.

This is forgotten richness
That half of Europe's history
Strikes from a local dark,
But still in the open day
Turk and Gypsy and Greek
Though separately set down
Where files and feelings speak,
Share here the shape and squalor of the human town.

And can we share it too?
By the stream at the edge of the town,
Dry except for the few
Brown fly-haunted pools
Of a buffalo-wallow, we stood
Last night with a bull-headed herdsman
And he seemed, relaxing his frown,
To seal with word and grin our common blood.

But under the Turkish tower
Where a sun of the palest brass
Gives violence to the dryness,
By the mottled plaster and wood

I examine the bites on my knees
Received in the sleepless hour
And to which in years I have never
Been able yet to adapt myself like these.

No doubt one would soon become
Used to the sour smells
That drift from the houses and streets;
But here in a stronger form
The minor problem is set
That the humanist often meets,
Striking all poetry dumb:
To balance one's abstract love against the bed-bugs.

TO LAUNCH THE SATELLITES

for B.I.S.

First it is fitting to name pioneers:
Tsiolkovski, Ganswindt, Goddard, Oberth, Esnaut-Pelterie.
Ley and other formed the VfR: whence in the war
Von Braun worked at Peenemünde, under the cold Baltic,
And the rockets fell, on Antwerp and London.

Peace turned some to vertical: they pointed at planets.
At White Sands and Woomera work went on.
Interplanetary and Rocket Societies
United the technicians and theoreticians:
And in their motives one of the integrities
Which are diffused in art, was sharpened to sheerness.

All of which leads to the time, not far from now,
When the frontier will be reopened, both to the farers
And, just as five hundred years ago,
In the mind too, on the fug of ideation.
Thenceforward not even the most hermetic in art
Will be able to ignore the situations of learning.

Under those unknown worlds, in believable Florida
Or deep in the larger landmass, intent on instruments,
This autumn are men assembled and urgent who have

Prepared a wave to break across the sky
And mount the natural cliff.

NON-ARISTOTELIAN POEM

    On the second night of summer
Visual energies of the air and eye
Seized cypress, stream and moon; and the tongue took
Perspective from a translator dream
Spread across the awakened, resting sky:
    This can hardly be put in a poem or a book.

    Yet I will remember
Heart, mind and senses finding one wisdom,
A single self not verbally divided
Nor rounded out rigid and wrong,
Remember the whole composition of freedom
    When the formal divisions subsided.

    On the second night of summer
Time stammered to silence under a generalized sky
As that dream dissolved through the interface
Of wordless and verbal. And the trees flamed with art.
For thus through the frozen levels is thought made free,
    And the self arranged in the poem's grace.

JET OVER THE PACIFIC

The 707 fumes into the sky.

Ocean Beach, a last long
Smear of apparent white,
Melts in that broad flurry
Of darker land, which soon fades too,
The great artefact gaining height.

A view, then, only of ocean
From thirty thousand feet. – More
Distance, merely? Larger amounts
Of the visual, to be filed
In dust, words? No, for

– Even without, finally
The white mound of cloud
Heaped on Mauna Kea,
The scatter of swart green
Island focuses – amplitude,

The simple peal of depth,
Extends the apprehensible,
In no gross measurement
But the scope of the long light;
Just because unusual

Only slightly, subtly, strikes
Undistracted out of this bare
Field of few properties:
Bluish, wind-blanched, a sea's surface
Through cubic miles of air;

Extends the sensuous!
A not yet known mauve:
Accumulation of the slight stain
On extreme clarities of air
Hundreds of miles, to a roil of wave.

And the sensed is a deep chord
Of revelation (not grace-
notes on a main music – me!)
My neighbour, twelve hours from Sydney
Is bored. I am not bored.

And I shall not be bored by the view from space.

SMALL HOURS

The warm dark room. High windows just imply
Two black, though less black, squares of clouded sky.

That too fades. In her arms the second time:
Pure night through which all constellations climb.

Abstraction at a pitch that's so intense
Black absolutes blaze clear to every sense.

The high elations shake him through and through.
And words break free, a sigh: "I worship you."

II

The rich ores of that barely conscious cry
Forge instantly, spear-sharp, to accuracy:

Not love, or not yet love, the sacred act
Speaks to that "worship", passionate, exact.

The truly human action which of all
Seems most material, most animal,

This rite of adoration, thigh to thigh,
Creates the star-strewn goddess, the deep sky:

What all those churches shoddily declare
When theologians smoulder, mystics flare,

The long-limbed, clear-eyed Stranger, worshipped in
Incense of breath or transubstantial skin,

But for its softness marble, you'd suppose,
But for its whiteness, tissue of a rose:

For once those marvels flame mere pharos to
The unconsidered, absolutely true ...

Through muffled glass, the not extraneous sky
Forms vaguely to his image-dazzled eye.

Sphere after sphere, the apprehensible
Shines light-years through her lips, or past the sill.

Harmonics of pure truth, slight noises spread
Around them, the soft breath, the rustling bed.

III

With gold so faint as almost to be grey
The windows hint of the impending day.

Passion of accuracy, yet no constraint,
As poetry sees it, makes the sage and saint.

What is the sex of meaning? What delight
Labours to loose it from the brooding night?

Here perhaps was accident, the Pythian voice
Drugged where the tripod's fumes blur chance with choice.

Futures may frame tough trainings, whole techniques
To make life language. Only poetry seeks

Meanwhile – as through jungles rank with myth
Intellect moves in speed and passion with

Pure instinct like a striking fer-de-lance –
The fluency and rigour of the dance.

GENERALITIES

for Celia Kirwan

Late April. Taking stock
Of love, a long year's hoard:
What can define that luck?
For love's a general word
Diluting brilliant essence
With seepage of other minds
And dead experience.
Who froze a fire that blinds?

– In winter poems he tried
For strictness, for the rough
Undecorated ode;
Now he'd be pleased enough
If sentiment were stated

Vaguely among these blooms
With his heart completed
And his words in his arms.

BAIE DES ANGES

For once a simple image: moonlight on
A strip of gently moving water. Love
Makes it a system of comparison.
The clear unchanging tone and lustre of
This light is emblem for the purity
Of love's obsession. Its protean dance
From smooth and shifting facets of black sea
May represent the endless play of chance
Where the love's sameness never shows the same.
And several other forms will have occurred
For this clear twice-reflected stellar flame
To those who counterchange the world and word,
Whose senses rule their passion circumspectly.
But it is getting cold when all is said.
    So now let love speak more directly:
        – Come to bed.

BARI HARBOUR: REMEMBERING DREAMS

    Light, light, light. The cool
    And shallow day returns,
    And into its refreshing pool
    The heart drops like a hot coal
And quenches its night-won burns.

    Yet in the shallow light
    Now, a cold crumbling stone
    And not as when it lit the night,
    It seems it could never be lit;
And I seem all the more alone.

    – Out of this summer bay
    Translucence laps the mole:
    But who would welcome day

Unless made ductile by
Flame from that midnight pole?

BIRMINGHAM

for D.J.E.

Enright country: his images
Suck the smoke through the sky, grow tall
Among pillars of fire by day and night
And roar under Snow Hill Station.
                    All that is left
Is a green park, voices of girls and birds,
The common undenominated roads, and glass
At heights and angles of impersonality.
                    And to speak quite simply, as in all of them,
Over the beer in the bar's corner,
In the ambience of women and their scent,
Under the sky's ochre or the sky's blue,
Whoever the poet, he must be seeking
The multiple vision he can make one

– One town, one life.

THE VIRTUES OF POETRY

I read in passing, or with killing thirst.
I take a draught of freedom or a sip.
The stiff dichotomies may slur and slip,
The faulty neural currents be reversed.

The tongue could be too salty or the tang:
It all dissolved beneath an actual sweetness.
Teaching no law and claiming no completeness,
It opened what we said to what we sang.

For it disbands all false habituation
That carves life up with language; it will not
Disrupt one brilliance into *think* and *feel*.

Body-and-mind's a fracture it can heal
In such a rush of luck and liberation
As grips a gambler when the dice are hot.

SUSQUEHANNA

Two hundred miles up the Bay
Here and there high bluffs impose
Of a miocene blue clay,
Beyond which, flowing east and south,
Sight finds the smooth and luminous
Sedation of the great stream's mouth.

And over it from Havre de Grace
A long bridge crosses where the slow
Grey-surfaced waters spread and space;
And the one tone of a locust-tree
Sways outlined for contrast to
The blurred greens of the various sea.

Humanity? Yes: this white town,
Those fishing-boats' cinnamon sails,
And on that pale beach a brown
Girl lies and another runs,
Moving so that one's grip fails
On the poem's abstractions.

And history: the British burned
This place. Or upstream Ewell thrust
Furthest, before that war-tide turned.
And so on. Life, sea, past are met
In no famous brilliance – just
This ordinary conjunction. Yet,

To the accepting heart unique,
It burns to a breath-taking cry
This Maryland, this Chesapeake,
Breeding no easy lyric. – Come,
More passionate for accuracy,
And grip that vision, poem.

THE APPLES

Good and evil. And afterwards flame-edged steel.
But some mistake seems to have drifted in.
A belly-ache was brought on by that unripe meal
At first, but soon the imperatives wore thin.

Well, nothing could be done with the rotting core.
But zephyrs polished the other apple to gold;
Then it fell by chance into sweeter mythical lore
And down the table, among the ambrosia, it rolled;

And none of us have any cause to regret it.
For daring the disapproval of Zeus Almighty
There was a bitter competition to get it,
But Paris finally gave it to Aphrodite

Who ate it.

MALBOSQUET

There are trees here, and water,
And the passing current of the poem
Takes them for its images:
The cypress and the goldfish pool,
The oak and the stream.
For attitudes must alter:
The fresh turn of the word
Has reached its own exhaustion;
Our obvious situation
Requires no strict report;
The verse seeks for a rule.

But some have planted their tree
On some low hot islet,
A salt waste's oasis.
On it the rains rave
Blown from the water places,
And vivid artificial salts
Compel involuted root
To draw its needs out of the damp

Recesses of the mangrove swamp,
Only forming the hot fruit
To a random passionless pulse.

And others have entered a dry
Desert of the intellect
Where dews of sand refract
The strict enquiring sun
And intellectual power by
Miracle makes a rose flower;
Still it is a desert rose,
And if a rose-branch strike
Crystalled water from the rock
The sap and the stream go to waste
As an abstract sand-wind blows.

But those dichotomies
Between the thought and feeling
Are carved by codes of error
In which the verse is caught
With all the rest of living.
To keep the concept purer
It fires those bitter boughs
And feeds the ashes to its root,
Lest words dismember knowledge
When mind and heart are one
– A tree of flame and foliage.

Inland out of Corsica
Wind blows into the poem
Bringing the real closer.
For neither fire nor form
Can hold his heart and terror
Who knows what depth of error
Slurs over love and dying,
Till only poems can fling their
Seed to the wind's four quarters
Like these sensed and real trees
By fructifying waters.

VISION

One sight I never happen to have seen
Is a naked girl by the sea's edge.
Photographs in a current magazine
Lead me to believe I've missed something.

In a field of corn, yes, and other places
– In the snow, half-naked on skis,
(Oh, very fine!); mostly with known faces,
And usually none the worse for that.

So if I do not mention Aphrodite
It is not for want of reverence.
Too formal, though. As one may find too flighty
All those cold-eyed nymphs of the sea.

Visual excitability, landscape, love,
Impose images: memory and myth
Will tend to coincide. Indulgence of
Mere whim, you think? No, pass at life.

A conscious pose would not be quite the thing
(In spite of those professional layouts).
Luck, spontaneity, must work to bring
The extreme result. This summer, I hope:

On a clear day, a blue but cloud-flecked sky,
Water sparkling: hair in a light wind;
Foam round her calves; eyes, limbs livelily
Thronging the sublime heights of the mind.

EASTERN SHORE

The orchard oriole sings in the sweet-gum bough.

The whole Virginian Tidewater flamed high
With qualities and climates to endow
That efflorescence of integrity.
This ridge of sand and swamp still bears them now.

For where, in Accomac, wax-myrtles shade
White portico against the hot sun's harm,
Wealth, birth and power lose all doctrine's aid;
The heart spells out tradition, kinship, charm.

The diaspora of that ancient race
Hear always in a commerce of confusion
Cities and standards of an alien face
Around them like articulate illusion,

Till, when they meet, they smell the Chesapeake
Breeze and see the humming-bird that sips
Magnolia bloom upon the ripened brick,
And the heart's language reaches for their lips.

The snapping-turtle drifts upon the swampland creek.

A GIRL AT SEA

Dawn on that classic sea. Pervasive light.
A timeless and translucent layer seems
To blend the surface into as smooth air.
Only the attention's far perimeter
Is touched by faint hulks of the Cyclades.

A sudden thrust of animal energies
Throws up beasts of legend and muscle:
Around the bow a school of porpoises
Cuts through the sheared and curving green
Against the turning moment of the wave.

I imagine her there, alone on the fresh deck,
As calm as these calm waters and as lively
And abandoned as those playful animals.

What stress of light, what trick of thought or passion
Can synchronize such images to one
Blaze of immanence round that yellow hair?

A problem for the eye, the heart, the poem.

EVENING ON LAKE GARDA

The sun sets. The lake grows calm. The mountains fade
Into a darkness round the hamlet's lights,
A darkness welling out of the sky and the waters
                    Until the world is full.
We can be calm now, but can we be more content
Than Catullus whose yacht sailed upon this cool
Water, than D'Annunzio whose rage was made

Brass at Gardone there, find further release
Than any poet who cooled his rages by
Apparently fruitful waters and calm nights?
                    Beyond that scattered shine
Of petals blown from a sea of starlight
Upon the lake, with accordions and wine
People are dancing through this dangerous peace.

And the water reflects the darkness like an art
As day and music fade into its glass.
But our poems hammer a no longer malleable time
            – Straining to keep our vision
Clear of a calm more bitter than those rages
They cry for unattainable indecision
As the ingot grows cold that took its heat from the heart.

A SORT OF ZEITGEIST

Smothered in imaginary flowers, correctly dressed,
He skims near the pavement on patent leather.
The clocks are astounded to see him. They click their teeth.
And the Demiurge worries,

For it hoped, in a vague inertia, to keep the cosmos
Intact, more or less, from such deeds as of this heroic
Bespectacled apeman clutching a handful of something
Probably lethal.

Nevertheless the man in morning dress
With butterfly wings is much too quick on the uptake,

His casual glance out of some bitter depth
Of power destroys,

Bites like a cobra; till that entirely sensual
And blockhead Creator, drooling an insipid ether,
Turns purple and dies. And Shiva walks on and on
Down Coventry Street.

THE ABOLITIONIST

The clear-cut, alien fault he understood.
Thinking he saw a universe of good
       A fruit within his reach
       He grabbed, and made the breach.

Upon his rock of faith the Union broke.
Five hundred thousand dead repaired that stroke;
       His own obsessions bore
       Into the risks of war

– War nearly lost at that, upon the free
Bayonets of Pickett's infantry,
       And almost worse when won
       Than if never begun.

For he brought on us, almost to this day,
The carpetbaggers and the K.K.K.,
       A running ulcer till
       Eased by the South's goodwill.

A sort of saint. And our own times can learn
How deadly such humanity will turn
       Which serves to decorate
       And justify that hate

Till it approve, in cattle-trucks and camps
Or under the interrogator's lamps,
       What treads its own first flower
       Into the filth of power.

NEAR THE DEATH OF OVID

"Now life alone is left me, to maintain
The matter of, and means of feeling, pain."
        And the stylus loosed the last couplet
            Into his Letters from Pontus,

Whose luminous, mythological resource
For nine years now had held a single course:
        To work at Caesar for escape
            From those gale-and spear-swept frontiers.

And now, ill, he walked slowly to the general store.
Inside, amid the smell of rope and tar
        Among the candles and sour wine
            He talked to the half-Greek

Proprietor, while under moon-cooled skies
The marshes glittered with the hint of ice
        Out beyond the skin windows
            And the stockpot's reek.

And he thought, over his barely drinkable pint,
As the evening thumped with a Sarmatian chant,
        Once more of casual Rome and women
            And his senses' long distress.

He, first, had honoured Lucretius; he had portrayed,
Welcoming poets to the Shades, Catullus's shade.
        Was their passion for sex or reason a sharper
           Edge to the great gift? – Yes.

WATERING PLACE

Through flowers fat after so much flattery
And pompous roses cured by tricky surgery
A rash on the garden's shoddy upholstery,

At the end of their six-hour parabola, the masters,
Careful as porcelain with consoling gestures
Return to nibble at their ancestors:

Fumbling with flesh beside the undrinkable ocean,
Drawing nourishment from the will's exhaustion,
The twin manna seeking under clouds of desolation,

Now (as they say that some whose breath is needed,
Spinning downwater, from black ships unthreaded,
Fear more than drowning the cold slime of the seabed)

Worse than war's open furnace of the null,
More frightful than all bombings, they must feel
The sulphurous fires of an inner hell,

And caught at last by the nude accusing ache
Freeze in that moonlight where, a measured snake,
The tongue bleeds out its metaphors of heartbreak.

BALCHIK

The sky is a pale water-blue
With the softest touch of gathering mist
    And ahead of us the road
    Twists and whitely climbs

Across the Deli Orman plateau,
A land of dry and fruitful stone,
    Across the former frontier
    And disputed territories.

Where writers find obsessive words
To construct a bitter symbolism,
    But we drive on down the gorge
    Into the little city;

Buildings and trees, a calm sea-garden
Set in a crumbling dry whiteness
    Like a greenish jewel
    Between the cliffs and sea.

Cicadas enrich the evening now,
A caïque loads at the little pier,

Birds swim in the harbour,
And the trees stir slightly;

I find in this more depth and meaning
Than in symbols of the frontier;
    And a sea-mist hides the town
    And flattens the clear water.

VARSHETZ

Where he is not, nor ever has been, but
Now holds her and becomes the centre of
All his imagination and his love;
Whether, like wolves, around the forest hut

The winds howl, a grey blur of frost and air,
Or pale skies that do not clash with white
Hold silence tautly to the glazed snow's light
Outside the plate-glass windows, she is there.

And this need only touch the blood, it stirs;
The body's pleasure fills that evergreen;
And verse pours out of a heart's arrogance,

Where love has freed the intellect and seen
A sky form round about it, clouds and stars:
Strong, natural art, a timelessness of trance.

A PERFORMANCE OF "BORIS GODUNOV"

The fur-cloaked boyars plotting in the hall,
The heavy splendours of the palace room,
The monk intoning litanies from old
Parchment in the great cell's timeless gloom,
Keep tense beneath the Russian music's weight,
Demoniac or numinous with doom.

Even the False Demetrius is caught;
The silver armour, dark-eyed paler face,
The Polish gardens and romantic love:

There is no weight or depth in all that grace.
Only the Jesuits are black and cold
– He knows them shallow, knows his doom and place.

Down in the church, vibrations scarcely heard
Beneath the senses tolls the slow, huge bell.
The silent, smoking candles give their gleam
To themes on which the holy paintings dwell
With artlessness that comes of certainty
– The terrifying crudities of Hell.

Even the drunken friars, the peasant dance,
The claimant's quick ambition, are a froth
On depths that pour into the dark Tsar's heart
Unlit by white Ionian or red Goth,
Where Athos, Sinai and the Thebaid
Glide darkly from Time's vaults, past secret Thoth.

But that dark river is the music now:
Not hope nor love nor thought can will it dry;
The priests and boyars stand round like a wall,
And as the anthems sweep him off to die
The drowning Tsar hears dimly through their voice
The hallucination of eternity.

SPOTSYLVANIA COUNTY

These green defiles through the green
    And tangled chaparral
In many fiercely run attacks
    Rang with the rebel yell,
Where Hill, where Longstreet got their wounds,
    Where Stonewall Jackson fell.

Detribalised intellectuals stand
    Bitter with fear of death;
They hone to principle the edge
    That ripped out the rich depth;
Offering countries to that knife
    Compounds their own thin breath.

Here, where the individual bud
    Blooms on the sassafras
Or bog-magnolia's special smells
    Rise from some small morass,
Men too made refutation of
    Pure system and pure mass.

Carpetbagger and scalawag
    Rule many old lands now.
Cultures stand gaunt against the sky
    Having no root or bough;
And cold constructions of dead thought
    Rise from the heart's slough.

But here the Orange Plank Road runs
    Dark between close-set pines,
Or through scrub-oak and chinquapin
    Matted with trumpet-vines,
Cutting, yet fitting, natural growth,
    Accepts as it defines.

Rappahannock and Rapidan,
    The rivers of that war,
Wash the fierce brilliances to peace
    Through life and metaphor.
Red cedars lean across their flow;
    Free people tread their shore.

ADDRESS TO AN UNDERGRADUATE SOCIETY

The Chairman forgets my name. I address them.
Half male, half female, one clergyman.
Few beards. The usual exhibitionist
In velvet or what-have-you appears to be absent.
Surely I'm talking down to these bright ones
Who must know at least as much as I do?
But there are no incidents; no complaints.
A nice girl asks one question about symbols.
A crew-cut politely doesn't share my views.
Why should he? And what, anyhow,
Is all this about? I form no impression.

– No, can't you see? The poet isn't sensitive
To human beings. I see a woman as,
Forgive me, a woman; a man as a voice
Expressing general ideas or limericks.
But fifty people have assembled (whether for
Disappointment or not is fairly irrelevant)
To look for something for which the young and poets
Alone retain their keenness. Something, comment
Or revelation, on the edge of that great light
Where joy and knowledge meet, ignite
And blaze so high that such tears start
As blur the vision of the heart.
Hunt through those tears into yet clearer sight:
Art in a crystal air, an essence of
(Let's not be too complicated) – love.

KEATS IN 1819

He does not yet conclude the psychic commerce:
The muscled mirror emptying the lyric.
Or corporeal roses turned hysteric;
Does not accept oblivion's lavish promise.

His body struck beneath concentric blows,
His love become a huge infernal fire,
With what strength does he call the mirror "liar"?
With whose endurance crush the tempting rose?

Dominion now they offer him to keep
Or sensual gardens, every *summum bonum*.
Yet – as such weakness never could expect –

O look, where in extremes for lack of sleep
The tough and bitter pride-of-intellect
Defends itself with vigour and with venom.

KAFKA'S "THE CITY"

They raised their city by the chosen site
In fierce dispute on how to build the Tower.

from

ARIAS FROM A
LOVE OPERA
[1969]

for my wife

SEAL ROCKS: SAN FRANCISCO

Quite close to the abrupt city
Set on a circuit of bay,
Rocks shrug off the Pacific
A cable-length from the cliff:
Non-humans inhabit that spray.

Last night in a North Beach bar
I was shown, by a fine poet,
Arrangements of syllables
To the levity of dance
And the labour of thought.

Which it's tempting to match with
The accomplished arc, all
The swing of the seal's dive,
His romping swim in
A sun-and-spray sparkle.

How can a real being
Float, tamed to another's
Symbol, though? The differences,
Escaping such aquaria,
Plunge superb. Yet reminders,

Connectives merely, may
Splash illumination
Over his hot solids:
If his tight fury is absent
May spin the wake of his action

Across the more often forgotten:
Arrogance of pure art,
And gross humour of enjoyment
The blue heave bans all dead
Choreographies, for a start.

Not trying to be, just being,
Subduing the willed; the poem
Living the poet; all that move

Amphibious, so emerging
Out of a dark, deep medium

Where they can live but not breathe.
Meanwhile, watching these
Big-eyed, unanxious sea-things,
We can enjoy the merely
Actual: a good thing for verse.

MEASURE OF ALL THINGS

                    Naked, she wants her shape
                In index numbers; starts to inflate
            Her lungs. A harmless vanity. "Don't cheat!"
        Her smile leans to his, a kiss. He takes the tape.
        Bends, only slightly so far. Over the sweet
                High rondures fits it firmly: 38.
            Two handbreadths further down,
                    Below faint white a streak
                    Still faintly brown,
                    A slight swell firmly
            Presses his hand. He lays a cheek
        Against it: love. He reads off: 23.
        Then, holding it loosely with thumb
            And finger, works it down, letting it slip
    Out between them, until a sleek, hard maximum.
        Breath shortens but richens, and perspective
        Grows warm. Kneeling now he can look up
                At differenced life. And down at: 35.

CHATEAUBRIAND'S GRAVE

The island holds into this big sea's surges
A nameless tomb to face the glorious rage:
But from that toil the image that emerges
Fades in the lost conventions of its age.

And when the tide goes down, and rock and sand
Join the high island to the trippers' beach

And melt those lonely grandeurs in the land,
The obvious comments snigger into speech.

– Silly or not, conventions cannot hide
The seas' huge swirl of glitter and of gloom,
Nor pour oblivion on the baffled pride
That thrust the memoirs from beyond this tomb.

THEN

Loudly the engines of the five Dakotas
Roared in a glittering glass air, ten thousand feet
Above the Macedonian rocks and rivers.
                                    Far below,
Minute among the clenched mountains a train
Pulled slowly down the Vardar's banks with field-guns
For the Germans round Strumitsa – no concern of ours.
– Now for an hour there was only a little danger,
A possibility of sudden Messerschmitts, but not enough
To build its alien life into our breath and brains
And sow the field of vision with its lethal salt.
                        No: that slight touch of fear
Was just enough to fill the glowing atmosphere
With extra strangeness and sweetness, and to help
The hypnotic engines and the natural brightness
To create in us a lucid organism
Watching the landscape and the future
Half-asleep in a mist and a dream.
                                    And now
I seemed at last to fade into acceptance
Of the knowledge of death's usualness: that light
Seemed to transcend, purely, inhumanly,
The warmth and softness of a summer landscape
In which some dying rifleman might find
A desperate heaven.
                            The engines' note
Changed slightly as we wheeled to avoid
The guns of Veles. Level with us to the east
Loomed up the huge and snow-topped ridge of Rila.
The world re-entered time. I settled down to bridge the gap
Playing pontoon with a signal sergeant,

My heart still cool and new from the stripped vision.
                                    And above the glowing rocks
The aircraft drove on, heading north.

ROMANTIC

He never guessed how much his roots could mean:
A people rich in beauty and in bluster
But swamped with flesh and dreamt into disaster
Through deadly fear of angel and machine.

All the long sweat of intellect and love
Amasses a safety where he could forget
That in him too the trap was always set,
The scimitar hung bloodily above.

How could they, stumbling past pits of fate,
At cold lianas of temptation hewing,
Break from their future's flowering of wrong?

Or he expect, already far too late,
To keep the will uncrushed beneath the ruin
By taking the whole tears' weight upon the song?

THE RETURN

He stood at last by the old barbed wire
And looked down the valley of mud and fire.

He thought of a girl and he thought of the war
But the past would no longer obey or adore.

Armistice day had come too late:
All he could do was sit and wait.

Perhaps time went on just the same
Until the demobbing order came.

The lorry rattled over the bumps
Past the graves and the wired-in dumps.

Back again in the old home town:
Some of the buildings had been bombed down.

"Darling, how your face looks strange."
"A man may change. A man may change."

"Darling, what's the bayonet for?"
"All's fair in love and war."

REVUE BAR STRIP

> *Nec fuerat nudas poena videre deas.* – Propertius

Undepilated beauty stands.
The Texan by my side
Stops talking about cattle-brands.
He looks fit to be tied.

The feminine! – He garnered it
From volume REF to SHU
Of the Encyclopaedia Brit-
annica (Plates II

To X, Article "Sculpture") – or,
Gazing at Russell Flints,
Found, anyhow, no Swedish shore,
No "pornographic" prints.

Those bronze nymphs in the entrance hall,
That oleo's pink shine,
He checked in passing, if at all,
On girls or eight or nine;

So boys condense their sacred haze
– Not everywhere on Earth,
No doubt, yet where white statues blaze
From Athens to Fort Worth.

With wives and so forth, later on,
Life, as it often does,

Coolness, to meet its charge,
Needs a strong weapon's aid;
And clarity is but an edge
To the great weighted blade.

READING COLERIDGE

Worse than to bear that albatross
    Humiliations have come
    Compromising my life
    In its search for a truth or a poem,
    As I think of the times that I have
Used prudent speech avoiding some
Material or social loss.

And when I find the excellent:
    As I look at the evening sky
    And the words in this book of verse
    I understand what they say
    Each in its special voice;
"Repent", all verities must cry,
"Although it is too late, repent."

BUDAPEST IN 1945

Looking through dusk and a very light mist
Over the luminous grey Danube and the lamps beginning
From that hill of broken palaces the ruins
Assumed an ageless beauty, hiding the terribly
Slashed city, one of the very rawest

Zones in which Europe's hatred went
Absolutely to the bloody whirlpool's centre,
Struck a cold thunder over
Every usual noise and thought, and carved
Granite to a formless monument.

Gold light shivered warmly from the water though the vague
Evening. For even there, among all that
Debris of brick, flesh and steel, the eye selected

Blindly its focus. And so no verse can ever
Express the essence of the deadly plague.

LOSS OF NERVE

Once again the roaring voice
Builds its tensions to the brain.
Across the European plain
Iron shears the blooms of choice.

And soaked in tragedy too much
A milk of useless pity drips
Down upon the singing lips
Become too sensitive to touch,

As the European arts
Sense that we must once again
Drag back reluctantly to pain
The busy bruises on our hearts.

And arts and guns consider if
Our minds can bear the weight alone,
While the days like rotten stone
Crumble from the future's cliff.

RIO NEGRO

At Manaus the two rivers meet, and move
Their different-coloured waters on ahead,
Which, oddly apt as symbolising love,
Go side by side unmixed, though in one bed.

The context too: life in a lush resilience,
The damp green forest glittering in those heats,
Dazed with a myriad birds' and insects' brilliance,
Screaming with marmosets and parakeets.

Even the small piranhas, wild for blood,
Stripping the flesh from bone, may savour of

The hidden dangers borne along its flood
By all the witless savagery of love.

Finally mixed, they last well out to sea.
Then dissipate beyond the coastal shelf ...
An image has its points, you may agree:
I hardly find them adequate myself.

MEMOIRS

In a square room he chattered with his staff
As reports came in to show his frightful error.
No longer could he work his well-known laugh,
But plucked his whiskers by the gilded mirror.
And, miles in front, men killed in fear or rage
Made individual tragedies that night
In scenes of horror Greekwise done off-stage
While his bright braid flickered in the limelight.

In some cathedral town his story closes
Arraigned more flatly as his blood grows colder:
Ink supplements barbituritic doses
As, like their limbs, his brain begins to moulder;
And history's dramatic intuition shows us
The strategist more tragic than the soldier.

YOU GET USED TO IT

The sensitive construct their screens of fantasy
And those who watch the world allow their hearts to harden,
     But there are always a few
The world's water always dripping on whose faces
Does not encase their eyes in globes of frozen stone;
     They accept as true

The terrible imperfections of which worlds and selves are full
And the poet has merely to be one of them, with an odd gift
     But not better or worse;
Unsimplified in the affective field

To feel the thousand radiations and vibrations
     And enter them as verse.

For the corrupt external triumphs and, in the heart,
The intolerable pressures of a racing engine
     Call for the ode
Of fascinating, purifying beauty which cannot
Be formed unless on waking every morning
     He swallows his toad.

COUNTY CLARE

Under a barbarous star the summer dogs
Our footsteps through this heaviness of light.
Wind squeezed from the sopping air a slight
Precipitation on these bone-dry bogs.

This land implies its literature in so
Delicate a strength from those blue hills,
Whence, through some woman, stone or swan, it fills
The shallow basin with old music's flow.

A weather quite rejected by the tongue
Yet forms into an unclear crystal's light
The little stream, the town, the broken tower,

Till we forget discomfort and the sour
Taste of fatigue and heat, and isolate
A region of the heart in one small song.

NEAR CORINTH

     O nymphs representing ideas,
     Come from that Platonic cave
     Into a blue-washed air,
     Or under the green of the sea
     Lie in the lapping wave ...

Believing them a false ideal image,
The poetic version of a metaphysic,

I yet think it would scarcely be more strange
To see them here beside me in the classic

Mediterranean light, real sea and place
With odour and sound (the citrus and cicada),
Than what we do so normally, but seems
No less unnatural as a view of matter:

The interpretation of her moving face,
Skin over bone and muscle, tinged with blood,
To intricacies of personality,
Pervasiveness or subtlety of mood ...

    O satyrs of a deeper cavern
    On whom those sweet nymphs dote,
    Say if such clear eyes can
    Invent the mind of a man
    Through the masks of a god and a goat ...

GEORGE ORWELL

Moral and mental glaciers melting slightly
Betray the influence of his warm intent.
Because he taught us what the actual meant
The vicious winter grips its prey less tightly.

Not all were grateful for his help, one finds,
For how they hated him, who huddled with
The comfort of a quick remedial myth
Against the cold world and their colder minds.

We die of words. For touchstones he restored
The real person, real event or thing;
– And thus we see not war but suffering
As the conjunction to be most abhorred.

He shared with a great world, for greater ends,
That honesty, a curious cunning virtue
You share with just the few who don't desert you.
A dozen writers, half-a-dozen friends.

A moral genius. And truth-seeking brings
Sometimes a silliness we view askance,
Like Darwin playing his bassoon to plants;
He too had lapses, but he claimed no wings.

While those who drown a truth's empiric part
In dithyramb or dogma turn frenetic;
– Than whom no writer could be less poetic
He left this lesson for all verse, all art.

FAR WEST

for Walter Bernstein

The tribes would follow the northward-trekking bison,
Flat-forehead Mongols with sandstone axes.
Winter brought bitter war, ice on
The lakes, and the scalped bleeding skull.

For a drunken moment the routine relaxed
On a sniggering continent of goldrush and vendetta
Till Methodists with revolvers and directed will
Clamped down the railroad like a fetter.

TONE OF VOICE

Out of the raw materials of verse,
Great writers' words, all nature, reason, women,
The poem resolves into the superhuman
The pure description with the praise or curse.

But often now he finds proposed a smaller
Problem the summer's brilliance sets an art:
In their relation to the sensing heart
To state the elements of light and colour.

Once more the river with the sunlight on it,
Willows, the glowing air – a usual scene –
Draw all his mind and eyes, compelling to

Efforts to fuse into some lucid sonnet
Marvell's absorption into local green,
Mallarmé's cry for supernatural blue.

HOUGHTON HOUSE

1

Behind the elms, sunlight on ripe grey stone,
The blue-green grass, the slow gold of the bracken,
A glow of ruined Jacobean fluting
Whose separate bricks have weathered into one.

The towers speak pride, intellect, devotion;
The grass-floored hollow halls direct to peace:
The whole great building seems, in stone and space,
A huge machine to generate emotion.

But slow the emotions rise, and incomplete
Roused not by beauty set in stone or phrase
But by the watching ancestors who raise
The creative past, the centuries of weight

On the formulating centre of my brain,
– And then the patterns of responses die
Caught in that unpredictability
Only the verse can hold and perhaps explain.

2

It is seldom that all the conditions are present together
To harvest the heart. It is seldom that chance allows
Suitable landscape, physical well-being, weather.
    But here by the ancient house

Emotive bells of nature and mind are pealing
And I should be, and am not, in this summer prime,
Caught up in a resonance of air and feeling
    An assuaging single chime.

And the rolling turf and trees, a vigorous vista
Down to the slow sweet waters of fenland stream
Somehow today can do little more than foster
An illusory tension of dream.

And at the carved lintel framed by this glowing view
I look half-expecting the fall of another stone
With a vague sense of fate, but of the ordinary too:
    As they might have done.

3

The emotions are truly there
But immobile, as it were.

No real tensions remain
From deeper thought or from pain

So I take my pen and write
To focus its fading light

And the energies disperse
Through the loose dykes of a verse.

FILM REVIVAL: "TALES OF HOFFMAN"

Occasionally obsession
Comes to its flower, grip and shine
From the soundtrack and screen.

Light sheer to the glazed dark limbs and the smooth pool.

Integrities of the automatic voice.

Florid, impenetrable Venice.

In superfluity of magic a single note
Shatters the glass jewels. A dancer's arm
Makes a gesture that is love: and art.

VASSAR

Petals on a fall wind, girls stream
Across the campus. – Now don't start thinking
Of "petals" as just a romantic
Property, the old dream-and-gleam
Of a delicate white or pink thing,
Choreographic, corybantic.

(Though there's that too: surely today
Censorious little shags might drop
Those screechings on How to Act Tough?)
But the immediate image rings free
Already in a fuller peal
Hard, white and smooth: fleshy;
– Camellia? Magnolia? – anyway
Veined with a spiced sap.

At the strained nodes of the real:
None the less subject to love.

A CHINESE PAINTING

Late Sung

Clarity! This bird, this branch of pine,
A gull-wing cloud above the cataract:
Unstressed felicity of space and line
And colour come exact.

The heart shows timeless in the unrippling mirror.
But our scalding epoch shudders, leaving me
To think of this: their time too had its horror,
But the art came free.

For with the silk's soft texture and its light
This dark-green branch, this red bird still unroll
An unemphatic lesson to our fright:
– Transcend the lethal Whole.

Images of desert, dangerous seas,
Still come unbidden to an unfree pen:
I seek instead that landscape's calm, that tree's,
And art made sane again.

MOBY DICK

Ishmael. He had once had paradise
And now had loneliness. A shattering music.
Not like that albatross of Baudelaire
Or Yeats's swans, a manageable symbol,
But hidden, patient, huge and dangerous:
Heavy with storm up where the great waves rumble
Or, in black deeps, from silent pressure's load,
With death and terror for its metaphysic
That loneliness became one sort of God.

MOTIVES

And must he always either sing of love
Or drone the incantations of some nightmare?
Honey and sulphur saturate his air?
His sun and moon be opposites above?

And, while an intellectual anger showers
Its filthy images of approaching way,
The pains of love be always urgent for
Their atmosphere of broken stars and flowers?

Or could one music hold the double weeping,
And let the sexual and the political
Illumine faces of a single love?

And through the fumes set all its fountains leaping
Into the passion of no bitter will
To break the one world open, make it move?

A SEATTLE PARKLAND

In memory of Theodore Roethke

To light winds, tawny sun,
Recrossing ripples stress
The pool with arcs of dark
– Simple and intricate
As the opening oleander,
The opening heart, the run
Of tawny hair, light dress.

What words make movement tame?
The bright elms hack down deep,
Roots racked through a rocked soil;
That endlessly exploding
Sun blasts through the crackled
Corona's harshest flame;
The glib aches in their grip:

"From the claws of a heart's crab
Loss tears the harmonies
Which make, which spring, which stun,
When the breadth of the breathed air
Freeze down to a clenched crystal
Pinching to one thin stab
Of twisted fire that sun …"

What says? Here's true! –This air,
Its warmth not wrenched beyond
To leave such shriek, such void.
That sun's a real all;
And a right concentration
Still laps the forearm's sheer,
Still lights the grove, the pond.

The rock, the long sun fade.
All strength must sparkle there.
I find the light and sweet
A bough on a tough tree.
Her skirt moves in a mood.

Power? A leaf that's swayed;
A shake of tawny hair.

    II

This sleek air sifts through green
Riffling lawn and leaf;
Or rubs up the rough nap
Of disaligning hair;
Or presses the green blouse
To scarcely need to mean
All nakedness beneath

– Though that's taut to transform
The day, tingling, young,
With extra wow, woosh, wahay
And sting of light, ache of
Something in the ribcage
That swarms and is warm
To what's so stressed, strung.

"Clawed iron of the burst
Bulkhead splits and rips
Where the drag of the drowned heart
Lugs up the cry of poem
That turns life inside out,
Cold tons sloshed through rust
On salt-peeled clammy lips …"

When's wreck? Where's bitter reef?
– Elms rinsed in a light haze,
The senses break with stress
And let me through to love.
I am wherever she is,
An image sprung to life
At the focus of green eyes.

Through blanks of scent and sound
Flame beats that pale sky off
The face that shows no mood,
The slightly parted lips:
Wildfire in the eyes

Looking beyond, beyond,
To love, to love, to love.

III

It hacked on through a rough
Year; grace groped at fog;
Love stepped in the town's slush.
The grey deposits of
Water, soot, sulphur,
Awkwardly wiped off
On air like an icy rag.

Momentum trundles love
Through years, lead in the scale,
Where under the weak violences
All horror boils around.
– Proportion, thighs and elms,
And all the delicate, tough
Clarities shall prevail.

And if the flame-front sweeps
That bellowing white-hot stain
Out from ground-zero's eye,
Or slit-eyed police-troops rave
More coldly through the streets,
The carbine in the ribs,
The arc-lamp in the brain,

If we fall, we fall.
But in the even-there
If live, live worse but with;
In filth of doctrine, flame,
Bone-rot or broken bone,
Best if that swamp recall
Its springs: bed, torrent, air.

The green leaves feel her cheek.
Light, blood, are equal things.
We enter the great words.
I take her voice, her touch.
The world is as it is.

What sings could also shriek,
But just the same it sings.

BYRON'S SEX-LIFE

On the knife-edge between actual and potential
Mere heat of distillation may abstract
An interface where everything essential
Plunges the great dream in as great an act.
Once through, that act's a pallid image of
Its dream; but here is art, perhaps, or love.

Where egoism and self-immolation,
At their extremest, border one full mood,
With almost equal warmth art scans a Station
Of the Cross or gawks at some Pandemian nude;
Yet all that awe and impulse may collate
Only the windy half-world of self-hate.

Pulses of lightning blaze, or break, eclectic.
Love, only, lets totality prevail,
When appetites grow calm, affections hectic,
To eat and beat and worship and inhale:
Till art stands purged, to grasp with full intent
The disparate violence of that one assent.

Crude images of tenderness and power
Are rafts swept down a deep but childish tide:
The phallus, or the mind, "thrusts up a tower";
The "wounds bleed dark" in some obsession's side:
Hysteria may intrude its postured "I",
Or calculation squeeze all affect dry.

What toil can raise its constructs equal with
The status of emotion or event,
Not standing slobbered with a mist of myth
But clear and real, ablaze with measurement?
For Sestos' ruins what Leander braves
A blue heave of unconsummated waves?

Up through that imagery of turbulence
The thundered peak strikes grandly for the sun.
What most transcends phenomena, each sense
Most firmly grasps as pure phenomenon.
Strong words, and stronger passions, stand at length
Mastered and ordered by that greater strength …

TOWARDS

The painter's pigments seem exactly matched;
Precisely true the violins are strung;
But verse comes from a more empiric tongue,
Ambiguous on the page its signs are scratched.

Its herbs composed to some correct infusion
The cauldron boils or the fire goes out
Unless a special discipline of doubt
Controls the winds of all the world's allusion.

For it is rich, too rich. It lays before us
Too lavish and too subtle images.
– How should such dazzled, fragmentary art

Halt its harmonics to a moment's chorus
Evoking none but natural purposes
Carved clear within the limits of a heart?

THEALOGY

Homage to Robert Graves

God the Father, brooding like a hen,
Builds a good fug round chicken-livered men.

In what dry caves of Sinai, counting kine
Lean as themselves, a patriarchal line
Imposed their bearded mania on the sky?
And what numb scholiasts would not let it die?

Yet poets have kept from that crass emblem's grip
A sharper, wilder, bright relationship:
Cool, glittering body, endless as their cry,
Goddess the Mistress arcs across the sky.

HIGH GROUND

On love: how should the poem encompass passion,
Express love in some systematic fashion
Yet bearing through its verses the full glow
Of energies below the images
In that still unmoulded stream of molten gold;
To clarify its purposes without
Their freezing in the analytic cold;
To watch its many-levelled structure show
        The fullness and the drive of doubt?

Not merely aiding in a definition
Deeper than those semantics of confusion
Which mutter "love" until the meaning blurs,
Nor as mere celebration or mere comment,
The exaggeration of the passing gust,
Nor in the genial warmth or dazzling heat
Of love's invariable surrounding climate
– Of that delightful summer which is lust –
        Nor taking less than love complete.

Though it is true that some sort of fruition
May form a verse out of the partial passion,
(When loss adds adventitious energies,
The single incident bursts into flames,
Or single aspect holds the fading light
In the illustrative moment of a lyric
Complete among its flowers; stars and streams,
Or in some undeep generalised expression
        Out of the immature empiric);

In this analysis of adoration
She brings his search for good into completion
In intellect, integrity, desire:
Not merely fire and flower, the form of love.

(Though as I write my whole heart sees her blazing
In all the beauties of her discontent!)
And then verse, sprung from all the meaning levels,
In turn helps integrate the heart, composing
        Its full perfection and assent.

Struck only from profundities of passion
It holds life's balance through that sane obsession,
Although the word reverts to its beginnings
When magic held the purposes of art
And naming cast the animistic spell;
Till "perfect" seems the definition of
One woman; "warmth" or "fullness" mean a heart;
And "desperate" lives only in some adverb
That qualifies a verb "to love".

EXISTENCES: ZURICH

Bad-tempered bastards! – Black
Swans on the Limmat hiss,
Cobra-necked, to strike at
Pochards by the greening
Buttresses of the bridge.
Such sleek ferocity!
Imagery loses track.

For that shape is assigned,
Those symmetries on water,
To lace, marble, snow, breasts:
Squeezed out of it like milk
A metaphysic of white.
Whatever we think we think,
Whatever we mean by "mind"

Machines, and those extreme
Machines the animals,
Engross in scoop or paw
The mere phenomena,
But we (where no autistic
Ideologies rave),
Seeing the jet plumes gleam

To rays of a G-type star
The colour of a black swan's eye,
Weave cocoons of echo
From the mist and shimmer of neurons
In their degree of freedom
Irrelevance and essence
Trick out things-as-they-are.

Philosophies and odes
Flinch at these graceful demons,
Black on a shaken gleam
Where waters disperse the day …
Flinch and are firm again
As that western light weaves down
Through white-swan-coloured clouds.

TWO ARIAS

1

The barely visible mountains
   Raise and round their convolution
      Into a dimness of height
         Over whose snow the small winds flicker
      While the dawn collects its light.

This outlined white contains
   Shadows without continuation,
      A colourless sketch on space
         Giving form and beauty weaker
      Than can bear the mind's embrace.

But the faintest rose returns
   Upon one slope of cloud and ashen
      Edge of the far snow's rime.
         And though day floods in ever quicker
      That faint flame burns up Time.

2

Once in a life the love that might
Strike out that whole life's chord
Plods him exhausted to its halt:
Dead brick and peeling board.

He sees the stinking bins, the blank
Wall of the cul-de-sac,
And with dry throat and blistered heel
Faces the long trudge back.

Love spits and claws inside him yet
While that numb toil begins,
As deathless as the alley cat
That slinks among the bins.

COMING ACROSS
[1978]

for Ann Smith

COMING ACROSS

for Ann Smith

Some miles north-west of
Calm St. Augustine,
The old Spanish city
With its fort and verandas,
As we run by the broad, by the
Estuarine waters
Of the older Atlantic
Spread out in the St. Johns,
We find ourselves launched upon
Interstate 10.

O Florida, Florida
(*Floride incroyable*
Was the comment of Rimbaud
Who'd never been near it),
White beaches, warm waters,
Pelicans skimming
Twenty yards out from
The white-fringed, the pine-duned
(The stone crab-producing
For that wonderful dinner)
Florida coastline,
We leave you, we leave you
As we swing to the westward
On Interstate 10.

On Interstate 10!
– The continent-crosser,
The ocean-uniter,
Through the States and the time-zones,
The clenching of mountains,
The seething of rivers,
The glaring of deserts,
The rumbling of cities,
Westward, still westward
Into the sunset
On Interstate 10.

For days we'd been driving
From Washington southward
By Williamsburg, Norfolk,
To the Great Dismal Swamp, then
The sounds and the islands
Of North Carolina,
The strange little sea-towns,
Calabash, Southport,
The great famous cities,
Charleston, Savannah …
Thousands of miles to
The eastward lay Europe,
And thousands of miles
To the west California:
An unresolved balance
Between oldest and newest,
An edge of essentials,
As we just savoured bays of
The homey Atlantic.
– A bit indecisive,
Not quite committed
To the great looming landmass,
Looking backwards, like children,
Across the old Gulf Stream,
Till we turn from the past into
Interstate 10.

But now here's the driver,
A woman beside him,
A dog in the back-seat,
As they bowl through the noon-tide
In a happy hypnosis,
A prospect before them
– Rolling before them –
Of light, cow-cropped grassland,
Of pond-fringing woodland,
Odd lakes, farms and meadows,
That seems at the present
To go on for ever
On Interstate 10.

And now the Suwanee,
Dark trees, Spanish moss-hung
Over marshwaters moving
In swirls, whirls and downdrafts,
Upwellings and foldings,
Spreadings and suckings
Smooth as molasses
Around White Springs jetty,
But we must head on along
Interstate 10.

Hour after hour, then,
Girl and hound drowsing,
My eyes scarcely open,
Hour after hour through
The State's long panhandle
– But we're not the purists
Who'd object to a detour
From Interstate 10.

Through cattle-land, forest
Down to the Gulf coast,
The motel-rimmed beaches,
The sudden vast oil-rigs,
And by Apalachicola
We're in a new time-zone,
Then blank sands, bare pine-glades
Till we run out of gas, and
Find a motel, seven
Miles from nowhere ...
Off at eight in the morning
Without any breakfast
Till in warm Pensacola
We get eggs, grits and bacon,
And are glad to be back upon
Interstate 10.

Very soon Alabama
For just a few hours now,
A low grassy plateau
Then, southwards and leftwards,
The greyly transparent

Light of the waters
Where Farragut shouted
"Damn the torpedoes!"
Then we're heading south and
We're in Mississippi
And here the coast road runs
A mile or two southward
Of Interstate 10.

And we turn to the beaches,
The long-stretching beaches
Right under the townships,
Colleges, campsites,
An island chain southward
A pine-treed horizon,
And down little lanes
To Waveland and empty
Skies and dusked water
Until we turn back on to
Interstate 10.

Now Louisiana,
And we're soon in New Orleans
The node of the highways,
The crux of the rivers,
– Maitresse of all waters:
A hotel in the quarter
And dinner at Antoine's,
Bourbon Street jazz-dives
(Where Yellow Dog Blues is
Played just in honour
Of the visiting basset),
And coaches and flowers …
Will we ever get off along
Interstate 10?

Once more we turn southward
Through white Cajun townships
On long, still, dark bayous.
The Bayou Teche leads us
Under intricate live-oaks

And then we are back upon
Interstate 10.

Another dull stretch
And we're both almost dozing
And then we're in Texas
– Long days, nights in Texas –
Unintricate Texas,
Huge, glittering Houston,
Then the Alamo draws us,
Bowie and Crockett!
Names that in Europe
Ring as deeply in legend
(Well, almost as deeply)
As Ajax or Arthur.
And these not very ancient
Walls cast a shadow
Like Troy or Tintagel.
But we must fare westward
On Interstate 10.

On Interstate 10
– On Interstate 10! –
We drive through a rainstorm
The road swinging smoothly,
The two of us singing,
The basset-hound barking,
The hills turning purple
As we swing down the passes
To Ozona, Fort Stockton.
Absurdly pretentious
The merest of two-lanes
(Till we're west of the Pecos)
Now takes up the duties
Of Interstate 10.

Flat desert with distant
Reefs, rims of mountain
Like the crumbling walls of
Some ancient arena
From which huge spectators
Might gaze at the movements

Of coyote and cougar,
Rattlesnake, scorpion
And men in their armour
Of automobile,
Caprices and Monarchs,
Furies and Mustangs,
On Interstate 10.

For hours before us,
They pass slowly round us,
But we finally reach them
And wind through the passes:
The Apache Mountains,
The Sierra Diablo
– Once more a new time-zone –
Then down to the banks of
The famed Rio Grande
A dubious ditch between
Parallel mudbanks;
We cross a small bridge and
Drive to the huts of
A Mexican village
Crumbling, lightless,
Which might have been built as a
Flat demonstration
Of the opposite culture
To Interstate 10.

A contrast more violent
Than that between Juarez
And adjacent El Paso
When we see them next morning
– And that's saying something.
But it's hard to remember
As New Mexico takes us,
The tumbleweed rolling,
A roadrunner skimming;
Up through the mountains
To the bright, hard-aligning
Continental divide, and then
Down the long canyons
Narrowly plunging

And soon Arizona
And in Cochise County
A ticket for speeding
On Interstate 10.

We drive on more slowly
On Interstate 10
Till, south of the highway,
The San Xavier Mission.
The towers of whiteness.
The vast baroque cavern,
The colours, the incense.
The columns, the icons,
For a few dozen converts
In mud-and-skin hamlets
Strung along the old trackways
Which long since preceded
Interstate 10.

A second reminder
– And far more impressive –
Of a consciousness different
From that which drove forward
The powerful conception
Of Interstate 10.

Different, impressive –
But in no way refuting
The opposite grandeur,
The endless achievement
Of the makers, the Marthas;
And only a clod would find
Merely material
The pure affirmation
Made manifest for us
As Interstate 10.

We drive through saguaros
Like an alien army
Frozen in stasis
Awaiting the order
To march upon Tucson

But soon they give way to
Thin ocotillos
Equally alien,
Far less intelligent,
At least in appearance,
Four-headed, antennaed …
Forty miles from Phoenix
We come to a junction
And once more make an exit
From Interstate 10.

Long deserts, thin rivers,
Once more looming mountains
Grey-black at the skyline,
Yuma, and over
The dark Colorado
To the last of the time-zones
– California and miles and more
Miles of bare sandhills,
Then Imperial Valley
Once desert, now fruit farms,
Then mountains like rubble,
Like a stone-quarry's dumpings,
Huge, barren boulders,
Pitted and ugly
As we wind ever upwards
And wish we were back upon
Interstate 10.

Then small Indian townships
And green Alpine meadows
A sweet air, a soft grass,
And then San Diego
And on to La Jolla,
The sea and the surfers.
And soon we are into
Los Angeles freeways,
Overhead and beneath us
Stems, columns of concrete,
A huge white acanthus
Taking root in the dry lands,
And at intersections

Troughs, aqueducts swinging
A fluid of drivers;
And just at the moment
We'd almost forgotten
Its very existence
We come to a knot in the
Midst of the city
And find ourselves back upon
Interstate 10.

For ten or twelve miles then
We head again westward
To the waiting Pacific,
Santa Monica's beaches
Broader, more golden
Than the Floridan edge
Of the almost forgotten
Ancient Atlantic …
But marking the finish
Of Interstate 10.

Right then, to the northward:
San Luis Obispo,
The Big Sur and Carmel
Till we're in San Francisco
– One cannot live always
On Interstate 10.

On our mudguards and hubcaps
The sand of the desert,
The grit of the canyons,
The mud of the bayous,
The salt of the ocean,
The dust of the meadows,
The ephemeral strata
Of Interstate 10.

Of Interstate 10
Which lies back behind us
Across a whole country,
A line on a map, a sharp
Brand on the landscape,

White cicatrice running
The length of its body,
A structure of reason,
A realised concept,
A white stamp of wanting,
A symbol of something …
Dawn shakes along it
As it leaves the cool beaches.
Noon beats on its centre
In the great stretching deserts.
Dusk strikes at its ending
Over Avalon eastwards.
And all of its lighting
And all of its distance,
Its curves and conditions
Accumulate into
Long weeks of image:
A section of life, yet
A respite from living.
So it's good to look back – and
Perhaps always will be –
When our single horizon
Our space-time, our world-line,
Our only perspective,
Our sole obligation,
Was journeying westward
On Interstate 10.

from

THE ABOMINATION OF MOAB

OF MOAB

[1979]

for Anthony and Violet Powell

TWO HOUSMAN TORSOS

Among the fragments discovered on the backs of the A. E. Housman man-
uscripts in the Library of Congress, there are two which have long seemed
to me to be fine and characteristic examples of his talent, only requiring
a few lines to be poems in their own right. I have here (in the passages
in square brackets) tried to provide material for making them available
as poems. There is no further pretension. The additions can perhaps be
regarded like the plaster of a restored statue: claiming no more than to
recreate the proportions of its original. I have naturally used John Spar-
row's readings, rather than those which have appeared in book form in the
United States.

This reconstruction differs, in two minor changes suggested by Mr
Sparrow, from its text as it originally appeared in *The Times Literary Sup-
plement.*

1

Stand back, you men and horses,
    You armies, turn and fly;
You rivers, change your courses
    And climb the hills, or I
    Will know the reason why.

Die down, O tempests brewing,
    I will have heaven serene;
Despair, O tides, of doing
    The mischief that you mean,
    For I will stand between.

Death, turn your dart and blunt it,
    Hell, take and break your bow:
[God's wrath, as I confront it,
    Shall fade, for He must know
    I will not have it so.]

2

Some air that swept the Arabian strand
    When the great gulf was calm,
Some wind that waved in morning land
    The plumage of the palm,

[Past Libya's red and Ocean's green
        Has sought our western glades,
To sigh the linden's leaves between
        And lips of Ludlow maids.

And lads, they know not why, turn south
        From toil with scythe or shears,
So soft it spills across the mouth,
        So faint about the ears,]

With odours from the groves of balm
        That far away it fanned,
And whispering of the plumy palm
        It moved in morning land.

HIGH DEFINITION

I hardly think that anyone
Denies the power of passion's sun.
From it all energies derive
And all that makes us look alive.
All bask beneath its potent blaze.
Some seek the essence of the rays.

And then it is disputes arise,
When, supplementing naked eyes,
Upon such heliac studies tense
The poets prepare their instruments:
Spectrometer and thermocouple
In skilled hands growing yet more supple,
Schmidts stretch out their resolving power,
Emulsions track the meson shower …

You'd think all would accept this rule:
The sun is hot, the lens is cool.
So, the corona's streamers pass
Unaltered through the object glass.
But there are some that think its heat
Their instruments should just repeat,
Until beneath a lens of jelly
The red sphere quivers like a belly,

Or, with burnt hands and shrill distress,
They cover up a molten mess.

Avoiding which, some hide the plate
Through all that sunshine, to await
The empty night and aim it far
Upon some distant, private star:
A useful exercise, it's true,
But hardly what they're paid to do.
Besides, such life, in such cold hours,
Deletes the habit of their powers.

You need be no astronomer
To check which observations err.
Nor are theirs brighter now who think
To write in fluorescent ink,
Or match the randomness of flame
By letting symbols act the same.
– Whatever way they fake or fail
Their own skins gleam too red or pale.
The firm hand backed with lazy bronze
Best serves the image orthicons.
The warm heart and the cooler eye
Best grasp the great gifts of the sky.
Poems, recomposing it to one,
Are yet themselves and not their sun.

LITERATURE IN SOHO

Gamboge neon BOOKS AND MAGAZINES
    Is a convention which means
        You'd be lucky to find

Eliot here, or Waugh or Amis – Lawrence
    Yes, but as reassurance
        Only, a kind of a kind

Gesture to the bourgeois, the genteel
    Who otherwise might feel
        Ill at ease, out of sorts,

(As, looking at that pile, they would be if
　　They noticed on top SIR CLIFF-
　　　　ORD'S MISTRESS, which, of course,

Purports to tell the consequences of
　　Chatterley's successful Voronoff
　　　　Operation and Mellors' sad

Midnight accident with the man-trap),
　　But we, under no such handicap,
　　　　Are free to wish that we had

The eight guineas necessary to horn
　　In on all that splendid porn-
　　　　ography – beautifully

Hand-tooled, morocco-glittering books
　　From the break-up, by their looks,
　　　　Of Lord Houghton's library.

VENUS IN INDIA on the upper shelf!
　　– The only work I've read myself
　　　　In the genre from cover to cover, (oh

Surely you're not counting FANNY HILL?);
　　It's Victorian, formal:
　　　　"... *at once*, Captain Devereux!"

An imperious girl completes instructions to
　　The hero, whose substantive portion you
　　　　Will have to take as read.

The whole book's very coarse and healthy fare,
　　Unlike the COLLECTED WORKS, up there,
　　　　Of (though I've only skimmed him) Sade.

"No expert, then? Don't read it much, eh?" Yes,
　　That's so, I'm sorry to confess.
　　　　But if I did voraciously

Absorb it, some would call my standpoint biased.
　　Either way, in fact, in my est-
　　　　imation, they could speciously

Discover an *ad hominem* to pull:
　　Arguing with a liberal
　　　　Attitude is difficult.

But anyhow, wait till we reach the outer
　　Salon. I know enough about a
　　　　Nude photograph to make them belt

Up on that one. – Sade, then: a Bastille
　　For a few years and you too might feel
　　　　A little frantic. A Thousand

Nights, (was it ?), of raving lusts, on paper.
　　Scholars find the dull old raper-
　　　　dreamer most significant,

But *I* reflect, in life he gave some smacks
　　To a girl's bottom; then dropped hot wax
　　　　On it: dubious, no doubt,

But hardly, you'll admit, the very worst
　　Type of sexual holocaust.
　　　　Illustrated? Well, don't pull it out,

For here, back from his phone call, Liberty's
　　Agent – not one of your Garibaldis
　　　　To look at, with those water-blue

Eyes and clipped moustache – in a polite way
　　Leans through the sort of plywood guichet
　　　　Blocking much of the view

Of the back-shelves. *Was it bondage, Sir?* Well, as
　　A matter of fact really I was
　　　　Just browsing. And the answer's no.

Nor do I get much out of this rone-
    oed short story, THE HUMAN PONY,
        Nor RUBBER-GIRDLED FLO.

– I detest what these chaps read; but I defend
    Their right to read it, and
        I won't think it does much in the

Way of harm till I see girls lassoed
    Out in the Charing Cross Road,
        What harm it does, moreover

Being negligible (in the very strictest
    Use of the word) against the best,
        Even, results of scotching:

Eunuchs, weasels, satyrs, zombies, goats
    In a frenzied scrabble for motes
        Might try some beam-watching.

So walk in, or (if a pony-fancier) ride.
    Meet, or beat, or be, your bride.
        Not your taste? But, for example,

Who never wants to more or less tenderly rape
    A girl of the right sweetness and shape?
        And that's a fairly simple

Case. "The obscene does dirt on life". – Come off it!
    Remove that robe, damned minor prophet,
        And get something into your head,

Whether you're sticking solely to the Bible,
    Or are one of the new lot, liable
        To call LADY C sacred:

Life is not so feeble. It can take it.
    It's also much more complicated
        Than you seem to imagine:

Freud, in his "A Child is Being Beaten"
  Says the most fantasy-ridden
    Most hate a cruel real scene:

While Himmler forced himself to be a brute. He
  Relied on a sense of duty.
    – In "duty", power, even fame

(That first infirmity of nasty mind)
  A mask quite like mankind
    Conceals genetic shame

Which twisted, in some long-past generation,
  To this unfavourable mutation
    – Sub-men in other ways, but

As successfully parasitic on
  The genuine social organon
    As the tape-worm on the gut.

And let's recall how keen the Nazis were
  On stamping out erotica
    (Like the Stalinists still),

Which makes it all more than a little hard
  To put the blame on poor old Sade
    – Who thought no State should kill.

As for "mere fantasy", well, would you feel
  Better if it were proved real
    – Or *became* most realistic art

But a bit belatedly, in retrospect
  As it were, through the imitation act
    Of nature (if you can call it that)?

As I'll swear on affidavit, I myself
  Was lectured, when eleven or twelve,
    By one of those clerical beaks

Who, starting, "Now, that part of you between
     Your legs – *you all know what I mean*",
          While explaining how sex

Was sacred and swinish, branded self-abuse
     But had the decency to refuse
          The old terror ploy still

Practiced elsewhere, that it "drove you mad".
     It's high time pornography had
          The same sort of acquittal.

No doubt you can get addicted to a book
     Just as you can (take a look
          At Hirschfeld there) to a fur,

A pair of shoes, a penknife or a bust
     Or even – a more recherché lust –
          To a nickel-plated boiler.

But even the boiler fan, (with his thousand-pound
     Fantasy to drag around
          In case he needed rapture,

Causing difficulties with hotels
     And a great deal else
          – You can recapture

The whole story somewhere in a back file
     Of the *News of the World*) ... Meanwhile
          Even that, and even odder

Things appear a minor nuisance matched
     With the manias getting hatched
          In the mind of a do-gooder.

Mightn't truth be better, in a way,
     Than trying to make humans obey
          The various regulations

Laid down, it seems, for quite a different species?
    Your little daughter? One day she'll see she's
        Welted by your tight-boned notions,

So if you're laurelled with excessive guilt
    Keep it to yourself: once spilt
        Its juice is deadly, dripping

Like Upas. And who – if character defects
    Do cluster around sex –
        Shall 'scape (excuse it) whipping?

Well, apropos, CRUEL NYMPH implies more action
    Than most of this. But for satisfaction
        The stuff's more promising

In the outer room. On which the complaint could be
    Not "fantasy", but "reality".
        But there's no pleasing

Some people. And, hell, what should I do?
    I don't propose to visit a stew
        Just to point some apothegms.

For anyone with eyes in his head and sex
    Somewhere will like the effects
        Of the (still vicarious) harems

On the baize table – MODEL, TITTER, SPICK,
    (Though not the SEXOLOGIC-
        AL JOURNAL, thanks). Oblique

Sex stimuli? Yes – except for beasts, or sailors
    Thronging down gangplanks of whalers
        Years in the Arctic, horned like

Narwhals; (even the real stuff in Soho'll
    Seem pretty good if a blowhole
        Has been your biggest thrill long.)

– I've been waiting to get out here all the time :
        Less to talk about, more to chime
                In about with sigh, snort or song.

But look, what luck, the very SCANTIES 8
        That a bench had to reprobate
                Last year as "absolute filth",

As a result of which seethings the judicial id
        Fined the printer nine hundred quid!
                Oh dear it's dull, but a wealth

Of evidence against – not of course the printer:
        Just nudes and semi-nudes, not a hint, a
                Gesture obscene (if you'll

Pass a certain vulgarity of style),
        Depilated, no single vile
                View of the sexual

Parts – unless the justices now count
        These as starting above the Mount
                Of Venus. And there's FEMME,

Equally blasted, just as innocent. Well
        Instead of the fuss about DHL
                The intellectuals should, damn

It, have defended these good causes first
        – Excuse the moral outburst,
                But perhaps you too have felt

Righteous anger? Well, let's calm our nerves
        With these unsinusoidal curves
                From which, as any gestalt

Psychologist would tell you ... Better now
        Already? I'll take TITTER. How
                Can we leave without a purchase?

Three-and-six? And anyhow the one
        On p. 27 seems to run
                Right through me. Phidias

Would have approved that as a major part
        In appreciating his art
                Even though wanting other

Components. Those who don't like icons of
        Women, for all their talk of "love"
                Don't like women much either,

Relying for their sustenance instead
        Upon vague creatures in their head,
                Simpering, sopping wet.

I don't say, spend long hours in this mart.
        There's not much about Life and Art
                To learn here really. Yet

Unless that bit is adequately mastered
        You remain a contemptible bastard
                Like those censured above.

– Beyond word's fantasy, or vision's pose,
        Through sex and the feminine one knows
                Oneself. Then others. And then love.

VERSE TRANSLATION

Sundance Mine Bar, Palo Alto

Tenebrous cave! I chew my pen in
Undifferentiated half-light:
Right rendezvous to take to transit
Two tongues, two poetries, two cultures.

I search for word, for rhyme, for tempo.
The tiny, graceful student waitress
Soon understands I didn't want ice
In my faintly watered bourbon.

And that's Anglo-Yankee contact!
Well, one does one's bloody best, man.
Hi there, Alex Solzhenitsyn!
– Bourbon? Oh, I'll switch to vodka.

FAR OUT

Lessons of Science Fiction

The poet on Sol III
Too often makes free
Of a jitter of jargon
All structure far gone,
While around it the images
Like a cloud of dim midges
Or blatant blowflies
Imply that the oaf lies.

One might learn this sooner
By a look beyond lunar
Pressure-domes' cluster
Out to the vaster
Sphere of the possible
Where anything's real.

The senses? Of course.
Take the simplest case:
"The grass grows red",
Yes, he meant what he said,
Beaming it straight
From Deneb VIII.
While each colour and flow
Psychedelicists know
Mira Ceti projects
As ion effects,
Quotidian sights
Of those counterflared nights.
Then, the howl of Hine "ice",
The Arrakis spice …
(You don't know what drugs are
Till you've hit Barnard's Star:

Interstellar Narcotics
Says heroin's for hicks.)

Mood? Touch of pure
Terror? Well, sure,
– A psychotransducer.
D'you feel it too, Sir?
Rigellian Thanatics
Go in for such tricks.
So give them a burst.
Sergeant! Your turret first.

Words? Any intense
Disjunction of sense
Is malfunction (routine)
Of the translation machine.
And that's with the simpler
Straight-concept transfer.
When it comes to amaths,
Time-twist telepaths
With Gestalt exchange
Beyond humanoid range,
Both species lock
In semantic shock
With half-crazed equipment;
(As for what that last blip meant ...)

Thus we hardly went all
The way with the mental:
It makes one too dizzy.
– But even the physic-
cal gets exorbitant:
Like a dinosaur-ant,
Like walking sequoias,
Thinking yachts (or destroyers),
Roughly humanoid entities
Who may have eight or ten titties,
And others like starfish,
And some polymorph-ish
By moments or eons,
And even Proteans
Who cause endless trouble

By becoming the double
Of Man at a whim,
Or half-you and half-him...

Well, all such perspectives
Are already correctives,
And we've not yet put forth
Those like nothing on Earth:
Rulls ("Perfect Ones"),
Ingesters of Suns,
Equator-long worms,
Planetoderms,
Mind-mists on Pyria
Like clouds of bacteria,
Dimensions-free Eich
And Riss and their like,
Thinking wave-patterns
(For example, on Saturn's
Ninth moon Iapetus),
And Energy-eaters
In crystalline strains,
And Sessile Brains
Sunk in fluorine baths,
And Ninety-G Laths
On a gas-giant planet
That twenty suns shine at ...

And their arts. One note plays
Through thirty-five days
For the whole of the Horsehead
Nebula Gorsedd;
While the Hectops who live
On Betelgeuse V
Take the Regular Solids
And launch them as bolides
In a dozen or more bits
To admire the orbits.

And their limits of culture
Might even insult your
Social capacity.
A pile of scrap a city

For motile shards?
Suicidal amoeboids
Symbiotically bind
An android hive-mind?
– As for strange kicks,
 All-species sex!
Tentacles, essences
Sting *your* six (or less) senses.

Enough? Well, go back
By the spacewarper track;
Take the images with you
Produced by the mytho-
poeic potential
Of the merely essential;
And ask, back on Earth,
What are images worth?

The extremes of verse?
– Just what occurs
Somewhere, or might.
What's so thrilling to write
Is in principle normal.
What's not are the formal
Virtues of art.
Try *them* for a start.

SOCIALIST REALISM

Barren and burnished
The air clangs angry
Above the political city;
Drums, statues:
The organisation of
Absence of love.

Shops, full or empty,
Are owned by the queues.
The police belong

To the frogmarched suspect.
The censors serve
The poem's love.

Where the social words
Are gnawed like carrion
In a blank, blinding light,
Poetry dies or defies
With vision to prove,
People to love.

POEM ABOUT A POEM ABOUT A POEM

" … often writes not about life but poetry" (a critic)

To ride on horses (or eat buns)
　　Is Life, and may be Song,
(To sink drains, or interpret dreams
Or listen to a baby's screams,)
But not to write a poem, it seems,
　　That isn't Life, it's wrong.

And yet – at least I thought so once,
　　The time I wrote those lines –
To ride a verse is quite a thing,
(Sinking a rhyme, interpreting
The wordless cry, the concept's ring,
　　The field of sensuous signs.)

But let the bays, the greys, the duns
　　Go pounding round the course.
Stallions may sometimes turn vicious,
But art gets so damned meretricious,
Horses are better than wishes:
　　I wish I had a horse.

VISITING POET

A letter to D. J. Enright from the University of Buffalo

Outside, scores of squirrels are scampering round the campus
    As the leaves fall one by one, a smoky gold.
And between the Isotope Room and the Office of Religious Advisers
    I talk of Modern Poetry and Creative Writing.
(For the moment this building copes with the overflow
    Of several what might be called disciplines:
The atomic reactor is still rising by the football field;
    The churches exclude; the Poetry Library is full.)
On the left, three types of Certainty; on the right one agreed Hypothesis;
    With us, something less definite.
"Radioactivity: Keep Out" is not matched by "Modern Poetry: Come In";
    It is right that they find their own way.
The promise of "Consultation" is too strong for Creative Writing;
    We simply say what we can: it may not be much.
I read a short story, leading up to reliance on God:
    It is quite astoundingly bad.
A poem-shaped object is studied, all about fall-out:
    The best you can give it is "poor but honest".
The Isotope Room bears the three-pronged sign of atomic danger;
    The Advisers have a four-pronged cross and a six-pronged star.
But Poetry has no symbols. Creativity must shift for itself.
    Come in!
                Well then, stay out, blast you!

AVANT-GARDE

He thought his singing could postpone disaster:
He spoke the thrilling formulae on love;
His tongue moved frightened down its secret groove
Clever with tiredness, nervously faster

Through fevers and horizons as it tried
To beat the images into a weapon:
Time was not on his side, it could but sharpen
Those blades of choice on which the hero died.

For though he was overwhelming at a moment
The enemy was patient and would hear
Unmoved all brilliant and disastrous song,

And then evoke such immanence of wrong
As could forever with some quiet comment
Squeeze the last note out in a fist of fear.

WASTE LAND PATROL

And though whenever the horizons broke
With a long gleam and flush of distant waters,
Long hours toiling down the stony wadis
Led only to another Bitter Lake,

The salt, corrupted fluids did not bring
– As to those other skeletons bleaching there –
Delirium's green dews or parched despair,
But moistened tongue and throat let him sing.

That energies might flower in his will
Forcing a challenge through his speaking action
To move the double spheres that are and seem,

And enfilade us in some hidden skill
With weapons forged from dark and cruder passion
That poetry mines for deep inside the dream.

BACK TO THE THIRTIES?

Marching Song for a Pilgrimage

Years when the struggle was decent, when the individual,
The intellectual, talked continually like back-seat drivers,
Expressed at conventions in the heart of some stricken country
Their private scratching emendations to poems and Utopia.

When the voice by itself had power, or seemed to have it,
And the semi-political play said solemnly, "Judgement".

The sweet-toothed gourmets feasted on jellies of conscience:
But cartoonists' dummies were nursing their sickening armament.

Even then the decisions were made outside the cell in the tower
Where under the spotlights the Writer spoke to his Soul:
A dialogue he knew perfectly well to be censored,
But with what flattering care, and even a dole.

Does anyone give a damn for him now, or even pretend it,
As power is openly out in its fighting formations
And the experts in self, still making their vows about values,
Pose like ridiculous statues, spattered with blood by the nations?

from

FORAYS

[1979]

In Memory of

B

1964–1978

CASUALTY WARD

On a green plastic stool beside the bed
She sits chatting tensely, smiling
At the white face under the bandaged head.

Thin, not-quite-yellow colournesses twist
Down from the drip-feed bottle
Into his forearm, just above the wrist,

Cold tendons, or tentacles of some malign
Marine organism. And what lies below
The metal hoops tented with white linen?

It was his strength she had most come to resent;
His being, as it seemed to her,
So unshakeable, so non-dependent.

Yet when she'd left him, after those five years
Together, of love then less, he was
(The first time that she'd seen him so) in tears.

He really needed her! She really did fill
The role she'd now rejected as false.
Curiously enough, that made her harder still.

Sullenly, she turned back to rehearse
Old grievances: their row over that
Greek band; the way he used to curse

At having to put up an aunt's friend's daughter;
His shunning picnics. Indignation
Soon boiled as hot as ever, even hotter.

And strengthened so, she finally went,
The suitcase snapped to, the door slammed.
– And, in a month or so, the accident!

Surely in no way suicidal? Still,
Some sort of desperate inattention?
Or even a dull erosion of the will?

And coming as it did so soon afterwards
What does it change? Can it really begin
To stir the hard strata, bring to light old hoards

Of laughing golden masks, their Mycenean
Age of benignly beautiful
Heroes and daughters of goddesses? A bed-pan

Is rushed to some curtained case at the other end
Of the long ward. Life and death
Keep their soft horrors. Her overloaded mind

Turns, unintentioned, to the fresh pile
Of problems in that supposedly freer
New life outside: job, shopping, flat. Meanwhile,

Though, to what high answer can she rise
As lips, once hers, now murmur numbly
"Don't hurt me. But don't help me with kind lies."

I KNOW NOT WHERE

Perhaps the best moment is when,
 His hand at the curve of her back,
 She comes in to their first kiss
  Like the bending of a bow.

– Near the height the old bowmen
 Would draw that fathom of yew
 Too. Lithe, hard, supple.
  Arching, giving … But no,

Wait a minute, how can
 That be right? The string
 Is what the archer pulls
  Towards him, and the bow

Curves the wrong way. Reason,
 The organising hand, eye,
 Must delete the false start.
  – In another sense, though,

It's too late! The greenwood in turn
     Generates woman: Marion.
     Then taut Athene, Penthesileia ...
          Images run on, winds blow

On, blow on, blow on, green
     Leaves scatter till through stripped
     Dryad limbs sight bursts into
          Such stars! The Pleiades, Virgo ...

– In fact as a background scene
     The whole phenomenal
     Universe! But at a strange
          Angle, by a strange glow,

Where even the flicker of an
     Imperfect imagery seems
     Itself a Light of the World
          – An arrow of getting to know.

AURORA: GULF OF ST. LAWRENCE

Already the low shore, the
Outermost context, drowns;
The sensuous receptors
Tune out locality, distance.
From the highest deck even the ship's
Blurred tons settle deeper in darkness.
Till there's only this flattened, stressed
Dome, with its writhings of white.
Merest phenomena:
A single mind and light.

Far from the screaming mirrors
(Sweats, secrets and pursuits
Where a sea licks the sand
And spits into the wind,
Or cadences tinkle and crash
At death or at citron hair ...)
Simplicity burnt white

177

Is all that's here,
But who can ride the light?

Not even colour. Form?
No flame-fronds, no shatter-planes.
– Ions, simplest of particles,
Stream, white and silent
From a radiant in the zenith:
Bursts of non-human art, tight
In the lines of the magnetic
Field … What grasps the light?

Knowledge? But that's the self
Or one of its sharp moods. What
Point in the streaming sky
Can lock it into circuit?
What long, intermitted, slight
Star, in a spray of lightning?
What thread, what edge of light?

From the dark behind the word then,
Cooler, extremer flame
Strikes through all senses and sentience
Till the great deeps focus right,
Matching the mind's tangles
To a rigour of the random light.

IMMORTALITY?

Cow Cow Blues – Bob Zurke at
The piano. I listen at first
– Abstracted, reading – with half an ear.

His solo starts. "Communicate"
– Is that the word? Anyway what's best
Defined as personal, near.

I might have heard him with
The Bobcats. Didn't. The grooves
Still catch him in the act.

"Dying amid the dark"? No myth
Arises. The sensuous moves.
The dead man comes exact.

Is it the "natural noise of"
Good? Solvent, anyhow,
Of the solids of gloom.

Nothing makes me think of love
Or virtue. Life? Joy? now
That's closer, I cross the room,

Turn up the volume slightly,
Close the windows and door,
And he's here. Here!

A simplish air, semi-boogie
Style. "Died 1944".
I'd lost the thread a year

Or two before. Even then
Used to prefer it slow, cool
Not so up-and-about …

Great things are done when men
And music meet – What a roll
Of echoes! Tune them out.

For the great composer or
Writer wins us instead
When attention's complete,

– And it's precisely this more
Gradual, unpremeditated
Entry into his mind, his beat!

I flip the lever to "Repeat".

TO BE A PILGRIM

We got away – for just two nights.
She'd booked us in at some hotel
Over in the Isle of Wight's
Western corner. Friends spoke well

Of it. The name just slipped me by
And only half-way up the drive
A revelation came, a cry,
"Farringford – Tennyson's old dive!"

Beautiful! Unchanged in mood.
The swimming pool discreetly far.
The kitchens (for quite decent food)
Hidden by firs. Thank God, a bar.

Beneath the boughs, the green-gold leaves
Of this most grand of whatsit trees
He wrote – that is, if one believes
Old Robert Graves – of drunk Chinese.

And Garibaldi came! – A plaque
Below a tall and swaying pine;
(And in the modern Visitors' Book
Just you and me and Phil. E. Stein).

The track he pushed his wife up, on
The downs' low edge, to see the sea.
– Could a Swiss or Paraguayan
Dream of writing poetry?

But now how piercingly my charmer
Yells! Above her furious gasps
I hear among the furze the murmur
Of innumerable wasps.

"You see, there's been no winter snow.
We gets them thick in such a year."
Did he get stung much? Well, if so,
His closest to the sure-thrust spear.

Our room. I gaze at sheaf and stack
While she's proceeding to anoint
The sting with sal ammoniac;
"This really is a pleasant joint!"

A notice opposite the bar:
The Tennyson and TV Room
– His cloak, his stick, some books. And – ah! –
Grandstand bright through Gothic gloom.

Those books though – classic, pastoral –
That taught his verse its solemn stride.
My head still ringing with the call
Of Hesiod, we go outside.

"Hera! Pylos' teeming great
Herds!" Unmoved the Jerseys munch.
"Kore! Maiden! If …" Too late.
The old words fail. It's time for lunch.

And then, why don't we drive across
To seek through scents of salt and rose
The chine-hid church where Swinburne was –
– Baptised? buried? – One of those.

ON THAT ISLAND

The etched Saronic's hardest blue
Lies back through miles of light.
The years' long lenses focus true
And on the heat-blanched height
The girl I see in the mind's eye
Trembles with actuality.

That lime-green thicket lifts again
Two pillars of bruised stone,
Black stubs of Aphrodite's fane,
Perspective of our own
Course through cracked arch, crushed architrave,
A sequence that includes the grave.

Intensities of light and love,
So urgent to revoke
The weed and thorn, the fading of
The white acanthus, choke
In that rank undergrowth, regret,
Clawed to life's stinging limits. – Yet

Goddess, or goddesses, you name
Them so to represent
The numen standing outside time;
Pure vision, abstract scent
Sear off the patina of pain,
Strike flesh and marble white again.

In which continuum the girl
Who climbs the slate-pink stair,
The lemon-trees behind her, all
That sea-wind in her hair,
Purely immediate, yet shakes free
The blind blue of eternity.

THE POET'S MORNING

Bleary with bed, the bloody fool's
First act's to fall between two stools.

His breakfast next, as things conspire,
Drops between frying-pan and fire.

And then to work, his every squib dis-
gusting Scylla or Charybdis.

Far better if he'd stayed asleep,
Betwixt the devil and the deep.

LATER

We asked him, did he really want her back.
This seemed to take him very much aback.
He spoke of her belled hair

Tawny against the hayfield,
Behind her voice the meadowlarks;
How by dolmen and fir
– Druid white, dryad green –
She assembled the phenomena
And became their rune.

The incurvations of her breasts, her back!
That sweet beast, each contributing a back,
Played on the silken sward
Through those summer nights
Never quite sleeping
As hounds belled, hinds leapt
Through life-turfed, legend-treed
Glades, in that chiaroscuro
Of dream that is deed.

And so he'd felt it when they married, back
In '68 – a hunch he had to back
With all his life. A great chord
Held, right through the million
Words, the thousand kisses,
Intricate veining of
Happiness and unhappiness,
Ephemerals to dip, gleam,
Fireflies circling
A strength, a theme:

– The loyalties of love, when back to back
They stood against the world. "Stabbed in the back"?
– He shrugged. At any rate
Cords of vision cut,
Ice-sharp, unexpected:
Collapse of green landscape
Under a doltish horror.
After the short shock
Stale erosions rotted
The sheared face of rock.

He knew the stream of time would not turn back
Where pike devour the teeming stickleback
In a white frenzy. Till even

The cruel clarities may
Grow gross, thick, (he made
A grimace); the sharp waters
Spill over sour roots,
Slump to oils of marsh,
Slow, confident rats.

And then, how had he tried to get her back?
– The worst ways with a woman, falling back
On pleas, argument,
As the fire guttered
In wet infirm wood,
Tears, everything known
As useless (another shrug).
Why? – A profounder skill
Herding the hurts' panic.
To his real will?

The load of loneliness upon his back!
Surely he did, would always, want her back?
But the cramped myth, memory …
Green days in the high meadows,
Mists, twists of icy passes,
Now one far, glittering range;
And in the foreground shown,
Galatea's opposite,
A girl turned to stone.

His lame conclusion, then: if she turned back
To what she was, of course he'd want her back.

TRY AGAIN

Things are terrible!
    Well, yes.
And the poem doesn't state
Or celebrate
Or give your own relation to
    The mess?

But perhaps its job is just
    To hint.
You may think, son,
Those are cries of passion,
But they rather look to me
    Like print.

THE RUINS OF CARTHAGE

Bou Kornine, the split hill,
Stands braced to the long frame
Of a parabolic bay,
And abstract ichors spill
From the bowl of a blue day
Into this bone-dry tomb.

A city dead in our minds,
Humps of disorganised wall,
Red striations of arch,
No livelier than the street-signs,
Place Hamilcar, Rue Baal:
The black butt of that torch.

No substance to its past:
Flickers of dead phosphorus
In delusion of deeps. Hanno,
A crucified sea-beast;
Augustine's cauldron seethes;
But the sharp umbra slams to.

Old images pulverised
By an inarticulate thunder:
To the blare of a blank sun
The desert numen burst,
And dry huts huddled under
The dust of Kairouan.

Night. No sound in the court
But the whine of the log fire,
No sight but the desert words
Clamped on a cut sky:

Algol, Achernar, Fomalhaut.
And beneath us, disorder of shards.

Like death itself. A black screen,
An impenetrability, rife
With brute abstraction. – Or else
Discarnate: she that is queen
Of Tunis, she that dwells
Ten leagues beyond man's life.

747

(London–Chicago)

After the horrors of Heathrow
A calmness settles in.
A window seat, an ambient glow,
A tonic-weakened gin.

The pale-grey wings, the pale-blue sky,
The tiny sun's sharp shine,
The engines' drone, or rather sigh;
A single calm design.

Those great wings flex to altering air.
Ten thousand feet below
We watch the endless miles of glare,
Like slightly lumpy dough.

Below that white all's grey and grim,
The wrong side of the sky.
Reality's down in that dim
Old formicary? Why?

What though through years, the same old way,
That world spins on its hub?
The mayfly's simple summer day
Beats lifetimes as a grub!

A geologic fault, this flight:
Those debts, that former wife,

Make some moraine down out of sight,
Old debris of a life.

(Only one figure, far and clear
Looks upward from that trough
A face still visible from here
– The girl who saw him off.)

The huge machine's apart, alone.
The yielding hours go by.
We form a culture of our own
Inhabiting the sky.

Too short? Yet every art replies,
Preferring for its praise
To Egypt's smouldering centuries
The brief Athenian blaze ...

That flame-point sun, a blue-set jewel,
Blazed blurredly as it went.
Our arguments run out of fuel.
We dip for our descent.

We drift down from pure white and blue
To what awaits us there
In customs shed and passport queue
– The horrors of O'Hare.

THE SACRED POOL, DZIBILCHALTUN

The rhetoric of love; some little lake
Planed by the evening ...
The image is a graft that doesn't take.

We slip into cool clarities, lie surfaced
Where, fifty metres down,
The bones lay late of virgins sacrificed

(Gold inlay long since broken through the slim
Wrists) to the Rain God.
It's raining now. Poor context for a swim.

SUNDOWNER

Gin and not much tonic is among
The moment's contents, certainly;
Also the implied relaxation
Specially welcome after his long

Trouble. But the sunset's passed
And it's that English indeterminate
Half-light, quarter-light. On the balcony
He sits, sips, sips again, his eyes fast

On high trees that edge the park, curving away
West, dark-muffled but still sensed
As green; engrailed, incredibly intricate,
Yet a long running unity against the stray

Faintly luminous sky – itself no
Monochrome, but just moisture-mottled
To hardly perceptible shifts of shade:
Smoke-blues and darker. The senses' slow

Recovery! Though all was abstract, yet
His body had felt lately as though
Suffering one great internal bruise.
Smoke from his Schimmelpenninck Duet

Spills upwards, spreading, to much the same
Grey-blue, then blue-grey, as the high sky.
From the open window a buzz-mute trumpet
Riffs softly affirmative. On his bare forearm,

Hard to say whether warming or cooling
It, a slightest movement of air burrs.
In fine, all the sensuous – unstressed,
Unhurried – is a calm tide piling

Up slowly in a closed cove. And as (back
Behind the still sharpening silhouette
Of fretted foliage) that peaceable
Sky, though not yet a blind black,

Turns now the opposite of iridescent,
Absorbing, not emitting, light,
He doesn't feel like a ruined man.
So perhaps he isn't.

THE PHASES OF VENUS

Defences a weak man may set
Against reality include
Ability to quite forget
A lost love in the nude.

A scorched earth policy? – you're wrong.
Not fire but salt: a waste terrain
Scarred sterile by such frantic prongs
That no seed sprouts again.

Yet, till that peach-gold truly blurs,
The marble index of a mind
May file such fruit, till it recurs,
In a hard Paphian rind.

Too far abstracted, stone to star,
Mere white transcendence eased our eyes;
Till now, hot poisoned pressures char
That last love from the skies.

APPALACHIAN CONVALESCENCE

Eastward, etched in purple by a sun
Invisible behind us, the Great Smokies
Loom clear through a transcendent unconcern.

In this valley nothing strong, no love,
No despair, no stabbing memory even,
Has had me. And yet, such a negative

Is false as saying that we do not see
The almost fallen sun behind this hillside
While we stare east through its fecundity.

All passion spent? No passions even start.
Yet here tranquillity's an active radiance,
The slow pulse strong from the unbroken heart.

So fade along the westering Tennessee
Light of all conscious feeling! Let the night-time
Confirm, as once it clawed, a mind made free.

IN NO TIME

    Wednesday July the 26th
Nineteen seventy-two,
Which mayn't mean much to you,
Was – at least on a Buddhist view
    My dearest, deepest day.

    Nothing whatever happened.
I didn't even breathe
– Literally! The whole seethe
Of love, hate, thought, faith
    In world or woman wasn't.

    We flew at mid-Pacific
In a flick – not even that:
No skip of the heartbeat
Or drop of the jet's note –
    From 25th to 27th.

    M 31 in Andromeda,
Northward blur of light
– The limit of naked sight
Declared distance right:
    But duration's by days!

    Metaphysic? conceit?
Then why the odd feeling
Of the missed, conceived thing,
An absurd soft sting?
    Ten thousand metres below

The International Date Line
Lay, abstract, upon a smooth-
looking, starlit wraith
Of a sea. Faintest froth
    Outlined unnaturally

    Regular walls – artefact
Of polyps, not thought,
Each, though, a seeming fort
Strung silent in support
    On the Tongan approaches …

    Well, what (which I've not done)
Of those who gain a day
Going the other way
With the same date twice? Do they,
    Would I, come to that,

    "Have my time over again"
At least that once? Correct
Retrieved regret, perfect
A little some lapsed act
    Of Nandi or Suva

    In Papeete? But that's a mere
Thought and I yet feel
As in a crazed way real
My lost unwasted shell
    With whorls of nothing.

    Days after one in the Nineteen-
blanks (or Twenty-blanks if I last
A little longer than most)
Will have the same taste
    Perhaps: sweet or insipid?

    What coronals of answers! …
As for that Wednesday the rest
Of you had but I missed
– Was mine really the best?
    We arrive at ourselves.

TECHNIQUE

To make this live flesh live,
Connect its irrelevant charms
To a central control, unravel
The tangle of angelic, magnetic
Shreds of metal, collect in your arms

With subtle fingers settle
Property and duty and position,
Tune the smoothly jointed segments
Into a firmness and a synthesis,
A whole precision.

And when she's warmly turning
Is the movement stiff and rigid
As the last? Or is there now
Delight and satisfaction? And if so,
Because of which new gadget?

GET LOST, GULAG ARCHIPELAGO!

> "The present Soviet generation is not obsessed with the errors of
> the past. It looks to the future ..."

For years those dreary old complaints
That we'd unfairly snuffed the lives
(We've never claimed we're plaster saints)
Of husbands, brothers, sisters, wives.

Thank God for the present lot!
They won't act up like those others.
After all, we only shot
Their fathers, uncles, aunts and mothers.

THEN AND THERE

When every block of every street
In Soho served one as a beat
Most tarts were awful. Still, there were

A nereid up on Soho Square,
An empress by the Caves de France …
But she who really took one's glance
Moved in the semblance of a bride
Along the sunlit stretch outside
That restaurant opposite St Anne's
(As if that's where they'd called her banns).
Not overplayed – just lacy-bodiced,
Wisp-veiled, white-nosegayed, modest …
    It's many years now since the nation's
Elected banned such decorations
To London – used their solemn powers
To screen from sight those fragile flowers.
High windows now may blur a face,
Illuminated bell-pushes
With "Marianne" "Marlene" and "Merle"
Obliquely offer some strange girl;
Advertisements pinned up, past counting,
"Beautiful butterfly: needs mounting",
"Wendy welcomes old and new
Friends at No. 32",
"Model", "Governess", "Masseuse" …
Such verbal emblems fade, while hers
Unspoken, rosy, pale – the Spring's
Bright sign – endures.
    Her image rings
With greater certainty of tone
Than girls' I've actually known,
Whose well-grasped lineaments disperse
Into that misty universe
Where memory, conception, form
Swirl thickly in too blurred a swarm.
    Recalled not even once a year
Why does her image curve so clear?
I never spoke to her, let alone
Went further. In fact, what "went on"
In this subliminal transmission
For me was vision, only vision.
What does it mean? I hardly know.
I think it rather goes to show.

TRANSATLANTIC, OLD STYLE

From a bar in the underbelly of the great
Machine, see through window's glaze and cloud
The immense Atlantic's dullest blue
(In a small, clear storm's rage
Barely perceptible at this height
And unheard what must there be loud)
Which divides and unites the two
Manifestations of our life and language.

The smooth horizon soon lets slip
Towards us cool Newfoundland
Dark beneath billowing nimbus, till
Pine-forest, lake and lake-like swamp
Surround the dawn as we dip
Through what is fresh – because beyond
That practised evocation's skill –
To Gander's airfield's breakfast, fuel and damp.

But over Cape Cod again emerge
The images that root in our lives
Like those green pine in their island. Yet
Thoreau, bob-whites, that salt talk
Are far enough from Europe's rage
To refresh our eyes and beliefs
As over earth's curve the sunset
Falls, and the plane sinks, into green New York.

HERALDRY

for Anthony Powell

Alone, or at any rate cornered in his heart
Like most of us, by a hot breath of error,
He pushes roots into a nourishing past
To find in depths of that receding mirror
What cannot fade or tremble
A symbol
Like some rare moment of unbitter art.

For he takes talisman against the storms
Not from the total history's stinking press;
But phrased in long-forgotten vanity
The timeless motto or, tricked in clear MS,
Quarterly argent and sable
A label
Gules: which are certainties, platonic Forms,

In what way differing from theirs who will
Hatchment of theory on the centuries,
Breeding not harmless talbot, wyvern, but
Beasts of abstraction? – From a field that lies
Goutté de sang in real
Blood, not enamel,
Hobbyists of dogma turn on us, and kill

A VISIT TO THE EVANS COUNTRY

(Rondeau for Kingsley Amis)

"Just one sip," cooed Evans. What he'd spent on
A bottle of crème-de-menthe at The Old Ship
Was worth it perhaps? "How old are you?", he went on.
"Sixteen." Thank Christ, this time no risk of Penton-
ville (an anxious point to bastards bent on
The work of Dai). Gwen let the green dew slip
Over the red rose of her lower lip,
And Evans buzzed in like a bee intent on
          Just one sip.

"No, that's your fourth, not fifth." Her left breast leant on
His shoulder as he moved to shift his grip.
"It's dark now." The sky gleamed, a pewter tent on
Rhydd beach ... But, Christ, he'd laid the sentiment on
Sufficient so it wouldn't sound too flip:
          "Just unzip."

195

NOTES FOR A WEATHER POEM

1

Italy: so bright
The shadows seem
Under the clear-cut
Carbon-arcs of night
And the blue lies so deep
That it imitates that sleep.

But out at sea the wind
Begins; across the mind
The blue-white broken seas
And the writhing headland trees
Throw smells of salt and pine:
A song like a sharpish wine.

2

Or Cambridgeshire, in the soft month:
Imprecision of the falling dark,
The overlap of colour, intermingling
Movement of leaf and wind;
A fading chime of undogmatic bells
On a breeze that smooths the fern and strokes the cheek …
– The autumnal riches that so often melt
The structure of the English poem:
Let it instead confirm the heart,
Its heavy and historic loot
Ballast the ship in the green
Swell of the absolute.

3

December: what landscape's tone
Rings clear when light is gone?
North and South accept the voice
Even of their winter ice.
The cold fen under the fog,
The alp-snow lashing Lombardy,

In the condensed or blown breath
Speak of pain but not death.

AFTER WRITING AN OBITUARY

Of course he's here. It's just his sort of party.
I think I hear him in the other room.
I'll wait until I've crawled clear of his doom.

Paralysed by a spider, wrapped in web-silk
Spun to contain the stung, the nearly dead,
His life seems just some clenching in my head,

A closed compaction to the sort of essay
About the famous dead one had to write
When one was still an undergraduate

– In his case well deserved: the poise, the spacing.
Fame now? Mine were no more than instant glyphs
Of death-called lightning, not the deep-carved cliffs

With their inscriptions rich in fuller praises
From integrating centuries – and yet in a
Fulgurous flash one stamps the retina!

"To no one shall we sell, deny" – our Magna
Carta runs : and then it adds *"delay*
Justice." Must he, beyond his dying day

Find court after court, appeal after appeal ?
Each century may overturn the rest.
– To hell with them! My verdict stands as best.

Another, older friend, (of cooler talent),
Once told me that he didn't in the least
Mind dying. Even lives that missed their feast

– Made do on skimpy rations of work, women,
Laughter, travel, suffering, drink – unload
In a half-reluctant "one more for the road …"

With him? One hardly knows. His writings conjure
Old melancholies, shaded to acceptance
With such a power as may refute their sense.

To grasp him fully? We commune in demotic.
After such flickering talk I have to try
To find the idiom of eternity.

He walks toward us with a mug of Irish.
A dead man walking? Well, but aren't we all?
My typewriter's not killed him past recall.

" – I never read such balls as Balbus' latest.
I'm a bit pissed … Christ, look! Those tits, that bum!"
– The nail of some colossal statue's thumb?

1944 AND AFTER

Pinned down in the little valley – in its way
A trap, or would be if they had the strength.
Not very dangerous, with a little care.
Still, a long day
Pressed into hollows in the rocky, bare
Untrenchable soil, without food or drink
Or anything much to think
About; damp, coldish, shiny air …
Until, near dusk, at length
A few guns, manhandled across the bridgeless
Black ravine, suppress
The enemy strong-points, in a thundering glare.

Later, lost love pinned him down for years
But the relief came up at last – again
Covered the breakthrough to the warm, wide plain.

Life itself, some say, is just such waiting
Hemmed in a closed cirque of one's own creating
As cramped decade after decade runs
Towards the dusk. – But where are the guns?

TWO AT LAKE TENAYA

Not far below the ten thousand foot
Tioga Pass – the Sierra's highest – on rock
And lake the light lies delicate.

Under intricacy of pine-needles and
Simplicity of darkening green shadow
We come out on to the white sand,

See grey-white of that planed rock-face
Slip without stress into the concentrated
Blue flame of the fluent surface,

Under pale, infinitely recessive
Blues of the sky. Fine air lets clarity
Range free, far. And yet if

You inhale pure oxygen
Colours around you brighten instantly, so
Shouldn't the lack of it deaden?

But the faintest shadings come through
More accurate here, no less subtle, (white
In everything, even that full blue).

Like the old ascetics, we gain
Attenuation's own intensity – rich
Vision in the scanted brain.

She's naturally the focus. Her eyes
So matching the lake's hot blue, contrasting so
With the faint blue of the skies.

But more – behind clear gaze, firm bone,
Fresh candours hold that serious face serene
In the light's trueness of tone.

So if you've brought love to the High
Sierra, don't let it sink to scenes below
The edge of the sky, the edge of the eye,

As you ride down from Lake Tenaya
Quickened beyond image, yet forever infused in
A white bowl half-filled with blue fire.

from

NEW AND
COLLECTED POEMS
[1988]

for Liddie

HALEMAUMAU FIREPIT

We scramble down sliding ashes
To a Lost World sunk under high grey-black
Bluffs: Kilauea caldera's hot
Mile on mile of lump-lava, scab-rock,
Satin-black or cinder-black
Around green sulphur-patches;
Sharp crumblings underfoot,
Sulphurous, silicate.
We cough, in the grey light,
At jetting steam, sputtering smoke,
Puffs like spurting matches.

Till we reach, by its Western side,
This broad near-circle, clear-cut,
And gaze down thousand foot
Blacker cliffs, at the slow writhe
Of fire-fluid. Red, red, red,
With blackness just turning to red,
Solids just starting to seethe:
A hump in the huge world-magma mass
Here breaking the surface, blood through skin.

We stand closer, her hand in mine.

The faint love-glow lapping the two of us
May not seem to compete
With the gross heat from the world's gut.
– How thin the crust over raving
Miles of flame! And yet this mere film
Of solid has saved, is saving ...

We still stand in the high realm.

And what's between us and that which opens
Everywhere, daily: the firepit
Of lies and terror – the flame-weapons,
The blood-ideologies? What but

Those small defences she and I
– Like others – may yet prove enough:
Love and sanity,
Sanity and love.

PORLOCK: ONE IN FOUR

Going up the hill in bottom gear
The engine labours, a rising scream,
Growing insupportable, like fear

Blind, staggering at an extreme
Cliff-edge of subhuman singing

So strange at last is this
Clatter of levers bringing
Easier breathing, loosened emphasis.

HIGH

The sun cried in the air, bleeding and blonde,
Its heavy assurances of eclipse.
But still the Sybil did not move her lips.
We felt the mountains ravening around
Us, occasion viciously sought
For avalanche. Far from the valley's fond
Babel of purple insolence we found
Astringent, unifying ways of thought.
We crossed the pass before the mad girl spoke
– An incomprehensible tentacle of speech,
A murmur from heart's mild and furtive convulsions,
Charring image to ash in the iris of each
Of us. Ice clamped the pools. The clouds awoke.
And the answering current flickered in our brains.

HERE'S HOW

From a passenger chopper on
The Santa Catalina run
Suddenly the Englishman

Sees, far below, the *Queen
Mary*, celled in her own
Closed concrete lagoon.

Was it thirteen years back
He trod, aft of that red-black
Funnel, down deck after deck

Of Tourist cabins to surprise:
A girl waiting, champagne, goodbyes
Drunk from two tooth-glasses? …

Now it's Pacific, the water.
Above, blades thrash and clatter.
Beside him the seat-belt holds her

Who has held him, whom he has held.
This too is a parting. They head
– With much that may stay unsaid –

To this island, to Avalon,
Close, alone, an afternoon
Before that London plane.

In between, God knows what. Well
Flats, deaths, jobs, travel,
A marriage and its debacle,

A basset-hound's whole lifetime,
A million words to his name.
Then, kindness waved from

The gangplank. Now, landing steps,
And out to a white-wood township's
Bay-circling steep slopes

Till, by eucalyptus at
The sea's edge they hear – 't 't –
The tiny, sweet-toned ratchet

As humming-birds sparkle, soar
Green up sun-excited air;
Hand in hand gaze down clear

Water round tall sea-trees, which
Tingles with the golden flash
Of quick Garibaldi fish.

Green bubbles in gold air, then
Gold bubbles in sea's green:
A world of champagne

In a bay-sized goblet
– To celebrate what?
Love and regret.

ON AN X-RAY PHOTOGRAPH OF THE POET'S SKULL

1

Strangely light, a filigree
Layered with what must be
Pale lamination.
A brain capacity more
Than appears through flesh and hair;
Not too weak a chin.

Not like the preconceived
Symmetrically curved
Symbol – solid, white.
A gibber like an ape's.
That the dead seem dopes
Sometimes, looks right.

2

Strange, first of all, like myth: a

Set piece, stylised portrait
Of some minor being of legend,
Blur-masked for what must be the
– As yet –
Not too appalling cold of Elfland.

3

A "gibber"? No, more like a grin
To outface the spot we're in.
The Jolly Roger! All the fun
Of a dance to the music of
Horror rather than love.
Let the full-toothed rictus prove

We still have time to find the
Rhythm, the accepting gaiety.
But you'd need, to hold that smile,
Hard training. So – not for a while.

4

Above all, how strange the bone-being looks!
One's seen (in Robert Heinlein's books
For example) the notion of the alien "sleeper"
In the human body, ready to take over.

– These miscalculated. Clearly the plan
Would be to let the fleshy form of man
Disintegrate, when the calcite android
Could emerge, to be reactivated.

In the graves, reserves to master Earth
Lay, confident in their own human's death;
But the force-patterns to replace muscles failed
In the rare stress of our magnetic field.

In their vigil, immobilised, they lie
To greet the great ships darkening the sky.
But Altair V, the signal unsent,
Has long since written off the whole contingent.

5

An object like a rock or rose ?
– Coolness we can't achieve!
But let's be better braced than those
Whose skull is on their sleeve.

The wild beasts can't be choosers
And innocently unknow;
It's these obsessed life-losers
That spoil their own show:

Animal again, snarling, foaming – less
Painful, perhaps, if they'd given a miss
To consciousness, or self-consciousness.

Stuck on their skulls, pity each twisted feature
– The bitten lips of the dishuman creature
Crazed with the bad news from the future.

6

The more one looks
The harder it grows:
The grip of its teeth,
The hypnotic blaze
Of its empty orbits.

Behind it a land
Grows coldly visible,
Silicon-scabbed,
With fumaroles drooling
A sulphurous smoke.

Outside, the green
Vitalities sway,
Sentience flies
Or swims the bright streams ...

But under this gaze,
In a ponderous light
The abstractions freeze.

    7

A shell of mind? But
The black dog hunts bones. Cave canem!
– The backbone connected to the neckbone,
The neckbone connected to the skullbone
And the skullbone connected to – what?
– The *summum bonum*?
Ah, if that were known.

    8

It brings too much fantasy
And too much reality!
Everything about it seems quite
Strange, or totally trite.
For once not whistling in the dark (the blinding
Light of knowledge or ignorance made complete),
I hold a brief and probing sample
Of this region with its alien microclimate:
Chart or silhouette of a nice simple
Memento mori. – But who needs reminding?

AS IT COMES

I stand in this universe
Seeking completenesses
Without great success.

I meet pretty feminists.
I hear strange erotic boasts;
I see (sometimes) breasts.

But to co-ordinate
Such into group or set
Passes my wit.

And that's only sex! Add
All the odd, myriad
Cosmic bits – and you'd

Surely agree with me:
Watch out for *category*!
Feeling that can't be

Fully "conceptualized"
Of sun, poem (OK, breast!),
Tends to be best.

– The trouble with theory
Is that you're hungry
A half-hour later.

One thingburger, Waiter!

ONE WAY TO LOOK AT IT

The huge aches they may pant beneath
Should not make poets grind their teeth,
Nor herd into the structured line
The panics of the rooting swine.
Terror and filth subsumed in verse
Must not fall back as shriek or curse:
Unvital and discharging rant,
The lazy egoism of cant.

The cipher of a broken speech
Leaves much beyond the infant's reach,
For language of the fullest themes
Is not disrupted into screams.
– The Greeks excluding from the stage
The squalid orgasms of that rage,
The essence of the bloody hand
Struck generalized, yet still more grand.

Women, knowledge, landscape, art
Make the good elations start.

With these for power the verse may thrust
Strength on the politics of lust;
View with, not blindness but contempt,
The stinking bilges of the dreamt;
Till, all proportions manifest,
All high potentials starred and stressed,
Consummately impersonal
Life clangs through art, one lambent bell.

IN MEMORY

The last notes of a unique
Voice ran by the dusked fir
Five years all but a week
Ago. Bones of the inner ear

Bore music and meaning (those two
Alleged contraries, alleged
Complements), sieved through
No metaphored, imaged

Confusion, but clear as that cool
Vista, full, as the globed cloud,
Particular as one pine-needle.
– Yet vocalization had

Imposed on the molecules
Of air between a profound
Interweaving pulse
Complex almost beyond

Wave-analysis. And how
(Framed in also appropriate
Elegiac sundown and winged bough)
Could such turn absolute

Those never-again-to-be-met
Harmonies of heart, cries
Of completion, where the straight
Fir frames now emptiness?

BREATHINGS

Caught in the long wind, draperies
Are lifted, white, round longings. The girl cries,

"Realize me, wind! Take me, Time! Pour!"
Oh how thirsty, in that sweet thirst for

– What? For life? No, rather a folding of
Every leaf, every petal, all love

In the unephemeral, the divine. Wind
Of the warm discontent ... But that other kind,

Frosty, through rasped chiton, envenomed blouse,
Sets in. Sour women fall from the boughs.

A MATTER OF DEGREE

The ice-thick blasts assault and shock.
We inch – exhausted, cold –
Up so refractory a rock
Our pitons scarcely hold.

The black North Face falls from us sheer
Into the mists below;
With one long overhang to clear
To reach the rich plateau.

Till, sprawled where mind and body break
Exhaustion's last extreme,
We gaze down where, across the lake,
The gold pavilions gleam.

Small figures stroll about that isle,
Snug sheepskin on their back:
Travellers of another style
Who took the southern track,

Borne on those mules they've loosed at last
To crop the clovered slope,

Up paths hacked from the gorge-side karst,
Plank bridges hung from rope.

Mere tourists! How they'll beam and boast
About their breathless climb.
But what's our profit, who have faced
Forced draughts of the sublime?

– Tempered to take such last lone treks
As somewhere lie ahead,
We tramp down, bowed beneath our packs,
To food and bath and bed.

IN MEMORY OF LIONEL TRILLING

What weaker disciplines shall bind
What lesser doctors now protect,
The sweetness of the intellect,
The honey of the hive of mind?

A GEORGIA GRADUATION

for Helen

Four hundred boys and girls – the girls in white
Gowns and mortar boards, a charming sight.
My stepdaughter sways up to take her scroll.
The valedictorian's speech now: from her lips
The innocent clichés fall
In a hushed hall.

Later, by blossomless dogwood, high cypress,
We sit heavy with green darkness
Where fireflies' intermittent, unflickering gold,
Silent as ourselves, sways and dips,
Cool innocence taking hold
Of a hushed world.

CLICHÉS

He said "You mean the world to me."
    She asked "Do you include
The fruit and corn, the soil and sea
And Ceres and Persephone
And even old grandmother Gê
    And all her endless brood

Of all the living things that be:
    – The elephant and deer,
Seal and beaver, ant and bee,
And dog and cat, and louse and flea ...
But don't let's take an inventory
    Of all the biosphere!

– The ice that's coldly clenched (and she
    Shuddered) about the Pole,
The storm that shreds up ship and tree,
The fires that fling the magma free,
The strata grinding into scree,
    The reeking oil and coal?

'World' in the broader sense? We see
    The endless parsecs fall
Through cosmic cloud and galaxy
– But let's forget totality
Because, compared with you and me,
    It hardly counts at all."

WALK THAT WAY

"To flatter beauty's ignorant ear"
Was how Yeats thought he and Catullus were
    Whipped up to the wild verses.

But now we flatter ignorant eyes
Of a deafer lot whose microscope plies
    Through the prints of the poetry presses.

Beauty at least was its own entree
To the art – a sort of complimentary
    Ticket to the mind's high places.

While in their Departments, trying to explain,
They deconstruct the love and the pain
    Into some sodding great thesis.

Beauties can't, but then nor can dons
Decide what's to be more lasting than bronze:
    And there's not much bronze around these days.

ON THE STREETS

Four or five blocks out of the Tenderloin
I see under neon-fizz as I pay my taxi
A tart, you'd say around seventeen, sixteen,
Blonde, black-hosed, one leg outstretched to lean
Against a lamp-post – a Forties movie scene.
    She looks both sexy and unsexy.

To me, that is. Externals! But how to judge
What exists, what feels, behind this epi-
sode from La Ronde? Across the grey sound-stage
Over a presentation of strobed cleavage
Slit skirt, lip-rouge, our eyes briefly engage.
    And she looks neither happy nor unhappy.

PAUL VALÉRY'S "GENOA NIGHT"

(October 4/5, 1892)

At first just stormwaters pouring
Down cobbles of a canted town
To the glaucous heave of the sea.
Prone on the bed he feels faintly
Distant flicker of lightning,
Subliminal thunder-purr.

His life has passed through a swarm
Of demoralizings – as (he'd say)
Earth runs through the Leonids:
The lost girl, the lost aims.
Reasons for not publishing:
Pride, fatigue, foul galleys,
Twisted to one skein.
Non-completion of self.
Egoism? The end of egoism?
The brute powers close in.

2

He's weak when the sky slams
Down, blinding, reverberant,
And the whole world, through the whole night,
Unspeakably blares and blazes:
Icy purities of lightning,
Hot savageries of thunder.
A huge inexpressiveness.
He is numb. He is nothing:
Unlanguaged, unminded.
Clenched teeth, arched spine,
Crouched hour after hour.
It blasts through closed eyelids.

Nagaikas of lightning
Lash at a bared heart.
White-hot pincers of lightning
Pluck at a raw conscience.
Long hoes of lightning
Break up the clods of thought.
And thunder – a huge blind golem
Whose mindless blows thud down
Missing his essence by inches:
His will pounded to powder,
Mind rasped in a hyperaesthesia,
Senses torn from the self …

Gored on tines of lightning,
Stunned or not, a concentration.

The beams of the sky break
And the world crushes his chest.

3

A hard mind to crack ...
But silenced for ten years now
He'll seek through intellection
Poetry devoid of ideas:
Uneveness the worst evil,
Chance accomplishing everything.

"At each terrible moment of history
Some man sits in a corner
Stringing beads": in Attila's time,
Or Genseric's, or our own,
In a corner chewing hexameters ...

Cramped extremes of reason:
Arithmetica universalis.
But beyond rigour – charm.

A cosmos all compulsion?
But the mind needs for image
Materialities: salt, rose ...
The storm slowly unravels.
Faint sunrise streams westwards.
And now he turns to endure
Sleep of exhaustion. But the springs click.
The warped wood of the sill whimpers.

HONEYMOON IN HONDURAS

Soaked in sweat
In the hot, wet
Mayan November,
Up the steep side
Of that pyramid
She watched him clamber

And pose at the top
To give her a snap.
Back in Maine they knew
It was all a waste
– Overexposed:
The marriage too.

CONTACT

To walk the dog and myself, in a long day's
Drive, we're pulled over on the hard shoulder
By wire against which tumbleweed
Lies stacked by the wind.
I muse vaguely on women's ways.
– Sub-desert – cactus, creosote bushes – beyond.
We're ten miles out of Carson City,
Far off the Sierra's bleak East slopes smoulder,
And, squatting twenty yards away, a coyote.
The basset hound stops dead.

Each gives the other
      – Close in origin,
      Apart in experience –
                          a long look,
      Without expression,
      With significance.
Strange concatenation: but I'm struck
With catching it elsewhere, just the other day.
The coyote trots off. We drive away.

THE BEACH-BOY'S SONG

Sun-scatter from the salt-plumed pool
Fills out your face, my honey;
And sometimes it looks beautiful,
And sometimes it looks funny.

The tinted shreds of day have set,
Smooth moonlight brims the bay full;

And sometimes you're so passionate,
And sometimes you're so playful.

And which of them's the "real you"?
Sweetheart, I don't have a clue.

THE OTHER WORLD

The river spins a sleekness through the bridge
And over it a curious figure leans
Pointing his walking stick like a crossed crutch
Into the pearly air and at the streams.

Close to the motionless willows and the cloudless sky
Struggles a world of water, flecked with trout,
And confusion of his images will neither die
Nor even absorb doubt.

He trembles more violently than his reflection,
Frightened not so much at the thought of defeat
Seen in this blue world's surface and cross-section
As for reasons he cannot repeat.

For here it comes: higher than obelisked duty
The flames spout from a heart turned red-hot coal
Yet cannot singe that loose, indifferent beauty
Nor scorify the bilges of his soul.

So on he goes: through solid walls of nature
He walks like a ghost as visions blank his eyes,
Who will never find clear thought or sexual pleasure
Or be able to distinguish poems from lies.

SIMILITUDE

He thought of himself as a widower.
It seemed as though his wife had died
And an alien in her likeness tried
Hard to pass itself off as her.

– Unsuccessfully, on the whole,
Lacking enough knowledge of
Homo Sapiens' stance, or its eyes' glow,
Let alone adjuncts like heart, soul.

Difficult to prove to a judge,
Unless by a transfer of venue
To a court on Aldebaran II …
His fourth Scotch went down like sludge.

BAGPIPES AT THE BILTMORE

(Air: "Strathfiddich")

Downtown Los Angeles:
In the huge baroque lobby
Like the hall of a station
Three men with kilts on,
Skian-dhus and sporrans
And all the adornments,
Stamp round in circles.
One bangs a drum and
The others play bagpipes.
What on earth are they up to?
And who are the people
Marching behind them
With badges and name-tags?
An occasional banner:
"UBEW"–
"United", for certain,
"Brotherhood", surely,
And W's "Workers".
What about "E", then?
"Electrical", maybe?
But what has the Union
To do with bagpipes?
And why are they here in
The bourgeois old Biltmore?

It's terribly noisy
But fairly inspiriting
– Except, I remember
How we marched as recruits through
The fog-frozen Lothians
With pipers before us:
An ear-splitting torment.
Till two brave English laddies
Put paid to the nuisance
With a long knitting-needle,
And the fights and the uproar
Around the old squad-room …

My highland great-grandsires
– Macandrew, Macpherson –
Though they much preferred Mozart,
Passed down an old story
Of the head of a septet
In a bare granite hovel
He miscalled a castle.
After plenty of skirlings
His hereditary piper
With a tattered old plaid on
Would cry to the cardinal
Points of the compass,
"The MacShagbag of Shagbag
Has started to dine.
The Kings of the Airth
May now take their seats."

– For that you need bagpipes.
Mere whisky won't do it.
So they do have their virtues,
At least of nostalgia.
But instilling a spirit
In Electrical Workers
To march round the lobby
Of the stuffy old Biltmore
I believe, since I see it …

Just one more blow from
The unreasoned, untidy

World we inhabit
Against our assumptions.
Good for you, really:
Shakes up your smugness,
Freshens your senses
(In this case your eardrums).
I expect that tomorrow
Will turn up with something,
Though perhaps a bit subtler
Than this too sharp reminder
To haul off from habit
And struggle with structure,
With a noise so enormous
I can bellow unnoticed
(And it's pleasant to do it
In the solemn old Biltmore),
"Oh belt up, you buggers!"

TRANSPOLAR

All that ice (he said)
Isn't as cold or hard
As this girl's heart.

Still heading north
We'd flown over smooth
White mile after mile with

Treacherous leads. Now
What stretched out below
Was gouged, scraped, raw

In high clenchings, clamped
With torsion, humped
To blunted fangs, cold-grimed

Nearer black than green:
Above all, alien.
– Pretty bad, then.

It started an argument.
We all said he went
Too far. But we knew what he meant.

SECOND DEATH

A ten-pound Life will give you every fact
– Facts that he'd hoped his friends would not rehearse
To an intent posterity which lacked
Nothing of moment, since it had his verse.
Or so he thought. But now we come to read
What his more honest prudence had held in:
Tasteless compulsion into trivial deed,
A squalor more outrageous than the sin.

Piss on that grave where lies the weakly carnal? ...
– Hopeless repentance had washed clean his name,
His virtue's strength insistent on a shame
Past all the brief bravados full and final.
Without excuses now, to the Eternal,
He makes the small, true offering of his fame.

PONT DES ARTS

(On the left the Institut, seat of the Académie; on the right the Louvre.)

A: The small bridge arcs in air under the dusk
        – That higher arc. What reds! What turquoises!
        The town, part accident, part artifact,
        Marginally basking, smoulders pale.
        A pale Seine parts those halls of art and language.
        Swifts skim ... All's still: not tranquil, which applies
        Only to that girl who leans against the rail
        With half-shut eyes. Not tranquil, only still.

B: Still? While in Louvre and Institut
            The abstract forges roar:
        Steel for grids to grip and shape
        Loose skies and vaguer cities, or
            For blades to slice them through!

223

C: Arced too, her back, her thighs.
            She gazes, grey-eyed,
            Into the grey glide.

A: Taken for granted, utterly grotesque,
            Lives blaze or sputter in the little rooms
            Behind oblongs of glass, now lighting up.
            – The hunt for rhythm may fail all melody:
            Who has not sat, high in a little room,
            Wrung dry and hollow with a press of love?
            As your girl there may remind us. All the same
            She's one small vortex among skies and words.

B: What though the great perspectives plunge
                Or great affections burst?
            Flame-green theory, jewel of frost
            Can orchestrate the mind-and-heart
                To the hard baton's lunge!

C: Sex, but her strangeness too:
            To modulate and drive
            The heartbeat's carrier-wave.

A: There's shredded cirrus, moon a blank lead disc …
            But "mind and heart"? What sort of orchestra?
            A few strings of a Strad, a tom-tom beat,
            Reeds matured or cracked by various weathers,
            As strange and disparate as that moon, those birds,
            The Châtelet's gargoyles, ochres of the air.
            Stone-muted stream! Regime of accident!
            – Your rigour fails the inexhaustible.

B: Your weak light drips, your hollow sky
                Is full of beaks and bones
            Unless the mind, the visual cones
            Direct the modes the spectra gleam,
                 The curves the phyla fly.

C: Eyes squeezed to focus? Better blind
            With a magnesium flare,
            With her lips, with her hair.

A: The tip of that Nilotic obelisk
    May seem to trail high scrawls of indigo
    Limning some glyph upon the tropopause
    – That's no more than the seizing of our eye.
    All speech implies philosophy or song?
    Yet there, more tritely, the Île de la Cité
    Cannot but echo in the skull's hard caverns
    As "a grey frigate breasting the grey waves" …

B: Art's wildernesses! Lion shapes
        Steam off its sodden ground
    – Which sharp zeribas can surround,
    Strict pruning bring to symmetry
        The ovoids of its grapes.

C: The worlds ferment, the words freeze.
    A way to the warm and clear?
    Through her, here.

A: Pigments of static iris, marble mask!
    The inexplicit arts that seem to make
    The foliage of detail one green smear
    Somehow accumulate fresh immanence.
    Can words be carved like the great Melian breasts?
    All thrashing fiercely in our neurons' mesh,
    Phenomena no less than those two barns.
    – Yet see them loom there, nudes, philosophies!

B: To that great gaze of art and thought
        I turn an equal gaze:
    Striking till planes of fracture crack
    And all essential emerald blaze,
        I'll learn. I'll not be taught.

C: Tsunami up that total beach
    She waits in art, and for speech
    … *Mademoiselle.*

B: Rhythmless melody?

A: Extreme crystal?
    And what of the sensuous skeins, the will

Hammering its harder task?

B: Mere explorer's risk ?
Bright-miraged sand and empty flask,
Kayak ripped by narwhal tusk?

A: Darkness falls on it all.
The answers? Well, at least we learn to ask.

CIRCUMSTANCE

The feminine ways
Of A – poised in grace
By the turret-banked Thames
Or else smart and snappy,
Shading an eye
From the sun, drinking Pimms.

Pure gold. Till he saw
In that waterfront bar
B's brassy display,
Like a caricature,
Malicious and sure
Of the good art of A.

When he met A once more
On the path to the bower
Some portcullis had shut.
He knew it unfair
– But even her hair
Was of similar cut.

They went separate ways.
He could not know that A's
Small gestures, quick smile,
She had modelled on B
– Picked crumbling scree
For ramparts of style.

THE PENINSULA

Like a finger pointing northward, San Francisco for its nail,
Set between blue Bay and Ocean flecked with white by spray and sail:

Coyote Creek to Candlestick, Pacifica to Santa Cruz
Run the coasts that hold its counties concentrated for the muse.

California soft and mild! Surely just as fit a nurse
As any rugged Scottish moorland for the child that's into verse?

Let him grasp our air and landscape, just emerging to the day:
Sunrise runs, one glorious ash-blonde, surfing into Half Moon Bay,

Over Millbrae and San Bruno, San Mateo, Burlingame,
Strung along the old Camino where the Spanish Fathers came.

– Stretches of the old Camino don't recall their mission bells:
Used car lots and drive-in movies, massage parlours and motels.

Never mind – and, while confessing there's a purpose each fulfils,
Two miles East you're in the marshlands, two miles West you're in the hills,

Heading through the open country where the Foothills Freeway swings:
Long lakes glitter under pine-trees, San Andreas, Crystal Springs.

Sun that bronzes without burning, air that's always fresh delights
Woodside and Portola Valley, Los Altos Hills and Sharon Heights.

Easy driving, easy parking, easy shopping, night and day,
In Los Gatos, Cupertino, Santa Clara, San Jose.

Yet there's NASA's installation, looming over Moffet Field,
Our Linear Accelerator with its record muon yield.

For we're not in some Arcadia, work is hard and minds are keen.
Lotus no – but abalone, meunière or amandine,

Washed down by some dry white vintage Santa Clara's hills produce:
Green vines – Novitiate, Gemello, Woodside, Ridge and David Bruce …

What's this restlessness we feel, then, where life runs so free and fair?
Like some instinct to migration thick on land and sea and air:

(Grey whales offshore by the dozen, heading for some Baja cove,
Monarch butterflies in millions swarming to Pacific Grove ...)

– In Redwood City, Palo Alto, Mountain View and Menlo Park
Some faint tremor warns obscurely from the deep inhuman dark:

Far down, grinding through the magma, Nature brews her huge assault,
And that rift we hardly notice marks the San Andreas Fault.

WINTER WELCOME TO A WEST TEXAN

So here you are, lovely:
Arroyos of Kensington
With pekes for coyotes,
Green street-lamp saguaros,
Swirls of fog twisting
Like sidewinders over
The desert macadam.
High boots keep the slush out
As they kept off the cactus
In this English December
    Of a coldish year.

Such high-stepping heels, then,
Such eyes deep-horizoned,
What can she give us
Who has London lassoed and
Corralled and hog-tied?
– A locus of laughter,
A good supple brightness
By pavements and lime-trees
With their ice-film sheer as
Ten denier stockings
    When the vapours clear.

She brings us the sunshine
Instead? Not exactly:
She holds her own climate,

Heat, not heat's prickling,
Sand, not its rasping,
No bare, sun-stunned ranges,
Shade without scorpions,
And no Gila monsters
But humming-birds sipping
Flowers of the desert ...
     Thank you my dear.

So sun's how it strikes you?
Then we in our turn feel
Cold, not its judder,
Snow soft on our faces,
December undarkened:
In a jacket as warm as
A sleek palomino
She treads the rime's crackling
With a high winter vigour
Through fog that sparkles
     Like ginger beer ...

OUTLAWS

"Maiden! a nameless life I lead,
    A nameless death I'll die;
The fiend whose lantern lights the mead
    Were better mate than I!"

She thinks, Oh just a macho stance
    By old Sir Walter Scott,
Yet feels ridiculous romance
    Run through her, sweet and hot.

So complicated, real life!
    All shifting shades are there;
But welcome, even to a wife,
    The spotlight's simple glare!

She muses on men pure and rash,
    Distilled to fauns or fiends

.

229

(More stylish than the toothsome trash
    In women's magazines).

She looks hard at the one she's got.
    With love and sense of loss,
Thinking that maybe Lady Scott
    Stood for her share of dross.

KENNEDY CENTER

After the concert I
Get a great hearty
Kiss from the mezzo. She's
Big, blonde. What energies!

Still lively after singing
Like the Colorado swinging
Through the ornate hall's
High canyon walls.

Such a magnanimous, calm
Air, too, as she pats my arm,
Sitting in the restaurant bar
To the TV's coarse encore:

A "group" – girls mike-in-hand
And looming there behind
A battery of devices
To boost their voices.

What's she got that they haven't
– Apart from voice and talent?
Instead of the sour
Forced frenzy, a power

Reined under rule
By as strong a rationale ...
Somewhere in the pit
Of the stomach's where *they* hit

– That is, if they hit at all;
Many would find the howl
Of a coyote more moving,
More musical, no less loving:

Their sobs are suggestive
But not sexy, except if
Your ears are wired to your sex
So that it's mere reflex.

So let's get back to the mood
I started in, to the good,
To passionate control:
Where she hits is the soul.

AIR AND WATER

Sassafras, Wye, Chester, Choptank,
Spread rivers of the Eastern Shore,
Are sunken valleys, lawned to the bank.
It's the Tred Avon we're heading for

Down lanes white-aldered, river-birched,
In my side-pocket today's mail;
I take out a card when the ferry's reached,
And read it, grasping the damp rail.

From a poet: "I liked your last book
– All about aeroplanes and girls".
I photograph her against the wake
That fizzes across those slow green swirls.

Background of oyster-stakes, soft light, low
Crab-boats, high skein of distant geese.
Her form's curved to the rich flow,
Eyes glow, hair lifts to the warm breeze:

Their colours not consciously recalled,
Just suffused through my life's lens.
The boat scuffs the pier now, oaken, old:
I'll do without the aeroplanes.

LATE PASS

The dying animal, one fears,
    Will take us when it goes:
This beast composed of nose and ears,
Legs, belly, heart, and blood and tears,
Will only last a few more years
    And then turn up its toes.

– A mansion that contains its own
    Self-demolition squad:
Brick by brick and stone by stone,
Vein by vein and bone by bone
Till finally the very throne
    Of reason gets the nod.

As we approach that rendezvous
    There's not much we can add
To dicta of the sages who
Gave, as they shuffled up the queue,
Much that is tried, and may be true,
    – At least, the best they had.

So what's our contribution if
    It's all been said before?
A change of tone's all we can give
Such as that the alternative
Of having aeons more to live
    Might be a bloody bore.

So if our years at board and bed
    Were pretty much enjoyed,
Close the account while we're ahead,
Next year we might be in the red;
So just forget about the Med:
    Strike out into the void!

And if we feasted cheerlessly
    We still must pay the bill,
When all the consolation we

Can find is that at last we're free,
Home from the sodding awful sea,
    Home from the fucking hill.

SO

The poem, calm,
Stands in the eye of the storm,
At most ruffled a bit
By stray residuals of breeze.

The poem, grim,
Is caught in the eye of the storm,
A world's deep, seething pit
Of dungeoning darknesses.

The poem, firm,
Sees with the eye of the storm,
Up and out through the starlit
Perspective of infinities.

from

PENULTIMATA
[2009]

for John Gross and Sam Gwynn

Defenders of the Faith

IGNITION

Perhaps a bird-call
No different from hundreds heard
In life, and the bird
Not clearly identifiable,

Or a high-stepping girl
Crossing a plank-bridge
Into focus rather than knowledge
Into accept rather than feel,

A seed, a sigh, a scrawl
On the back of an envelope
To attain a full shape
Later, if at all.

IN ATTENDANCE

The small park, May, calm moment in their wooing.
On the face of it everything's theirs:
Pear-blossom only half conceals
Faint haze round the Western hills
Clear blue above southward spires,
Over town-murmur uninsistent cooing
As the touch of a warm breeze
All but skirt-liftingly moves
Across the rose-gold of her thighs
And ruffles the appropriate doves.

Doves? But there's something wrong. Their gait
Jerky, piston-like, a tick-tock
Inconclusive strut, male after mate,
Puffed-out plumage, ill-tempered look,
For all one knows lice-ridden ... Hardly part of
Aphrodite's train. Nor like some great
Artist's sky-projected Descent of the Dove
As the extreme white wingspread of a religion's
High point. The less satisfactory type of bird
Among these flower-beds can only rate

A less emotive, more objective word.
– So make it pigeons.

But perhaps, or even certainly,
We cannot quite break the cypher
That links mood to reality.
If this breeze is not the Cyprian zephyr
Nor this sky the nest of the white numen,
Their own mutuality must transcend
Even their own imperfect selves.
She is as much goddess as any woman,
And their own warm day dissolves
All attributes other than love's.
Grey-blue feathers glow, bird-voices blend,
Let's call them doves.

TWO OCCASIONS

1. Beached

A sweep of greener-than-azure sea and
A stretch of paler-than-gold sand
Hemmed in by shore-shadowing pines
From under which, just out of the sun
He looks down at a supine woman
Shapely, even beautiful, but one
On whom he has no designs.
Her bikini, taut between thigh and curved abdomen,
Shows soft fronds of her
Dark intercrural fur.
And he's suddenly overcome by an access
Of tenderness.

2. Heard Melodies

Moment, and then memory
May be stamped deep with a dreamsight
Some faint sound reifies,
As when tides of night run high
Round lifting breasts and thighs:
On a girl lit faintly by

Curtain-muffled moonlight
Love breaks like a wave, then dies;
And she gives a little cry
Or a series of little cries.

ONLY NATURAL

A huge moon sits on the reef.
Half-aware, he turns away from
Its power inland down from the cliff
Path towards her parents' home

Descending out of the direct
Beam on the track through the treed slope.
It's not even that they reject
Him. Too young: but they don't know how deep,

How far … And now, half a world
Away, their sudden posting will take
Her at just the moment the love-meld
Has not yet set firm. Will it break

Or hold? In this early hour
Of the second night that should have been
Theirs, he moves under cypress, cedar,
Their high leafages ungreen

In the cool lunar ashlight's white-gold
Glow, perfused from the parallel
Sweep down on his face's controlled
Expression at the doorway. He sounds the bell.

2

Now he prepares to endure
The night that should have been theirs.
Her father comes beaming to the door.
And she's behind him on the stairs:

A smile's quick complicity. Her
Hair, her ear-rings so set out that oval

Absolute … He pulls himself together
As her mother, too, vaguely greets his arrival.

Tonight was to have been theirs
Like last week's stolen, complete
Modulation of thirty-six hours,
The days fruitful as the night.

He can't blame them celebrating
The new job overseas. And she'll
Be back in late spring.
More guests. In to dinner. They file

Under the motile glitter
Of chandeliers, in a warm
Welcoming familial chatter,
The same bracelet on her bare arm …

How can he stand this? She's the far side
Of the table, two down. Why can't those
Others see that they're all black-and-white
While she's in full colour, jade, gold, rose?

She leans forward, managing to say
Across the grapeglow-filled glasses,
"Never mind – I'll be back in May,"
Spoken without any emphasis.

Then her eyes brush his lightly like the thin
Electric thread that precedes
And guides the lightning, in
This case broken off … He needs

To think in different terms. Reality
Is around them like barbed fences
And for now he has to remain physically
Passive inside his senses.

And these have sharpened – even taste:
The smoked salmon, the delicate
Moselle, and after that the roast
Duck, the burgundy, beset his palate.

The fruit, the port. Eventually
It's over. Cheeks just kissed
Formally, he hopes feelingly.
Then he's free and unfree at last.

Outside. The moon's gone: but his
Sight after a few moments adjusts
To the underbrush's intricacies
Of shade, the high overcast's

Smooth smudged charcoal, the upflung
Foliate antennae edging more sharply
Their arched life form, as he treads along
Its track to the cliff-top, to descry

The northern ness's distant chalk-face
Now an almost livid non-pallor,
And West the sleek panther-black sea's
Slow pulse. He's hurt. But the phenomena

Distract, if not quite soothe, the way
They seem to command acceptance of his place
In this random, uncompelled display
Of different darknesses.

ON THE VERANDA

"The girl-losing experience …"
His voice stirred up the soft silence
Where, sundowners in hand, the men's

Attention – mutual, serene, content –
Was over the warm, quiescent
Sea, under a dark blue firmament

With brush-stroke mistiness out westerly
As the good sunglow resumed slowly
Into the waters. A touch of melancholy

Imbued the ambience like a dash
Of angostura. "A longish
Time since that sort of anguish

Hit me. She was my very first.
She left me for one older, more self-possessed,
Richer – sure! – better-dressed.

– I was only a scruffy, last term
Student. Much later she told me what scum,
What a swine, he'd been. – Well, some

Consolation. Not enough to reverse
The long loss, the intolerable years
Of – I expect much the same as yours."

"Mine perhaps worse, since all my own fault.
Divorced, I thought that I'd play the field
With two girls, often three. I felt

Safe from the love-trap. Then one day
No. 1 switched to a fiancé.
Part of the deal – you'll rightly say

A miscalculation – I've learned better since.
The nights! I'd take four or five aspirins
With large shots of bourbon in half pints

Of milk, drunk quick to stop curdling, slept
If at all, with my right big and second toes kept
(With no erotic feeling) round my left

Achilles tendon. – I mention this
So that we wouldn't perhaps miss
Any pointer to full diagnosis."

"Sleep, yes. And drink. This smooth rum
Recalls how, when her bad letter came,
Stationed in Orkney, I couldn't get warm.

Before, I'd not minded the scything cold
But now four blankets – and rum – left me chilled.
– Another symptom of getting ungirled?"

"Well, here's a memory I'd quite long striven
To repress. We'd been married more than eleven
Years. All was dull – was depressing, even.

No adultery on either side.
Wanting more operas, cruises, she'd
Left from a boredom I thought I'd shared.

But in the event, the parting tore
As jagged, as barbed as any before
When young. A wound that for long stayed raw ..."

Turning now from the sea and sun
A drier voice, "Well, my contribution
To, I suppose, this panel discussion,

Since I imagine that between you
You've covered every important issue ..."
He paused for a sip, "here's a minor clue:

I had made love to her just twice,
The bond hadn't clamped down like a vice.
Then she went back to her rather nice

Chap. At the wheel on the Brompton Road
My tear-ducts all of a sudden flowed.
The traffic light was luckily red.

Yes, a close escape, which may illustrate
The problems posed." "What we still await
Is how, and why, can our psyches get

Gripped till almost as fused as steel?
There's surely no good biological
Reason?" "An unfavourable

Mutation?" …
                    "What have we exorcized?
In each mind-vault now perhaps a weaker ghost
Walled up, but not quite put to rest?"

– A last strongish drink then, toasting the bronze
Sunset and the warm, gentle ocean's
Uneasy effacement of demons.

BEYOND THEM

"*Perfect*'s a word you mustn't use",
She said (softly, strongly)
That evening after the long fuse
Of their love had finally

Brought shattering release
Of their imaginings into reality,
And with it, like all realities,
Some imperfection, incongruity …

Well: out in bright cirrus-sifted noon
Drenched by a sudden shower-spray;
At lunch her brief choke on a fish-bone,
Rather too sharp a Chardonnay.

Even bodily, the odd glitch
In their so overdue rites of union …
Still, little more than snags in the rich
Damascene of that attuning;

Like the one distracting flaw
In an old Persian's carpet-weaving
To appease what he saw
As the envious eyes of heaven.

But she'd chosen the wrong moment.
Lying, with her head on her right hand,
Her eyes livelily, lazily, intent
On where he happened to stand

(About eight o'clock from the end of the bed,
Some five feet distant). For through her smile's
Full calm there glowed, quick, unexpected,
A coherence of irrefutables.

Not just her cream-bronze candour displayed
On the coverlet's cream-citron
Chenille as early eventide
Gently shone through the soft curtain.

Not just the high, hand-filling breasts,
Or vision sweeping the tactility of
The smooth, hand-soothing thigh-and-waist's
Concord of curves. Not even love.

More as if a great painter (Venetian
School?) had stood and sought
With a life-trained concentration,
Grip of genius, toil of thought

To fix the exact point, the fulcrum
To raise beauty-scatter, love-breath
Up out of the natural world, to some
Cool altitude of truth

Which would, he already knew, lie clear
Unfailingly, unfadingly engraved
In the scan of his mind's eye, year after year.
And so it proved.

LOOKING UP

How have things changed since Romeo
Sang under Juliet's
Window of opportunity?

When you're so much older
And have been so often exposed
You might develop immunity …

Light, lighter than snow
Falls on the Savernake
And streams down the upper Stour

As she too leans from a window
Of a friend's context of cottage
Through thatch matching her hair

Undeniably evoking
Verona and that moon-viewed
Honey-voiced Capulet

Visioned through years and distances
And heard now above the high
Thrum of a west-winging jet …

ANNIVERSARY

How should I write it?
How not to sound mawkish
When thanking a wife for
Another good year? How
To set up a trophy
Or cut a new notch in
The tally of gladness?

Images? Well, then,
I see you this summer:
Sunrise and sunset
(We did see the sun rise?)
Then a great moon to southward
Air heavy with fuchsia,
Driving and loving,
Swimming and dreaming …

As for your faults, well
The way that you sometimes …
But I'd better not spoil it.
Just the same when … however
We won't let the public
In on such wrangles

And it's wholly forgiven
(It's even forgiven
That you forgave me):
The merest of jolts on
The smooth-swinging freeway
On the drive to wherever.

Once or twice seeing
At dawn with you sleeping
Your face on the pillow ...
But watch it! I'm getting
A bit sentimental.
I'll tell you in private.

What a year, what a life! I'll
Just close by moving
A vote of thanks – carried
Without opposition.
And now we'll move on to
Next year's agenda
(Where "more of the same" will
Be strongly supported).

AFTERWARDS

"recollected in tranquillity"

Is it so necessary
For a wild memory
To fade and blur
Before the full charge
Of an old love or rage
Can really register?

With a life's long perspectives
The changed picture gives
More depth and scope
As twisted faces shrink
To little more than pink
Blobs on its landscape ...

A passion, sharp and hot,
Might once have seized the heart
To rip or scald.
So far as this can be
Recalled in tranquillity
It's not recalled.

THE LAST DAY (EMBARKATION LEAVE)

Squeezing the water from bright braids
She stumbles, almost gracefully, towards him
Up the steep grass of the cove's brim
To their alcove under the colonnade's

White and westward curve to the ford's
Almost awash stepping-stones
Among a scattered flush of rhododendrons …
She smiles. Her towel clings. And he hoards

This among other images: asleep on the sand;
Doing a little jig at a bus-stop;
Quiet in half-dark with a wine-cup
Nursed in both palms; and; and; and.

   2

Dry now, suffused, mutual, they sit:
A time of slow knowledge, as last
Night was a time of precipitate trust.
And so the wide gaze opens to admit

The deep view, deep as their mood: soft airs;
Comforting waters; calm light – except
Where frayed fronds of a thin cataract
At the cove's head scatter small flares;

Salt-scent; thyme-tang; transsensual skies.
And it's not that the outspread scene
Is no more than props for their stage, the sun
Its arc-lamp. But it amplifies.

3

They aren't alone. There are others who murmur
Or stroll at the edge of their felt range.
But that's not why they exchange
No more than a few looks, and fewer

Words, in the mere now, the extreme now,
Where love sustains the near-silence
As our furthest, profoundest ocean's
Swell might lift a proa's prow.

And it's not that particles of a shared air
Drift away gently from one's lungs
Into the other's, over tongues
Which have touched. It's more

That what surrounds them seems to be
A stress-fluid, a field of force
With gentle but diamond-forging pressures.
Mind-sparklings leap from the quantum-sea ...

And the day dwindles. But still love
Glows through the globe's turning
An unappeasable yearning
For what they already have.

4

Evening smooths out every surface
Of water, of vision. The low sun's
Presence strikes up to them bronze
From the hard refracting grasses.

Above which a flight of doves
Having banked and twice circled
Is absorbed into the flickering dark-gold
Dome of a sycamore. Mauves,

Magentas, dim down. They must leave, not just loving
But even more fearing, into the imminent

Death-fogs, where today may have meant
What? Everything? Nothing?

They rise. Some quality of the late light
Takes the edge off the squared
Stonework of the crossing. Muffled cloud
Vaguely pervades. The moments concentrate

And confuse. And a low blue demilune
Is all that's left of the sky as from the day's
Depth they take their separate ways
– To merge again? Not certainly. Not soon.

LOST LOVE

"The climate of the heart"? – Young men
Who think they won't survive it when
That organ takes the icy blast
May find that once the winter's past
Their blood's been only slightly thinned
By the unprevailing wind.

PHRYNE

"It's such a pity that we don't have
Anything like a photograph
Of her about whom the ancients rave …"

He'd been talking about the well-known tale
Of her lawyer at her blasphemy trial
Baring her breasts to gain an acquittal.

Now, it wasn't the "beauty" of what they saw
That made the judges unloop the law,
But what's been described as "sacred awe".

Would visual be better than verbal, though,
Projected into the long-ago
Till we think we know what we'll never know?

Fragments, copies, museums still hold
Of statues she modelled, or so we're told
(Though not the Delphi one in gold).

Well, at Thespiae how did they feel as
Praxiteles, daring celestial malice,
Set up together, on equal pillars

Statues of her and of Aphrodite.
A girl and a Goddess damn-near Almighty
With a temper not to be taken lightly?

He could only pre-empt their sacred fear
With what could unarguably appear
As spillover from another sphere

On to physique made partly free
From the pressures of externality
Which is all that the subtlest lens can see.

(And Marilyns, Sophias, the very cream
Of our time, aren't sewn without a seam
Directly into the fabric of dream.)

But she's gone! Long gone! Gone to the grave
And left us, instead of a photograph,
The residual glow of an ancient grief.

IN BOTH SENSES

Scarcely discernible at first
Faint peachlight spills through blinds undrawn:
A soft susurrus from the East
Gently proclaiming dawn.

The sun, a single cymbal still
Ringing from some cosmic beat ...
Noon's loud light that seems to fill
Our minds with throbs of heat.

251

The red-brown dusk bays like a hound
That greets its master's late return:
That is, translated out of sound,
Kind warmths that do not burn.

Then Leonids streak across the sky
Without a whisper … Frozen tears,
High deeps, with senses tightened by
The muteness of the spheres.

DEEP DOWN

Guides to a City church (All Hallows) note
Dug up from Roman levels of the crypt
"Fragments of a figurine of Venus."

How young the city was then. Not so long
Since Virgil had recited to Maecenas
Those lines on "Britain from the world cut off."

One's first thought is, how far into our past,
The sixty generations laid between us
In clay-borne sites to which the mana clings

Imprints in twisted strata grinding down:
Cracked tepidarium tiles, a copper bowl's
Merest outline oxidized to greenness,

Flakes of crushed plaster, chips of paving-stone,
Grains of sand perhaps blown from the arena's
Killing floor some half a mile away.

– It was a violent age, a brutal age:
Seen too in smeared black streaks from the Iceni's
Burning of London (61 AD).

2

How could this cool and gentle image then
Make headway in the presence of a queen as

252

Ruthless, and as wronged, as Boadicea?

Or with such other claims to goddesshood
As all those pompous busts and bas-reliefs,
Deified tarts, Poppaeas and Faustinas?

And then Priapus, not so much obscene as
Coarse, crude, with phalli cut in street or wall
As signposts to some squalid lupanar.

Yet skill and sentiment carved out this calm
Recruit to Aphrodite and Athene's
Alliance against manic, smouldering lusts

– Though, shaped and smoothed, the young divinity
Is physical in presence, and the vulva's
Delicate notch does not debar the penis,

Giving Pandemian and Uranian love
Conjoined as with the writhing amphisbaena's
Two heads – transcendent dark, transcendent light.

3

But more immediately, this figurine is
(Something about the thighs) as if dug up
From strata of memory, a personal past

Distorted, crumbled, shifted in the mind
Out of that year when they were both nineteen, his
Life a daze of flared limbs, starspun hair.

A quiet kiss beside a Cotswold mere
In the erotic's earliest novenas
Eyes focussed far beyond the possible.

Muffled with rugs against the salt wind's keenness
Side by side on a ship's upper deck
Warmly together, half-asleep, content.

Yelling a chorus in a rowdy bar
Somewhere off the Rue des Feuillantines, as
Bright-eyed, red-cheeked as a female clown.

Pub bedroom, Kent: slipping from crêpe-de-chine as
Sleek as the figure now displayed in all
The reginality of Renoir's girls.

And not much else. Distanced, displaced, diminished,
What's left of love and beauty just survives
Like fragments of that figurine of Venus.

GOETHE IN 1816

Sunlight breaks dazzling from the stream
    But he is not deceived,
Nor when the young breeze shakes that gleam
    From trees gone golden-leaved.

But as he turns, with eyes undimmed
    To watch that warm sun sink,
A young shape, deep-eyed, golden-limbed
    Stands poised upon a brink.

Declension into saint or sage
    Is not worth thinking of:
Into the cold pool of his age
    She dives and brings up love.

THE IDEA OF VIRGINIA

It lay in the minds of poets: coasts fronting Arcadias
Sprang from the parchment map Doctor Dee in his study
Scanned for likely lodes of Philosopher's Stone.
But the land was also real: rivers, meads, mountains.

Deer and pumas ranged its high plains. Beavers
Toiled in its streams. Bluebird and mocking-bird,
Blue jay, redbird and quail filled branches and air.
In its woods poplar, walnut, cedar, mulberry grew green

Round glades clear of all undergrowth but the grape.
The dogwood blossomed in white clusters, the Judas Tree
In purplish buds. Clumps of sassafras, sumac, persimmon
Variegated the lush savannahs. From swamps

Rose up the sharp scent of the bog-magnolia.
Overhead, miles of canvasbacks arrowed the Chesapeake.
The runs were full of trout, shad, sheepshead, the bays
Of oysters. And among this abundance were men.

In spring they ate turkey and hare; in summer venison,
Terrapin, oysters on dry leaves, strawberries;
In winter tuckahoe, fish on fire sticks, hominy.
They drank a brew of hickory nuts. They smoked tobacco.

In his wooden palace in Werowocomoco,
His vassal werowances round him, Powhatan sat.
At each corner loomed a terrible image in wood:
A dragon, a bear, a puma; the last was a man.

The barbarian emperor had fled his faraway clan;
Hacked out a realm, seen two generations die.
No Atahualpa or Montezuma in gold-clogged pomp,
He had strength, subtlety and a few thousand braves.

He wore a grey raccoon fur. His wives moved in mantles
Of bluebird feathers, or heron or swan, embroidered
With animal figures. He lived in his treasure of weapons
And his two daughters: the elder was Pocahontas.

– And so great spaces, feelings, fruitfulnesses poured
Their warm potentials over a fallow landscape.
Its other affluent brimmed in a far-off island:
Liberties, laws, the strong consensual state.

2

As the *Susan Constant* approached the Capes, even before
The pine-tops of the low coast pricked the horizon,
The smell of the land came from behind the sand-dunes,
Blown from the miles of forest, the flower-pied grasses.

They built their Jamestown, triangular, wooden-walled,
On a fevered island – for protection from Spain,
With skimped corn-fields – not to hide Indian scouts;
A miserable lot, they would have starved amidst plenty.

But among them a secret strength, the conquistador
For this godless small land was ready – John Smith,
The man of no birth and no name, a century after
The spear-proud Spaniards awarded his king no empire

But a few thousand acres where a few hundred English
Could scarcely hold. Yet was as strong, as subtle
A village Cortez as Powhatan, his friend, his rival,
Surpassed in cunning the lords of the treasure realms.

He had fought in France, Holland; thrown overboard as heretic;
A privateer; a soldier in Transylvania;
His own pike felling the three Turks' heads of his arms;
Captured, enslaved, killing his Pasha, escaping.

Now seized by Powhatan, his head on a stone
To be brained by tomahawks, but Pocahontas springing
Between – if the tale be true, and even if true
The rescue not a charade of Powhatan's guile.

He saw her again. On some mission to Werowocomoco
He and his men sat by their fire in a meadow.
Pocahontas slipped from the woods with thirty maidens,
Leaves on her thighs, an otter-skin round her waist,

The horns of a deer on her head. She carried a bow.
A quiver hung on her back. Her skin was painted;
Her companions' too, each in a different colour.
They circled in an impersonal, passionate dance.

They chanted, but did not speak. They ran to the woods.
He did not see her again till she slipped to his camp
To warn of threatened attack. "Next to God, the instrument,"
He wrote, to save them all from famine and slaughter.

3

When he went the colony crumbled. Dale saved it.
Amid riots, hunger, false reports to London,
Conspiracies to assassinate the Governor. Yet,
"If you give over this country and lose it," he wrote,

"You with your wisdom will leap such a gudgeon
As our state has not done the like since we lost the Kingdom
Of France. I have seen the best countries in Europe …
Put them all together this will be the equivalent unto them

If it be inhabited by good people." They came, good and bad.
The Assembly's Speaker was Pozy, late MP at Westminster.
The same year the first black slave was sold by a Dutchman.
Settlers trickled in, and women: the poor and ignorant,

The rich and inquisitive, Sandys, poet and traveller,
Wyatt, the old poet's grandson. Plantations spilled westward.
Powhatan died: his heirs launched massacre twice,
But it was too late. The indentured servants arrived,

And, from the war in England, the younger sons
Of the defeated faction, ensigns of Rupert's Horse,
Of the Bluecoats of Naseby. Two new styles of toughness.
– And the first generation too of the native born.

All sought liberty, word of so many meanings.
All recognized, however reluctantly, law.
Freedom was a fresh breeze down from the Blue Ridge Mountains;
Slavery a stench up from the Great Dismal Swamp.

So through the varying centuries the land lived on,
Flawed in the stone of its cracked foundation, frayed
By the quotidian wear of the generations;
Its Form flickered and faded: but never died.

And the frontier rolled inland, Tidewater to Piedmont,
Piedmont to Shenandoah. Spotswood, sounding the passes,
Gave small golden horseshoes to all his companions
Richly engraved, "*Sic juvat transcendere montes*".

And in the townless miles the great houses glowed.
Self-confidence; trade and toil; duelling and horses;
The frontier code honed the aristocratic code.
A legendary generation approached its moment.

4

Haydn, prose, elections, deism, architecture,
Bred the leaders of battle, governance, law.
Washington, Marshall, Madison, Jefferson, Henry
Defended a heightened England from an England lapsed.

In a capitol later modelled on the Maison Carrée
The orators talked down tyranny. Fifty miles away
Their general accepted the English commander's sword.
– But then the new state grew stagnant, its fresh colour fading.

And the next efflorescence was war. All the red scars of
The Bloody Angle, the Crater, a hundred battles.
Great regiments faded on Cemetery Ridge;
Great captains lay crushed by the heavier guns.

With the best of the young men dead, the country ruined,
And the sourness of Military District no. 1,
The War was an after-image, a dominant lightning
To dazzle the stunned eyes of a generation.

But Lee in his college office in Lexington,
The man beyond criticism, spoke reconciliation.
Slavery at least was gone. Over yet one more century
As the wounds heal up, the flaws start slowly to fade.

The dogwood blooms, the cardinals perch, the lean hounds hunt
Where Pocahontas danced, where John Smith scouted, where
        Spotswood rode,
Where Washington marched to victory, Jackson to death,
By the slow rivers, the cool woods, the mountains, the marshes.

The Idea, never fulfilled, was never abandoned;
The free order only approaches its goal.
The land lived on imperfect in city and forest,
Its Form half-remembered; as it lay in the minds of poets.

PLACERVILLE

(California mining country)

After the temblor the strata settle
What was gold-dust in a slowing stream
Falls from that suspended gleam
Into solidities of lode-metal.

Shock, aftershock – over in days,
Consolidation of gold – eons:
But on our conceptual screens
Time knows its place.

In ten minutes a couple buy
At the store where such are sold
A ring struck from that gold
Engraved *Eternity*.

BELOW THE BELT

In an essay on seaside postcards Orwell
Found one was "obscene" without being "immoral"
– Inciting to nothing that's extramarital.

Broad bawdy, of course, cannot quite claim
Such fine amenity as its aim,
Yet it does seek to warm, and not to inflame.

Laugh-shaken, relaxed, subversive, a taste
Brewed up from humanity's seething yeast.
For some, that appetite's sadly decreased.

– Your seven-legged octopus may survive
(perhaps only six-legged, even five)
Not fully operational, half-alive.

So spare us the frigid, "transgressive" sorts
Of obscenity, with po-faced graduates
Jargoning away like juggernauts

259

Bargaining away … and we're rotten-ripe
With comics replacing mothers-in-law, tripe,
With a tedious tart-and-genitals hype.

To be fair, one must distinguish that from
The steaming Rugger Club's sonic boom,
The snigger of the Senior Common Room.

And the eighty verses of Kirriemuir
May not be rated as literature,
But still, their tone overlaps with the truer

Craft of the limerick, a serious game,
Wild fantasy, taut epigram,
Polished and cut like a five-line gem

Plucking the sensuous and mental strings
Giving the rhythmic structure wings
To stir up the psyche's happenings.

   2

They say women wince trying not to envision
Every organ, act or emission
While men just enjoy the verbal sedition.

That delicacy must be fairly addressed
(Though many exceptions might be pressed:
The Wives of Windsor and Bath, Mae West).

Still the genre seems somehow to correspond
To what they say about how men bond
The *mâle gaieté, si triste et profonde*

De Musset noted – and while we're abroad
There's Pushkin's shameless Gavriliad,
Voltaire's Pucelle, – and a gasconade

Of "Gallic salt" songs: (Bishop Dupanloup
Won immortality – though it's true
Not the sort that he had in view).

Well, back in England, from Chaucer on
In public (and privately Tennyson)
With Shakespeare, as ever, standing alone.

He "shocked"? – Not with sex. For that he'd use fright, as
With, perhaps, a bunch of first-nighters
Taking a drink between acts of Titus

Andronicus, and hearing the management's
Calling out to the audience
"We're expecting a little turbulence

Please return to your seats." Then the theatre's
Dead silence. – But with Hamlet's country matters
Their guffawed complicity shook the rafters.

Coarse tastes he reluctantly drifted with?
– That has long since been exposed as myth
For instance by Logan Pearsall Smith

Who makes it clear that a lot of his double
Meanings could only be caught by the subtle
Wit-epicures of the Mermaid circle.

Critics also note his obscenity
Exceeding other rhymesters' in quantity
– A side effect of genius and sanity?

So one hardly needs great scholarly probes
To show that, his patience being less than Job's,
He'd have said that the prigs and the anthrophobes

Were bit-players talking a lot of Globes.

CAMPANIA

"One party among us made the ascent of Vesuvius, while oth-
ers preferred the fertile valley (source of the famed wines of the
area). P., however, chose neither, visiting instead the barren region
north-west of Naples, known mainly for its repulsive character.
V., in his dry way, suggested that this reflected P's taste in artistic

The Arts that seriously address
The raising of the consciousness
Bloom in a spread of themes and tones
– Geology of various zones.

Some scale the great volcano – sky,
Flame, precipice, immensity.
While some tread, in the charming vale,
The villages-and-vineyards trail.

The grandeur group (though kindly) tends
To mock at its more modest friends,
While they, in turn, are quick to spot
Pretensions in the peak-proud lot.

But both despise one who resigns
The glorious vistas, the green vines,
For Phlegraean Fields that gall each sense
With flat glooms round mephitic vents.

A matter of tastes and temperaments.

AT THE REBIRTH OF ST. PETERSBURG

for Yelena Afanasiev

White nights of the northern city,
Blue eyes of one of its women.
Light brims up over the Pole, limning
With surfaces of serenity

Gold spires, green squares, grey river
Where today's dusk is tomorrow's dawn.
Sheets of light under the swansdown
Sky sweep through, around, over,

Unsilting every dulled sense,
Flexing every frozen mood

Of the stranger from a lower latitude.
Peeling from lulled waters, sky-silence,

How can such fineness run so rich?
– Laminations of light, ermine, almond,
Dissolved into the wholly transparent:
A fluid purity to leach

Out the crass, the quotidian,
Mind blanched to take stronger hues
And above all her eyes'. That blue's
Even more confirmatory than

All those wide-winged whitenesses:
With an unstinting radiance
Of acceptance, of endurance
Inexhaustible as the rich skies.

Profound plenitude, then:
Not the thin blue of the shallows,
– Unripe innocence that knows
Little of hate; nor like the alien

Flat amethyst ovals of sprites with
Snake-fascinations, snake-fears
In the cold springs, white-birch-hidden meres
Projected unfeeling from myth.

– And yet the inhuman has firmed
The depth and strength of that blue:
Here life's been indentured to
Troll, golem, the undead, the damned,

Mean fury has raved, ravenous
Down these streets, with claws of torture,
War, famine, lies, slaughter.
Terror-hammer, falsehood-furnace

Crushed the selfish, or just weak, to mere
Clinker, to twisted scrap; but
The fine, the firm, with eyes half-shut
Was forged through years in that fire

To a gentle strength, to a charm
Against all that's false and cruel:
And that blue is the sheen of a steel
It took white heats to anneal.

But now the white night is cool,
The eyes upon mine are calm.

IN PLACE

Six Malverns cluster round the hills
From Malvern Link to Malvern Wells
    Great, Little, North and West,
And, high above the ridge upthrown
From North Hill down to Raggedstone
    The Beacon's windy crest.

Where Langland, as our language woke,
Saw a fair field full of folk
    Past Teme and Evesham vales,
Where Auden like an admiral stood
On the old rocks, from which he could
    Scan storm-clouds over Wales.

Where back in the Armada's days
"Twelve fair counties saw the blaze
    From Malvern's lonely height",
My grandfather would say thirteen.
The toposcope which shows the scene
    Appears to prove him right.

The Assembly Rooms: those summer days
Of Festival – its concerts, plays,
    The strange crowd it would draw:
One incident I well recall:
My sister on her bicycle
    Knocked down George Bernard Shaw.

High, dominating, half way down
The slope of the steep-streeted town,
    The Priory's grey mass.

Its old font I was christened at
And outside, by a buttress that
        Shaded their patch of grass,

Some wooden crosses from the War
With aluminium strips that bore
        Both my uncles' names.
The younger with the Worcesters fell
Aged nineteen at Passchendaele –
        The shadow nothing tames

Deep in our elders' eyes still hung
But never thrust upon the young
        Though sometimes, nothing said,
A look that seemed to scan one's face
As though one could in part replace
        The irreplaceable dead …

The ghastly prep-school where I went
And all those winters that we spent
        With chilblains or with flu
(Or both). And where a gross cuisine
Of gristle stewed in margarine
        Sustained us as we grew.

The little Malvern House Hotel
Where I was born, and St. Anne's Well
        Among its elms and firs.
The bookshop off the Promenade
In which the choice was sometimes hard
        – Astounding or New Verse.

And so we felt our minds expand.
Not only that, as when the band
        Played at the Hydro Ball.
Paul Jones starts. With luck one wins
Esme or Pam, the lovely twins,
        Or Wendy, best of all.

Memories clear up like mist:
The second girl I ever kissed
        (The first was out in Wales)

The very first whose breasts I bared
– But on the sentiments we shared
    Is where description fails …

A sweet tryst by the British Camp
– Strange interweave of ditch and ramp:
    What if such history's died?
Or if, as that old poet sings,
"We shall not see the holy kings
    Ride down by Severn side."

For yet at Powick by the Teme
We'd meet; or down on Severn stream
    In gun emplacements for
The final fighting and the worst,
As Powick skirmish was the first,
    In England's Civil War …

Back to the Beacon: to the East
There is no higher ground at least
    Until some Ural peak.
The wind off all of Europe's ice
Scrubbed clear the granite and the gneiss.
    We hugged, too cold to speak …

– Some of the fragments that I shored
Against my going off abroad
    When I had turned eighteen.
And looking back across the years
I hardly think it all coheres
    Nor grasp all it may mean.

WHENEVER

This age requires "a tongue that naked goes
Without more fuss than Dryden's or Defoe's."

Thus Wyndham Lewis – let me check – a long
Half century ago, in *One Way Song*.

Our age requires … But first we should expound
What sort of age it is. Just look around!

An age that thinks it knows, what's known to none,
Just how societies and psyches run.

An age of terrorists and absolutes:
One primes the missile and the other shoots.

An age of intellectuals talking balls
Picked up in gutters or in lecture halls,

Illiterate nomads in their urban tents
And ideologies of virulence.

An age when creativity's essential
And people realize their full potential,

An age of people who're concerned, or care,
– With schemes that lead to slaughter everywhere.

An age of warheads and the KGB,
An age of pinheads and the Ph.D.

When churches pander to advanced regimes
Whose victims fill our nightmares with their screams,

Age that ignored the unavenged Ukraine
"Imperialist Britain" seething in its brain,

An age of art devised for instant shock
An age of aestheticians talking cock,

With education – but let's cool it, lads,
And say, a means of inculcating fads

For Loyalty's in bourgeois ethics set,
Taste a mere mirage we must all forget,

Judgement to Progress must incline its scales,
And Truth ensure that Prejudice prevails

Until, as Harry Harrison would say,
With us it's always Bowb-your-buddy Day.

– Suppose it is. Some think we need a verse
Disrupting the disruption ten times worse:

The vulpine howl; the ill-corrected proof;
The mumble from the mouth that lacks a roof;

Strumming a single toneless string will do,
Or else a *mélange adultère de tout*.

Well, plural decencies come down to this:
Our queasy tolerance extends to piss.

– Yet let our clarion of conclusion sound,
That, even more than Lewis's, we've found

Our age requires a tongue that naked goes
Without more fuss than Dryden's or Defoe's.

DEMONS DON'T

Demons don't
                    trust anyone, anywhere. So on no account
Trust them yourself. If you have one pent
Safely (you think) in your pentacle, a faint
Steam rising from its coarse integument
Fixing you with its single yellow flint
Eye, apparently acquiescent,
Never relax for a single moment.
Across vast voids, your formula of constraint
Has brought it you, compelled not compliant
As the occasional twitch of its blunt
Black lobster-like claws may hint.
One crack in the diagram, one error in the chant
And in a howling strike you'll be sent
Spinning down the dark dimension-vortex river
To a terror of dreary torment.

Demons don't
                    laugh. That long crescent
Gash below the eye doesn't show enjoyment.
Nor do they weep – a mode of the plangent
Their solid-state physiologies prevent.
But they are glad, even briefly, to be absent
From their own sphere's stifling environment
And melancholy at their too imminent
Return there: flat, infinite in extent
Uniform but for the odd lava-drooling vent
Under a pallid, sagging firmament:
And the nullity – no event or incident
Except the occasional entrapment
Of a human victim – of which the whole point
For a while at least, is to relieve a
Tedium otherwise total, transcendent.

Demons don't
                    love. And it's what they resent
Most, as an intolerable affront
To negation, when they detect the sentiment
In victims long exposed in the ambient
Horizonless, endless exhaustion-effluent.
In such, that is, as really repent
And not merely unwish, their arrogant
Distortings – from some of whom we've learnt
What we know of that realm: they are revenant
Because the realm regards even a remnant
Of that feeling as so indecent, so repugnant
That sometimes, cramped in a visceral, violent
Spasm, it hurls them back earthward. Gaunt,
Eyes clenched tight on both frost and fever,
They wander among us, saved but soul-burnt.

Demons don't
                    die; hence the astonishment
They feel when faced with a quite frequent
Wish, which if they could they'd gladly grant.
Immortality may be what humans want
But knowing what it's like to live for ever
Demons don't.

I. M.

On this Memorial Day
I remember a basset hound:
Bluebell (such was her name)
Died on the first of May.
Her ashes lie in the ground
By the lawn where her favourite game,

Chase-your-master, was played
Through the warm afternoons.
Sweet-natured, stubborn, afraid
Only of wasps ... One of those
Almost unalloyed boons
That life sometimes bestows.

Uproarious welcomes! She'd streak
Down the hall, ears trailing with speed,
Her melodious bay ringing out;
She wouldn't lick, but she'd
Gently nuzzle your cheek,
Then escort you back through the flat.

Her voices: that bay, sweet and deep;
The long coyote-like peals
That Satchmo's horn would evoke;
A crescendo of make-believe growls
As she swaggered up with a stick;
Her contented sigh before sleep.

In the morning, when she awoke
After lazily taking note
Of your presence, she'd always roll
Over for you to stroke
The silky white hair of her throat.
Then off for our morning stroll.

Philip Larkin she knew as a friend
– The closest description of
The affable contact it was.
Every letter from him would end

"Greetings" or "regards" or "love
To Bluebell" … It passed across

The small interspecies gap.
Once, out in Battersea Park,
He observed that, much unlike lots
Of dogs, even having a crap
Her back made a graceful arc,
Not one of your squalid squats.

A critic once said "Here's the deal:
You see her and old So-and-so
Being swept over a weir,
Which would you rescue?" "Her."
"Sentimentality!" "No,
That's when you fake what you feel."

Well, whether or not you agree,
She's gone as we all must go,
Comrade and comforter.
It's some consolation to know
I did my best for her,
She did her best for me.

On the move, she was always game.
She sturdily ploughed through the snows,
She lolled in the lukewarm meres,
She barked at two oceans … Then those
Almost idyllic last years
Here in her final home.

Whence she's gone as we all must go,
In her case leaving behind
A heartening afterglow,
A lasting awareness of
Those modulations of mind
We lump together as love.

THIS BE THE WORSE

They fuck you up, the chaps you choose
To do your Letters and your Life.
They wait till all that's left of you's
A corpse in which to shove a knife.

How ghoulishly they grub among
Your years for stuff to shame and shock:
The times you didn't hold your tongue,
The times you failed to curb your cock.

To each of those who've processed me
Into their scrap of fame or pelf:
You think in marks for decency
I'd lose to you? Don't kid yourself.

VESPERS

Dusk in St. James's Park, late May:
Soft serenities still play
Round the mossed margins of the lake.
I watch three mallards, one a drake,
Stall skilfully in flight, to drop
Mere inches to a splashdown stop.
Then ... But "Hullo!" – to wreck my mood –
Unreal as ever, there he stood,
No, more unreal, cheeks tighter still
And pallider, eyes yet more chill.
I hadn't seen him for some years,
Had vaguely followed his careers,
Art committees, book prize votes,
Backstabbed colleagues, TV gloats.
His first faint spark had long since gone,
He must have known, but carried on ...
How life had faded from his face!
My answer seemed to meet the case,
"Hullo. I thought that you were dead."
"Well, really, I'm alive," he said.
"In what sense?" He looked aghast.
I watched the landing of one last

Grey goose. And when I turned around
He'd gone. Or sunk into the ground.

ON THE SOLENT

I met her one day on the ferry
That runs to the Isle of Wight,
A girl who appeared to be very
In fact you might almost say quite.

But as it turned out she was barely
In fact you might almost say not:
She left me one day, most unfairly
For a wealthy young man with a yacht.

And as a result I was highly
As I saw their wake streaking the sea
But I said to myself rather wryly
"There'll be more on the mainland for me!"

A TASTING

One should satisfy neither
The emotional heavy breather
Nor the uptight, unsexed
Sniffer of dried text

Half seas over
Or ostentatiously sober
Themes served tartare
Or grilled till they char

Clashing with primary colours
Or nuanced to nothingness
Gross satiation
Or scrawny alienation.

On offer: the homey and wry
Or the slaughterhouse-steamy

Twisted simile-scraps
Or muddled news-clips

Evading coherence
Down a trickle of type-fonts
To sink without closure
In a flatland of posture.

Yes, above all the ones
Who, for whatever reasons
Hype their transcendence
One up on us peasants.

You'll drink to that? Well
Who'll be your clientele?
Only the strange lot
Who don't care what

It says on the label:
But seek deep, indefinable
Savours – much the same
In a wine or a poem.

THROUGH PERSEPOLIS

One of those best days:
Everything smiles, satisfies.
Lunch with an editor,
And you'd seldom find brighter;
She's smart, good-looking, we discuss
A great difficult success
We've worked on together,
Over a brisk Sancerre
And a sole meunière ...
And then out past Covent
Garden in an ardent
High autumnal sunshine
Too strong for the Reality
Principle, at least mine.
Yes, bells peal briefly,
But no real trumpets

Sound through gilded streets,
No one really scatters
A richesse of flowers,
And there's no glass coach a-glitter
To hand her into, to lift her,
Now that all's settled and done,
Into the sky, over the sun …

QUANDO DORMITANT

Among the century's most quoted lines
Are some that don't send shivers up our spines.
Either a good poet, briefly, has foresworn
His talent with indulgence in pure corn
Or, high-prestiged, demanding our respect
Slams down fool's gold and dares us to object.
Examples that your critic designates
Are Auden, Eliot, Lowell, Thomas, Yeats –

"We must love one another or die." Clearly the writer forgot
In the end we must all of us die if we love one another or not.
To do Auden justice, when he went through it
He gave it a questioning look, and then he withdrew it.

"April is the cruellest month." We chose
For that spot, February, when we froze;
Though back indoors we managed, by the fire
To go on mixing memory and desire.

"The lord survives the rainbow of his will"
Rings quite impressively – that is until
Found just as good ripped up and then restored:
"The will survives the rainbow of his lord."
Or, on the Quaker dead a Catholic shrives,
"His rainbow of the will the lord survives."

"Do not go gentle into that good night."
– But if it's good, acceptance should be right,
So perhaps he'd better have reserved his rage
For his discomforts at an earlier stage.

"A terrible beauty is born." – shocked thought
With partisan rhetoric overwrought
– Not used when his own Free State lot
Had seventy-odd republicans shot.

But still, the bards are far less to be blamed
Than those who've kept the public spotlight aimed
Askew. – So amnesty's hereby proclaimed.

TWO TRANSLATIONS FROM ANDREI VOZNESENSKY

1. You Live at Your Aunt's

You live at your ballad-studying aunt's.
She sneezes and wears men's underpants.
The damned witch! How we hate her.

We're friends of the barn, like a good bear;
It warms us like hands stuffed in a sweater
And smells of bee-hives.
 And in Suzdal it's Easter!
In Suzdal, there's crowds, laughter, rooks.

You whisper of childhood, as we touch cheeks.
That country childhood, where horses and suns
And honeycombs glitter like icons.
And look at your hair, its honey tints …

I live in Russia, among snows and saints!

2. Evening on the Building Site

They nag me about "formalism".

Experts, at what a distance
You're stuck from life! Formalin:
You stink of it – and incense.

You've got that virgin plain,
But not one pearl of grain …

Art's dead without a spark
– Human rather than divine –
For bulldozermen to mark
In the taiga's trackless zone;

It comes to them raw and salt
To straighten them up at once,
Unshaven like the sun, pelt
Peeling like bark from pines …

For some girl of the Chuvashi
Brushing a blue tear away,
Brushing it – sweetly, sluttishly,
Brushing it – like a dragonfly,
To clap hands at rowdily …

So to me they mean little,
The lances of libel,
The furious label.

MUZAK IN THE MEN'S ROOM (BEVERLY HILLS)

Eliminate the Negative
Is more or less appropriate:
But what reaction should I have
To this new (to me) phenomenon
– Camellias too, soft light, gold carpet? …

Well, why fuss with opinions on
Each oddity life may present?
Don't Fence Me In is the next tune:
Strumming the pink ceramic shine
I hum "no comment" as my comment.

DISTANCING

The dream recalls: "53864
79, Private Conquest, R.
Is that your name and number?"
"Yes, Sir." "Charged, in the field,

While on active service, that you failed
To …" what, I don't remember.

Come to that, the things I've failed
To do since then, if they were piled
Up, would make quite a heap.
Why would I dream of that particular
Grey skylight, walls? Just because all so minor?
Dismissed! Get out of my sleep!

REGRETS AT BEING UNABLE TO ATTEND A SOHO POETRY READING BY MR SCANNELL

Dear Vernon,
                When St Anne's sweet chime
Gave notice it was opening time
In we went to drink and rhyme,

Afternoon men come alive
From whatever club or dive
Had seen us through from 3 to 5.

Not much more than a pint or two's
Enough: you needn't think the Muse
Floats in on a sea of booze.

In the French Pub the merest pong
Of Pernod swung one into song,
Ripely the evenings rolled along …

Let's hear it for, and from, you! Cheers!
In Soho after all these years
With high-proof poetry for our ears.

FAR AND AWAY

[Epsilon erídani – so pronounced – the nearest sun-type star then known to have planets]

Philip Larkin (a mind immune
To cant) called the notion that feeling can
Thrive in short lines that rhyme and scan
"Remote as mangoes on the Moon."

A century hence: in Luna City
At Café Larkin a poet drinks
Mango juice fresh from Moonfruit Inc's
Tycho Dome orchard, and says "A pity
That the idea we all can heighten
Our sensibilities by schemes
Of sound and syllable structure seems
Remote as tamarinds on Titan."

After another century: Saturn's
Sky-filling rings, and there beneath
With tamarind-pods for a laurel wreath
A bar-bard mutters "To make word-patterns
Distil a radiance that would rid any
Sub-solar soul of emotional fogs
Seems distant as worlds where they'd serve eggnogs
Out round Epsilon Eridani."

A hundred years later: under Epsilon,
Humanic, high-gened for thoughts and tastes,
A three-point thrummer sits down and wastes
Cooltime with his chattering son,
"A great egg-fruit! Did your off-mate grow it?
The tests that our roboteacher's screened!
– What's a mango? A tamarind?
And one real puzzler – what's a 'poet'?"

SOONER OR LATER

Changed, when the great equalizer
Has played its black joke,

279

To a few pounds of fertilizer
Or a few puffs of smoke,

Some ways of such a passing
Strike you sharp and clear:
A van on a zebra crossing,
A vein behind the ear.

Or, with worse scenarios,
A slow melt-down that bores
And exhausts, till dark's victorious,
Not only you, but yours;

You feel the days dismantle
The billion-neuron hoard:
Love sputters like a candle,
Small facts go overboard,

(The mercy speech by Portia,
The words to Gershwin tunes,
The Roman Forts of Yorkshire,
The names of Neptune's moons.)

Anyhow, brain and body,
Here comes a new recruit
To much-missed ranks already
Long since gone down the chute.

What's helpful. Not much. Nothing?
But to fill in the time
There's little harm in clothing
Such nude truths with a rhyme.

ELEMENTAL

More swum than the stream
More breathed than the breeze
In all the great scheme
Of things somehow she's

More wholly there
Than their essence could be
More flown than the air
More sailed than the sea

Over and above
What is or occurs
Located by love
On this world of hers.

IN SUSPENSE

Mist-murked, a swollen moon protrudes
Out of the West, and brings to mind
– Gibbous, askew – the bare behind
Of one of Stanley Spencer's nudes.

Suet-hued, lax limbs outspread,
Eyes glazed, as if they didn't know
They were being watched: indeed as though
Caught in the dark on infrared.

A dead fly on the canvas web,
Some old cave's supine stalagmite …
Even this gold-starved, furtive light
Plumbs the pulsed ocean's flow and ebb.

His concepts hardly seem to mesh
Into our more reactive space
– Not just an inexpressive face
But even inexpressive flesh!

Clearly no sex or shock was meant
With genitalia on display
Like organs on a butcher's tray
Quite untransgressive in intent.

With tissue samples cut from time
He sought a fixed, unspurious pose
As truthful as the tightest prose
– Velásquez more like rose-blurred rhyme …

Moonset: that unorganic sphere
Rolls on; and where we live and breathe
Likewise the sensual spectra seethe
Swept down the irreversible year.

EQUATORIAL

Espèce de soleil! – Laforgue

Sod of a sun! your photon-spew
Is more than flesh can stand
Your glare sticks in our eyes like glue
We feel we're breathing sand

Hour by hour you braise or bake
Our lungs, our throats, our brains
But still our nostrils, though they cake
Can smell our simmering drains

So smug you hang there overhead
Time hardly seems to pass
As in our shadeless square you shred
The dry and desperate grass

How viciously you beat on down
(It's no excuse that in
St Tropez you gently brown
Those beachfuls of bare skin)

Downwards at last you start to dip
You redden, swell and throb
Like the intrusive glans or tip
Of some huge sky-bloke's knob

Swine of a sun! Still spitting bile
At last you sink from sight
Good riddance to your flashy style
Here comes the tasteful night

A breeze, and then in close pursuit
To soothe our mental burns

The slim moon, cool as she is cute ...
(But soon the sod returns.)

OFFSHOOTS

How can this Apple be defined
By red-green scrapings of its rind?
The sensed blurs with what went before,
Taste, texture, pips and core.
Then, imperfectly, close to sheer
Abstraction, shapes it to a "sphere",
While, deeper yet, our memories scan
Brush-strokes of Chardin, of Cézanne.

Try "Water": the slow stream, the pond
Stirred faintly by a flurry of wind
Evoking all that's cool and fresh;
Then vapour-trails; then maelstrom thresh;
Swum seas; tides pouring into verse,
Drenching the pale philosophers.

Just samples of such stimuli
As seethe through every instant. Why?
They ask us, burrowing like moles
Experts on nervous systems, souls ...
But how does that mind-moment meld
With no strange resonance withheld?

As in some bright, tempestuous dawn
All that dazzling detail torn
From sensed, remembered, thought – somehow
Churned up into this single Now.
Such stark asymmetries to blend!
How can the ego apprehend
Its wholeness when that overload
Kicks in, or crack some deeper code?

Behind that bone-curve crowned with hair
The consciousness's rushlights flare
Whose quarter-million hours awake
Stir memories that blur and break,

Half-worn tapestries woven of
Old colour-chords of loss or love.

So best shun any master scheme.
Eat that apple, cross that stream,
Chewing one's best to neutralise
Nude Aphrodite's golden prize.
There'll be no naiads in that rill
So let's forget about them. (Still …)

NOCTURNE

"Broad Daylight" – words you speak or write
Imputing narrowness to Night?

        •

Night's only moonlit, starlit, yet
See from that delicate palette
The crested wave that brims the cove
The breeze-blown-blossomed apple grove.

        •

Even when deepest dark has spread,
The lovers on the unlit bed,
In a deep sensuousness embraced,
Enjoy touch, hearing, scent and taste:
All the senses except sight
Providing adequate delight.
– While outside, champion of the dark,
The nightingale outsings the lark.

        •

That sweet bird's spectrum? Perhaps instead
Of Day's " … green, yellow, orange, red"
She, other creatures of the Night
Take in "… frost, steel, silver, white"
For all we know, these are no less
Compelling to their consciousness

As rich on their subjective screens
As all our diverse reds and greens.

•

And then, look up! The clear Night is
Home to all deeps and distances
Where ritualled constellations reign
Like some scored musical refrain,
Voids vivid there with planets, stars,
Diamond Vega, vermilion Mars,
The pale mesh of the Milky Way,
The meteor-shower's high, silent spray.

•

– Just match their breadths and depths and heights.
Night's limit to our naked sight's
That faintest blur M 31
In Andromeda, two million
Light-years! – Rather different from
Day's ten light-minutes maximum!
In fact Day's narrow limits are
Mere suburbs of one G-type star.

•

How would humans be if they
Were strictly creatures of the Day?
Asleep at dusk, up after dawn,
Night's treasures would have stayed unknown,
Those vistaed vaults would not have brought
Awed feelings, challenges to thought.

•

"Broad Daylight's commonly the time
Allotted to some loathsome crime
But let's concede, more cause for fright
Lurks in the narrower "Dead of Night".

EXTRAPOLATION

The thin crescent to the West:
Lit outline of a single breast
Of a sky-goddess otherwise
Wholly in shadow, and the size
Of half-a-dozen constellations …
Our imagery's impatience
Distorts the real sky
– But closer, and equally
Part of the universe,
There are such shapes as hers.

GRACE NOTES

The embarrassment of
Childish words of love,
"Blossom queen", "honey dove".

When girls (an old sage said)
Strip for a man's bed
Shame too should be shed.

And now? – As words get
More infantile yet:
"Baby lamb", "angel pet".

RECONNAISSANCE

On a clear night, we may look up at the All
As if standing at the central
Point of a huge flash-freaked black opal.

Then, past our vision, the mind supplies
Metagalaxies, immensities
For those impressible by mere size,

Well, we're nearing technologies that could scan
Cities on planets of Aldebaran,
Oceans as far off as M 31.

– And the forward edge of the far future's
Wave'll sweep right over those frontiers
For our heirs' almost endless voyages and ventures.

"Almost" because the very universe
Must in the end darken and disperse
Or so say our current cosmographers.

They plumb near the Big Bang's first nanosecond
– Though that may be only scraping the rind
If the full fruit's forever beyond.

2

We've always trolled for implicit patterns.
Lucretius interwove a sleet of atoms.
Some Greeks stamped number on reality's phantoms.

Random stars fell into constellations
Imposed on the celestial regions
By the ancient craving for aggregations

And, centuries later, the Hereford Map
Gave the world strict, but spurious, shape:
Jerusalem at the centre, a mental warp.

Now: seething quanta, dimensions, a spate
Of force-fields round which intricate
Equations weave their dazzling net.

But unobserved arrhythmias thresh
Around and soon break out of the mesh.
The massive computing starts afresh

And, as the phenomena froth and foam,
From our polders we toil to divert and dam
The oceans of the continuum.

3

William James once wrote of how temperament
Determined each philosopher's bent.

With the data so weak, we can only assent.

Though surely only the most rigid doctrine
Solely depends on (say) the endocrine
Balance or what's in the brain-dead groin?

There are, of course, many scenarios,
Quite a collector's cellar of curios.
We can only go where our thoughts will carry us,

Which mayn't be far – the point's Robert Heinlein's –
Any more than a collie has much of a chance
To grasp how its dog food gets into cans.

4

Some ache for those worlds beyond the voids
With appropriate orbits, the needed fluids,
To commune with minds of non-anthropoids.

But, above all, there's the heavy artillery
Of instruments, the tempestuous flurry
Of equations tearing through thickets of theory

And why shouldn't sages with minds like prisms
Probe the intergalactic chasms
Enjoying their new-knowledge orgasms?

Still, tracking the trail of the Big Bang
Is a waste for those happy with Yin and Yang
Or leaning back into the Allfühlung.

5

If to peter out is the lot of the All
Its tenure is longer than ours, but still
We may find some sort of parallel.

As wavelengths flatten to infinite
(Or are crushed to minima less than nought)
Existence fades into total night.

Meanwhile minds bred up from matter
– At once their prey and their predator –
Are faced with various ultimata.

Of the whole, we've only the thinnest slice
Just a brief tangle till we're torn loose
From the thorns of time, the weeds of space.

Does that last wrench, as the body-link goes
Or almost so, fill a timeless pause
Where the unflake falls and the unstream flows?

6

Research-hounds, trained to be untranscendental,
In two different packs hot on the scent will
Flush out the mood-modes, material, mental.

Some trace the intense billion neuron torque
That the crimped folds of the cortex spark;
Others strip the viewed psyche stark.

But concept-cantilevers somehow don't solve
The bridging of the spidery gulf
Between the nerved senses and the self.

7

Half-free of the clumsy cosmos-grope,
As if not quite woken from non-REM sleep,
Wisps of totality may take shape,

Mist moments smooth as chiselled stone,
Sweet Agnosis, sculptor Anon,
With all of the undivine withdrawn,

And, faintly felt through the near-alive,
The softest touch of a tendril of love
Too light for leaf or belief …

THE FELLS (MID-19TH C)

Fuzzy white cords of snow intertwine, trailing
Down from humped cloud-mass across his eyes:
A low light jostles unsteadily through
Ripped rags of the West horizon – paling

Backdrop to regretted decision.
Feet, mind trudge on between barbed hedges,
Numb fields. Boughs hang soggy black, any green
Trace supplied more by memory than vision.

No real colour, then. No reds or pinks
No holly-berry, flicker of robin-breast.
A fatigued yellow only, from the windows ahead.
But flakes feather about him. He huddles his senses. And thinks,

As he plods on to the place where he shouldn't go,
That after all the world could be worse. For at least
The spinning dark in the depths of the cumulus
Doesn't weave black snow.

LAST HOURS

The coast cools down the afternoon
And slowly a sky the colour of corn
Peels away round a reddening sun.

That creamy monotone dispersed,
Lime and umber, roan and rust
Well up out of the ored West.

Old vaults polish extreme song,
Intense vintage is smooth on the tongue,
The mind warms to the subtle and strong;

And pressed out of a dying sky
Sweeps of coloured profundity
Fill the heart as they fill the eye.

Sophocles and others, so we're taught,
Showed old age gather such glow of thought
To plenitude. Was it still too short?

Over this dim broadness of bay,
Pale tuberose, crimson ray
Brim over, and start to seep away.

The great sunset loses its strength.
The cloud's black that was hyacinth.
(Sophocles crumbles on his plinth) …

The thick hues, the transparencies:
It all devolves into a darkness,
Folds back into the cool abyss.

Dead in the water, the day is done.
There's nothing new under the sun,
Still less when it's gone down.

BLACK SEA

Lynx-lithe, a concentrate of light
Swoops, sudden, through the headland firs,
Claws slashing the soft lens of sight.
Even the thewed slope shakes and blurs.

The sun's outflanked the earlier shade
Of foliage with a horizontal
Blaze. Half-blind, we turn and wade
Through photon-seethe to our hotel

But soon we're over the effects
Of the harsh cosmos breaking through.
Fish from the bay, dry wine, sweet sex,
Then the veranda, whence we view

For now, a dimmer, different world
That wildness tamed; – while over there
The ground beneath the trees lies curled
Up like a hibernating bear.

CHALET

The wild wind, the white wind ...

Inside, in their long weekend,
Perhaps their last,
There seems no season
Only exhausted obsession
With their past,
Like a film in colour
Perversely techniqued to black-and-white,
Their unfeeling set in the pallor
Of a stiff glaze.

        – But now
Suddenly, a frenzy of love-hate ...
The wolf-wind howls through the snow ...

GETTING ON
[2010]

GETTING ON

Into one's ninetieth year.
Memory? Yes, but the sheer
Seethe as the half-woken brain's
Great grey search-engine gains
Traction on all one's dreamt, seen, felt, read,
Loathed, loved . . .
                            And on one's dead.
– Which makes one's World, one's Age, appear
Faint wrinkles on the biosphere
Itself the merest speck in some
Corner of the continuum.

Too extreme a distancing?
So let a nearer focus bring
The strange gaze of a sloe-eyed doe
On a cave painting from Lascaux,
Rock reamed by eons upon eons
Of such extreme, intense
Water-pressure as finally
Broke through southward, leaving high
Smooth-bored complexities.
                            And then
Up through those darknesses climbed men
Working towards each masterpiece
Lit by candle-wicks dipped in grease
Brought up there in hollow stones.

After five hundred generations
We have no other knowledge of
How they would feel, or think, or love.
Their speech – lost. Surely they'd curse and bless.
Their chants? Alas, we can only guess.

In faintest clues to that lost future
How might our meanwhile outlooks feature?
Dim distillation that releases
Endless potentials for the species,
Though all too soon perspectived on
Dark outposts of oblivion?

Back from those caves, at least we find
A muse-mode in the human mind:
Part poetry emerging now, part history,
The message it seems to impart is, "Try
To filter realities, out through past blunders
To a smooth flow". Is that beyond us?

***

Of course one's read a lot of memoirs
And always found the trouble with them was
Their pasts remained a jungle – viewed
From afar, from above – in any case skewed.
So try one's own experience,
Deploy some data, sense by sense,
Strange, fluent input from behind
The flat stage-scenery of the mind.

Visual. – In various lights displayed
Solar and lunar, shape or shade,
Their fine particulars all found
In the sky and the sea, by the stream, on the ground.
So it's not just the mind's eye that follows
The weaving flight of swans and swallows,
Starlit horizons, sunsets on
Plynlimon or the Parthenon –
And women – sometimes in the nude
Or other poses of pulchritude
– One of them keen to show she owns
White pearls like satin cherry-stones.
(Miniscule? Yes – to balance the huge
Spurts from one's cranial centrifuge …)

Sonic then: the ears like the eyes
Swing through the todays and the centuries,
Nor can one complain of the lack of any
Melody or cacophony:
Striking a bell, striking a chord,
The thundering charge of the Golden Horde,
Susurrus of oars in the Golden Horn,
The lovely lilt, too, of Goldie Hawn,
A sea-lion's bark by the Golden Gate …

But gold's too visual? So resonate.

See, Hear, now Feel – the sense of touch
Stroking so little, striking too much:
From silky skin that soothes one's fingers
To swimmer's flesh that's torn by stingrays.
Extremes? Yes, But there's also sex and love
Those two non-identicals, fused enough
Into a skin-and-psyche blend
That insistently cries "transcend!"

Let it simmer awhile – Mature?
There are some minds that take these newer
Insight gleams as giving perhaps
White-hot mountains for value-maps,
Whose failing volcanoes leave lava-clogged vents …
Yet, should such flow-depth somehow condense
And philosophy-lyric be seen as the aim
Some future archpoet might one day proclaim …

Till then, one can probably not do better
Than a quite superficial scatter
Of notes towards that perhaps eventual
Meld of the subliminal and the sensual.

***

Some would start with those well-tried stocks
Of monosyllabic building blocks,
Inflexibles which, for what they're worth, are
Hardly such as to take us further:
Out of control high words become
Off-putting, pretentious, numb
Whose marble platform soon rejects
One's futures and one's retrospects.
Yet personalities carved in stone
Somehow preserve stress, feeling, tone,
Leaving cool clarions to approve
The higher notes of Life and Love.

But first, as through murmuring minds it sweeps,
Remember how Life plays for keeps

– A game that one can only lose.
Hearing the sputtering of its fuse
One needs to concentrate on Time
(And tomb, its natural pararhyme).

Stroll through those earlier sheaves of verse,
As soon an old harvest-hope recurs
And throbbing with the pulse of years
Through the cleared mist Love re-appears
The sort of love that holds distilled
Those sweeter essences that yield
Flowers, lions, meteors – everything
About which one might dream or sing.

So far we'd barely touched on love
– And first in speechless contexts of
The wild heart racing, with the mind
Dragged half-helplessly behind.
Yet mind and body both survive
Largely through a superlative
Memory-wisdom of heartfelt care
Pervading one's always, one's everywhere,
Out beyond these short verses' scope
Vistas through which one can only grope.
While as they each of them possess
Good halves of their joint consciousness,
The beds and memories they share
Leave little other life to spare ...

    ***

And if one's asked can one recall
A slight acquaintance with the ALL,
Challenged so, one's muse-mind sees
How, in potential symmetries,
The poem beats time in several ways.
Some harmonies that it conveys
Come close to the intrinsic? No.
A pause for meditation, though.
Moments of calm closure?

But
As an imagined voice cries "Cut!"
Unorchestrated cyclones blow
From above, from beyond, from behind, from below,
Raising a brain-cell fog that blurs
Muse-moons – and brings new cosmographers
Who tell of near suns crushed so tight
Older reactions can't ignite,
While our far probes no more respond
From that faint featureless Beyond …

"Dark matter" next, "dark energy" …
Where is this darkness none can see?
An arid stretch of times and spaces
With human life its lone oasis?
Have galaxies failed to interbreed?
Is every mind-stream choked with weed?
While one's ready to disavow
Philosophy's Why, psychology's How,
Perhaps one's shown too little patience
With all those symbol-thick equations?

***

Let one just say that one prefers
To their pretentious Universe
How skill or accident deploys
The rich depth of the human voice
Come strongly out up from among
Lung-thresh, throat-clench, on to the tongue
That special instrument of thought
With which lost futures can be caught.

Always leaving one free to choose
What portion of the mind to use.
– Take human history, an immense
Portfolio of theres and thens
And check that Personality Cult
(With Unpersons one sad result)
While some who'd fought against the odds
Sought recognition as Ungods.
Then off to others that await

Contexts in which to replicate,
Free from each single obsessive train
Of thought, leaving an open brain.

For yes, these verses have ranged wide,
Caves, word-worlds, spectra – with the tried
And truly personal defences
For which the mind attuned the senses.
"Subjective?" – yes, say some who'd seek
To average out what's quite unique,
Whose winds and words can still outface
Negation with one warm embrace,
While lifespan, whether of days or years
Somehow up to a point coheres.
With open skies, hearts almost fit
To represent the infinite,
But no perspectives that suppose
Mind-maelstroms calming to a close.

***

Validities do not depend
On how their bearers fade or end;
With no conclusion on the way,
One needs the briefest holiday.
Inputs accumulating still
Find yet more questionnaires to fill.
And all these rhythms to satisfy …
One takes a breath …

    And then – a sigh …

from

BLOKELORE &
BLOKESONGS
[2012]

for Wendy Cope and Lachlan Mackinnon

The High Tribunal of these two
  Faults those omitting Fred
From status in (as is his due)
  Our culture's A to Zed.

FRED MEDITATES ON NATURE

Fred's always envied butterflies
    – Not for their sips and flits,
But the unfair advantages
    Their life-cycle permits.

At first on fuss and toil intent
    In caterpillar guise;
Then chrysalis retirement;
    And last, the sensuous skies.

And why the human species too
    Aren't programmed just the same
Seems slipshod (though Fred's not sure who,
    Or what, should take the blame):

To get the plodding over first;
    A snooze, and then to fly
Into a crashing sexual burst,
    And go out on a high!

It's not that his own love life's grim –
    Fred just finds nature great
To give philosophers like him
    Footnotes to human fate.

UNFAIR TO FRED

Quite early on Fred noticed it:
    A girl finds that, for her,
A chap behaving like a shit
    Is "showing character",

Or "challenging" the girl to see
    What she can make of him,
While those behaving decently
    Are left out on a limb …

One girl who dealt Fred blighted love
    Then went and wed the blighter,

Much later came to tell him of
　　The spasms of rage and fright a

Glimpse of the sod – by now her ex –
　　Induced in her for years;
He'd also been a dud at sex
　　– All music to Fred's ears.

A tough kid: now she frankly said
　　That with her youthful blooper
She'd dished herself as well as Fred …
　　The honey still looked super.

Things had turned out to validate
　　Fred's views in model fashion;
And yet he felt they'd left too late
　　A re-run of their passion.

A waste of time, a waste of what
　　We don't have too much of,
Fred doesn't think of it a lot:
　　But yes, a waste of love.

FRED FORGETS

You well may say a long-lost girl
　　Should now be cased in nacre,
An irritant become the pearl
　　Only his mind can make her.

But Fred so seldom thinks of her.
　　It's long ago. – And to be
Honest, he would now prefer
　　A sapphire or a ruby.

FRED'S FANE

Of course Fred's often heard the claim
　　A religious ex-

perience is much the same
(Or *just* the same) as sex.

Fred's known times when, in seconds flat,
    The female form divined
Brimmed up so high with mana that
    It nearly blew his mind.

But sometimes bedding down with such
    Turned to a playful game
While one who's not impressed so much
    Fair lit the night with flame ...

Perhaps among the mystics too
    Such paradoxes reign.
Of course, on a more general view
    The parallels are plain.

FRED ON MYTH

Though Orpheus won the laurel crown
    He drank the bitter cup:
Eurydice first let him down
    Then Maenads tore him up.

An Orpheus Complex? Fred won't fuss
    With such an ancient tale
(Unlike old Freud with Oedipus)
    – The thought, though, turns him pale.

Mere myth? – But that old Greek (thinks Fred)
    Who told the tale as true
Had some material in his head
    On which he later drew.

FRED'S PHRASEOLOGY

"Soft breasts, hard heart." It does sound quite
    A general apophthegm.

Fred meant it only to indict
  One girl, not all of them.

Yet gets the blame when girls find that
  Some bitter chap who'll not
Observe this careful caveat
  Applies it to the lot.

FECKLESS FRED

Woman's mentality is not
  (Fred holds) clear about man's.
They think us a seducing lot
  Who lay cold-blooded plans.

He takes a girl, say twice, to lunch,
  Then makes a dinner date.
That night, just rolling with the punch
  He might, or might not, wait.

And if he does consider how
  To get her to his flat,
It's only, as they put it now,
  Because that's where it's at.

Chaps may, what's more, fall madly in
  Love, as Fred once did,
His mind short-circuited by gin,
  Committed by his id.

NOT FRED'S STYLE

If you are wanting to annoy
  (As Fred hopes that you're not),
Nowadays there's many a ploy
  To make girls' cheeks go hot.

One method Fred has sometimes struck:
  With eyes half-shut and grin

Of patronising homage, chuck
     A girl beneath the chin.

"Well, well, my little one" will serve
     To aggravate your crime;
But even if you have the nerve
     Fred doubts you'll have the time.

Because, meanwhile, the chance is high
     That, when the penny drops
You'll rapidly be silenced by
     A smack across the chops.

Meekness, in fact, has had its day
     (If it was ever found),
But still nostalgia for it may
     Give chaps the runaround.

If so, to realists like Fred
     Their compensation seems
Only attainable in bed
     – That is, of course, in dreams.

ONE OF FRED'S FANCIES

Fred knows that, in their sexual stint,
     Breasts stand as stimuli
Designed by Nature to imprint
     The male's obsessive eye.

It may be just a whim, but still
     Nature might now, he feels,
Evolve, on the same principle,
     Extensible high heels.

FRED GOES INTO DETAIL

Women distinguish many a hue
     Far beyond men's scope:

"Teal" it seems is vaguely blue,
    A muddy shine is "Taupe".

"Minutiae from which," we groan,
    "There's little to be learned."
But Fred's not one to leave a stone,
    However small, unturned.

Well yes, we say, the colour sense
    Differs in him and her;
So girls' minds aren't the same as men's?
    Whoever thought they were!

Fred replies that what we've known's
    Been attitudes to love
And shops and time and telephones
    – All superficial stuff,

But now he feels he's found the key:
    Whoever thought a girl'd
Be structured to not even see
    The same objective world?

Yet Fred approves of Nature's plan,
    (From which we can't escape):
Who'd want a woman like a man,
    Merely of different shape?

FRED IN A MUDDLE

Though lots more logic would be nice
    It's even clear to Fred
He doesn't take his own advice,
    He takes the plunge instead.

Consoling him for such a lapse
    We tell him that we think:
His lore may be of use to chaps
    Who totter on the brink.

But Fred can't stand the ruck at all
    Who look before they leap.
What's more they're just the ones who call
    His "cynicism" cheap.

FRED PUTS THE CLOCK BACK

Fred muses on those eras when
    A woman would "confer
Her favours on" some lucky man
    And he would "pleasure" her.

"Have sex with", "have it off with" – this
    Jargon gives no sense
Of all those warm benignities,
    That sweet beneficence.

FRED, FILM CRITIC

"Explicit Sex": Fred says that means,
    In cinematic terms,
Humans set in carnal scenes
    Like pekes or pachyderms.

Nothing's less like the act of love,
    As those inside it feel,
Than such a representation of
    Its semblance on a reel:

On filming how a couple screws,
    With camera panned up close,
Silly's a word that one might use –
    Another one is *gross*.

So, round by round and blow by blow
    With false or faulty touch,
Their lenses' scope can only show
    Too little or too much.

Some erotica Fred's known
      – Exceptional, it's true –
(Indian, for instance) has a tone
      Truthful and tender too.

But, on film the whole thing (which
      Sometimes has occurred)
Can only reach us real and rich
      If adequately blurred.

While Fred hates in the average show
      Intrusive action by
The male partner ... and no,
      He can't "identify".

Even the pure, romantic screen
      Never exactly charms
Old Fred, with some young honey queen
      In someone else's arms.

FRED FILLS ONE IN

Check one: Success □ ; Health □ ; Feeling free □;
      Fully requited love □ ;
Your chance of immortality □ ;
      Or none of the above □ .

Fred's answer? – Well, it seems (though some
      Would take it to denote
A mind unsalvageably dumb)
      Love still might get his ☒.

FRED AND THE FOUNDING FATHERS

By "prejudice" we understand
      A blend of common-sense:
The wisdom of the ages and
      Life's experience.

Similarly with "stereotyped",
        Much used by trendies when
They want all knowledge quite wiped
        Out – then start again.

A base camp in that hard-won lore
        Serves Fred and others who
May move out from it to explore
        Whatever's strange and new.

FRED THE HEALER

Fred doesn't harp on it a lot
        And yet this thought persists:
There can't be many men who're not
        Part-time misogynists.

So he's devised this therapy
        To make the strain grow less,
Such feelings abreacted by
        Being brought to consciousness.

X X X FRED

Some find – what may unman the best –
        Although she freely strips,
A girl, quite lavish of the rest,
        A prude about her lips.

It puts in question, straight away,
        How far the union goes:
Mutual surrender, Fred would say,
        Must stretch from head to toes.

And when a couple's loins press tight,
        Locked in the act of love,
A formal handshake mayn't seem right
        To link the parts above.

That's why not only Fred – for this
    Applies to lots of males –
May find that if denied a kiss
    Their whole performance fails.

FRED AND FABLE

Some chaps are like the fabled frogs:
    They get, when they re-wed
In a reaction from Queen Log's
    Regime, Queen Stork's instead.

Who knows what Aesop had in mind:
    But politics of strife
Or compromise are not confined
    Only to public life.

FRED AND FIFI

Old Fred's imagination has
    In its conceptual net
A honey whom he thinks of as
    Fifi LaFollette.

French maid, or can-can dancer at
    Folies or Moulin Rouge,
She may best serve to indicate
    A really not too huge

Array of varied images
    In vision's repertoire,
Exotic with her flashing eyes
    And her unfloating hair:

One of a princely harem? Well,
    For accuracy's sake
Let's say, of the material
    From which a lad can make

A sort of sensual symphony
    (Blonde Swede, Circassian slave …
Sometimes a mix of two or three,
    At most of four or five).

A film across reality?
    A meld of metaphors?
A symbol of humanity?
    A condiment or sauce? …

When actual girls come into play
    The tactful little pet
Just waves her hand and trips away.

    Her perfume lingers yet.)

FOOTNOTES FROM FRED

1

"Si la jeunesse savait, si
    La vieillesse pouvait," yet
Fred brings up an anomaly
    That aphorists forget.

He finds that, with the years he's spanned,
    In his not special case,
The savvy's finally to hand,
    The pouvy still in place.

2

Of course, the knowledge has its gaps,
    The power sometimes fails,
And, as with all imperfect chaps,
    Incompetence prevails.

In any case, he'd hardly claim
    That spoilsports like La Roche-
foucauld would ever mark his name
    "Sans peur et sans reproche."

FRED INVESTIGATES

Do chaps find life with ones that scold
    Worse than with ones that sulk?
Well, of the sample Fred has polled
    The answer is, the bulk

Just vote against the mode from which
    Their present sufferings stem
("Don't Knows" have pasts containing each
    But now are shot of them.)

"These weighted questions," experts prate,
    "That ill-constructed curve …"
But Gallup won't co-operate
    So Fred's will have to serve.

FRED FACES FACTS

If *Blanc de Blancs* and *Blanc de Noirs*
    (Fred muses, rather pissed)
Are possible, as most things are,
    Can *Noir de Blancs* exist?

His reason tells him in a tick
    This is the merest dream.
But is his intellect so quick
    When women are the theme?

Not without effort. For he'll let
    His fantasy grow fond
Of, let us say, a blonde brunette
    (A sort of *Brune de Blondes*),

With eyes of blackly hazel-blue
    And skin all ivory-tanned;
Tall, tiny; slim and buxom too;
    Huge breasts that fit the hand.

– Such dreams he can return to store
    (Albeit with regret),

But others come which lure chaps more
    Insidiously yet:

A temperamental and serene
    Bohemian home-girl type;
A *poule de luxe* of modest mien,
    Mature and not yet ripe;

Demure, farouche; unspoilt and chic ...
    Of course the lesson is
He shouldn't actually seek
    For contradictories.

So when he toasts a girl in *Brut*,
    From Ay or Avise slopes,
Fred take the realistic view
    Or so he says he hopes.[1]

[1]

Girls aren't exempt. Their dreams evoke
    (Fred hears it every day)
The strong and independent bloke
    Who'll do just what they say.

FRED AND THE FRIGID

Some girls, from stuff they've heard or read,
    Embracing, think they must
Dig their long nails right into Fred
    To prove untrammelled lust.

Old Fred's recourse, such as it is
    – Just cease all movement till
They've ended such barbarities,
    Then work your mutual will.

But even odder female lore
    Fred's heard of, though he's missed,
Is girls who think a man gets more
    Excited if their fist

At the most sexy moment claps
    An ice-cube to his – Oh
Think of the suffering that chaps
    Go through that we don't know!

Fred's back soon heals. But when he'd see
    Things like the ice-cube hoax,
He'd long mourn girls' credulity
    At some sod's heartless jokes.

FRED AND THE *ARS AMATORIA*

Of course Fred's read the *Art of Love*
    But Ovid always seems
(To him at least) the picture of
    A cynic sunk in schemes.

Fred finds the whole approach unsound,
    As tasteless as it's trite,
Though he concedes a cynic's bound
    To get a few things right.

FRED ON FASCISM

"Fascism is," a learned don
    Once told Fred in a bar,
"A feminine phenomenon."
    Fred wouldn't go so far.

The phrase might sound, Fred would admit,
    Felicitous and fine;
The chap was perhaps too struck with it:
    Where should one draw the line?

"The ruthless certainty they're right …
    Such parallels are plain.
And yet their tactics are not quite
    As easy to contain."

316

"And when our lads, who'd laid it low
    In Berlin and in Rome,
Marched back they found it wasn't so
    Simple a task at home …"

Watching him stagger off, Fred thought
    Only in academe
Does one find such a fancy sort
    Of way to blow off steam.

FRED AND THE DOUBLE STANDARD

A double standard? Fred would say
    (In confidence): well, yes,
The universe is built that way
    Which one can't second-guess.

They win, say, three times out of five
    (Some chaps would make it four):
A truly just alternative
    Would hardly give them more.

And while a woman never doubts
    (As Fred observes these things)
Her losses on the roundabouts
    She just forgets the swings.

But Fred won't openly apply
    This test of them and us:
To raise the double standard high
    Provokes a fearsome fuss.

FRED SEEKS GUIDANCE

Philosophers might help? Although
    Fred sees they mainly stick
To how we know the things we know,
    What makes the cosmos tick.

There could be good stuff all the same
    In some old sage or seer,
And Epicurus seemed a name
    That might make all things clear.

Well, that old seeker after truth
    Said prudent chaps had best
Avoid the "fine, exciting, smooth
    Movements" of thigh and breast.

And what's the good of that to Fred?
    – Or Plato's two-backed beast?
Impatiently he shakes his head
    And tries the mystic East.

But they just tell him He and She
    Are merely Yang and Yin
Implying total symmetry ...
    Well, one can only grin.

In some ways Fred's a bit naive,
    It seems to be his fate
To take what deeper thinkers leave
    And try to set it straight.

Hurrah for Hume and Locke and Hobbes!
    And yet, when all is said,
– Except from intellectual snobs –
    A brief hurrah for Fred!

FRED OUTFLANKED

Our mores, so Fred used to feel,
    Should just be strict enough
That less than his own sex-appeal
    Would not tempt girls to love.

The competition thus cut down ...
    But soon he found, of course,
Girls so mad keen on clod or clown
    This logic lost its force.

FAIL-SAFE FRED

Some people think, though it's not true,
    Fred's nature is inclined
To take too sceptical a view
    Of love and womankind.

Addiction to the other sex
    Is praised, and shared, by Fred,
He just thinks there are side-effects
    On which light should be shed.

And though explorers can't be safe
    There's one rule they should keep:
Don't use a leaky bathyscaphe
    To probe the dangerous deep.

FRED AND FATS

"Your feet's too big!" Fats Waller sings
    As Fred turns on the tape
And wonders why supernal things
    Depend on women's shape.

They do, though, don't they? Still, it's crude
    Put in this Waller way:
Fred plays, in a more highbrow mood,
    La donna è mobile

But belts out Waller's words (no prig
    Or purist he): the pause
He puts before "your feet's too big"
    And after "hates ya 'cause".

This sort of melds, so Fred would say,
    Their physique and their mind;
Both, this time, in a tasteless way,
    Still, he might try to find

– For the same treatment – tunes on those
　　　Whose temperaments are sweet,
And bodies fine down to the toes
　　　Of pretty little feet.

FRED ON FEEDBACK

Girls look prettiest when they're sweet
　　　Entailing the reverse:
That when they know they're looking beat
　　　They start behaving worse.

Fred's read some cybernetic stuff
　　　– With systems acting so
Even in principle it's tough
　　　To stabilize the flow.

Not that he has to turn to books,
　　　Or scan the printed page,
Never to tell one that she looks
　　　Appalling in a rage.

DEAR FRED

Fred's boasted to us once or twice
　　　And only half in jest,
That were there columns of advice
　　　For men, his would be best.

One of the problems that arise:
　　　If you've contrived to poach
A party girl, and there she lies,
　　　Her eyes crammed with reproach,

When you – perhaps because of hormone
　　　shortage, psychic block –
Have been unable to perform:
　　　There's shame, and even shock.

Fred would advise you thus: Don't say
    "It's not occurred before,
I don't know what went wrong today,"
    Upsetting her still more.

Don't say "I've had too many drinks,"
    Don't blame a lack of nerve.
(Being let down once or twice, Fred thinks,
    Is what we all deserve.)

But hang your head, and say "My dear,
    You have such lovely eyes!
This happens all the time, I fear,
    I do apologise!"

And if the rumour gets around,
    As well the rumour might,
Then some advantage can be found:
    A girl may stay the night.

– "I feel so safe with (let's say) Fred"
    Yet get a nice surprise
When things build up a storm instead
    – What kudos that implies!

So any parfit, gentle guy
    Should bear the point in mind
(While more concerned with courtesy
    Than smugness at being "kind").

FRED TRIES TO HELP

When a friend of Fred's obsessed
    With some quite ghastly girl,
Fred takes him lunching at a rest-
    aurant, where thoughts of her'll

Lose some allure. It's slickly posh
    With female clientele:
The carrots' crunch, the yoghourt's slosh,
    The chintzy drinks they sell.

Tiny glass tables glint too bright
    From pit and mezzanine,
At one of them he sits cramped tight.
    But heard is worse than seen:

Across the lettuces and leeks
    Which dreadful dressings souse,
Echo the chattering, the shrill shrieks,
    As in the Parrot House.

Aversion therapy, in fact.
    Is it of much avail?
Fred thinks that in one case he tracked
    It seemed to turn the scale.

FRED ON LITERATURE

A "woman's magazine" is where
    Yeasty emotions rise
And thwarted love and hearts' despair
    Grip throats and soften eyes.

A "girlie" magazine's effect
    Is, on the other hand,
With methods rather more direct
    To give old Fred a stand.

Women may shake their heads in scorn:
    How low can our lot get?
While Fred just thinks how overdrawn
    Those wet romances; yet

Still grants her vision's higher tone
    While staring himself blind.
A difference – not the only one –
    Between two types of mind.

FRED GIVES UP

On marriage, Fred has things to tell
    Culled from many a friend
– But is it all reliable?
    And whither does it tend?

One pair on which Fred thought he'd check
    Had won the Dunmow Flitch:
The husband was a trembling wreck,
    The wife a raving bitch.

One pair was prone to public rage:
    Outside their house one day
Fred listened as they seemed to stage
    A sentimental play.

Marriage is such a strange affair
    That no one really knows
– Not even Fred – how any pair
    Stack up the cons and pros.

FESTIVE FRED

De minimis non curat Fred,
    Or so he'll often boast,
But some things send him off his head
    That don't loom large to most.

Christmas comes but once a year
    And as to what it means
To Fred, he's often made it clear
    He sees two different scenes:

The first is when at Christmastide
    And not engaged or wed,
Girls go back to their parents' side
    And leave a lonesome Fred

Who, with stout, claret, whiskey, hock,
    With Melton Mowbray pies,

With tins of tasty tongue in stock,
    Stretched on his sofa lies.

He doesn't shave. He reads a lot.
    Soft jazz relieves the hush.
He hugs himself to think he's not
    Out in the sleet and slush.

Holed up in his basement flat,
    Such simple joys suffice:
The thought of all the mishaps that
    He's missing adds the spice.

Viz: Christmas trees, charades, church – this
    All taking place amid
A rat-faced brother talking piss,
    An ankle-kicking kid;

And worse! – Some solace, as he can't
    Deny, may perhaps be found:
A bright and bodice-bursting aunt,
    A sympathetic hound.

Fred's fair, so mentions this relief
    But adds that, truth to tell,
Such interludes are rare, and brief,
    And all the rest is hell.

He daren't drink suitably. Instead
    His brain gets out of phase,
He doesn't follow half that's said
    He drags round in a daze …

Weeks or months, you'd think to hear
    Old Fred, are thus misspent
Instead of just three days a year
    – Not even one percent!

Which a less fine-bred chap might stand
    (Except when matters seem
So balanced that a grain of sand
    Would make them kick the beam).

FRED FOR THE DEFENCE

"My wife's a bourgeois philistine,"
    A lefty said to Fred;
Fred stopped him: chaps who take this line
    Make him see fairly red.

This was a girl it chanced he knew:
    No lowbrow Tory but
Bohemian, intellectual too,
    And merely not a slut.

FRED ON FEMINISM

On Women's Rights – what should one say?
    Does Fred have any tips?
Fred's usual answer is to lay
    His finger to his lips.

Pressed further – here there's no safe line,
    It's bound to leave you limp;
Object, and you're a macho swine,
    Enthuse, and you're a wimp.

"Of course, in general I agree"
    Is used by cagey chaps;
But can you stand the strain as she
    Looks out for any lapse?

The best (which isn't very good)
    Start off with "What the hell!"
Then say, at last you've understood,
    She puts it all so well.

Better seek other subjects of
    Which couples may converse:
Her beauty, soccer, Larkin, love
    – At least none could be worse.

FRED LOOKS BACK

Fred's lived through various epochs and
    Having no patience with
False retrospect, he takes the stand
    That contrary to myth

The Sixties weren't much good for sex:
    In order to play fair
Good-looking girls wore hideous specs
    And grew long greasy hair.

Fred grants "sex" happened, even that
    Its quantity increased,
But plates piled high with mutton fat
    Don't make a gourmet feast.

FRED GETS IT WRONG

Oh no, we never mention her.
    – Because her name might make
Such hellish images recur
    As even Fred can't take?

For once your guess would turn out wrong:
    This time the problem is
Not letting Fred go on too long
    With happy memories.

She was his secretary, and more;
    And so they went away
To take off March and April for
    A working holiday.

A peasant hut, fixed by a friend:
    From nine Fred would dictate
While she took shorthand and got tanned.
    (As Fred's now keen to state,

Such work together may enrich
    Vacant vacation days

To a good intimacy which
    You miss if you just laze.)

Then, sour wine and canned corned beef
    And next, an icy swim
From the sea-urchin-studded reef:
    It all seemed fine to him.

A stroll down to the little port,
    A trudge the two miles back
Heavy with provender they'd bought
    Between them in a sack.

At dusk she'd do the typing up
    While Fred set to and strove
To stew the stuff on which they'd sup
    Upon the butane stove.

And so to bed. It seemed to him
    The soft play of desire
Sank through a salt-aired sleep to brim
    Contentment each day higher.

Then home. The recent victim of
    A marital affray,
So still too numb to mention love,
    Fred let her get away.

Was she a rose without a thorn?
    Fred asks as one of those
Who's more than once been scratched and torn
    By thorns without a rose.

And if they'd wed? Though Fred will say
    Well, thorns are bound to sprout,
And petals fade and fall away,
    One sees he's still in doubt.

FRED AT A WEDDING

Fred's been to marriages before
    (Though mostly to his own).
He stifles, if perhaps no more
    Than other chaps, a groan

At tedium, cramp, a shirt too tight …
    But shudders as he spies
The awful air of triumph bright
    In all the female eyes.

And his discomfort grows profound
    As if he had to view
A lot of lionesses round
    A poor sod of a gnu.

FRED HAS FAITH

"The right true end of love" said Donne,
    Is taking girls to bed,
And now three centuries have gone
    He's seconded by Fred.

Dean of St. Paul's? – Not when he wrote.
    But many a modern Dean
Writes stuff on sex Fred wouldn't quote
    (So soppy and obscene).

ET FRED IN ARCADIA

The sort of life Fred tends to lead
    May seem to suit him, but
Sometimes, he'll readily concede
    It drives him off his nut.

And when he turns to metaphor,
    He puts it that he hacks
His way through thorny jungles or
    Up icy mountain tracks.

Of course he'd grant that this is how
    To gain experience:
– He's had enough of that for now:
    A break would make some sense ...

So, more than once in his career,
    Fred's copped right out and spent
(As other chaps might) half a year
    In unrelieved content,

Preferably in rural shacks
    With just a bit of ground,
Where he can work and then relax
    With hobby, hearth and hound

– A basset (say), its muzzle on
    His knee – he swigs (say) Scotch
Curled up contentedly to con
    (Say) *How to Mend a Watch*.

Drip-dry shirts, washed in the shower,
    Booze chosen to his whim,
Shaved when he liked, bed at an hour
    That simply suited him.

Celibacy? Not quite. He'd seek
    For the odd far-off peach
For just the odd weekend or week
    In travel or on beach.

She goes. The parting's bitter-sweet
    – A savour that goes well
With '62 Château Lafite
    And Veau aux Chanterelles.

(He tells himself the point with pith
    Until he gets it plain:
His house can't be his castle with
    A live-in chatelaine.)

But these brief cats-paws scarcely stir
    The millpond of his mind,

No nightmare memories recur:
    Those scenes are left behind.

And when he starts to find the pace
    Too slow, and summer fails,
His stamina's built up to face
    The equinoctial gales.

FRED COUNTS THE WAYS

Sometimes sex is glorious fun,
    And sometimes sweet delight,
Dark deeps dissolving them to one,
    A sort of feral fight.

In some moods Fred will make it more
    And talk of five or six
Such options. But he'd settle for
    The second (or a mix).

FRED AT THE FINISH

Fred is of service to his kind,
    Or so we all must hope,
And those should bear his points in mind
    Who plan to (say) elope.

His views are quite consistent (but
    He'd plead a change of mood).
His touch, though sometimes delicate,
    More often's pretty crude.

But if his warnings sound too stark
    It's only thus one schools
Chaps who might otherwise embark
    Upon a Ship of Fools.

He doesn't always come out well
    From stuff that he relates:

– He waives his self-conceit to tell
    What may affect their fates.

The good things about girls, Fred says,
    Are clear to all who've looked:
He could go on like that for days
    – They really have him hooked.

He's lots of evidence to prove
    Only with them you'd find
Such lovingness when they're in love
    Such kindness when they're kind.

And if the tributes thus bestowed
    Are seldom here expressed,
It's that they fit a lyric mode
    That other chaps do best.

Though most men hope, if perhaps not soon,
    Eventually to lie
At anchor in the blue lagoon,
    Their chances don't seem high.

Mourning all those who've come to grief
    On stormy seas of sex,
He seeks a passage through the reef
    Guided by previous wrecks.

from

REASONABLE RHYMES
BY TED PAUKER

GARLAND FOR A PROPAGANDIST

(Air: The Vicar of Bray)

In good old Stalin's early days
  When terror little harm meant
A zealous commissar I was
  And so I got preferment.
I grabbed each peasant and I said
  "Can there be something *you* lack?"
And if he dared to answer "bread"
  I shot him for a kulak.

        For on this rule I will insist
        Because I have the knack, Sir:
        Whichever way its line may twist
        I'll be a Party hack, Sir!

Then Stalin took the Secret Police
  And gave it to Yagoda.
Many a Party pulse might cease
  But I stayed in good odour.
At all the cases that he brought
  I welcomed each confession,
And when he too turned up in court
  I attended every session.

When Yezhov took the vacant place
  And blood poured out in gallons
Thousands fell in dark disgrace
  But I still kept my balance.
I studied, as the Chekists pounced,
  The best way to survival
And almost every day denounced
  A colleague or a rival.

When Yezhov got it in the neck
  (In highly literal fashion)
Beria came at Stalin's beck
  To lay a lesser lash on;
I swore our labour camps were few,
  And places folk grew fat in;

I guessed that Trotsky died of flu
      And colic raged at Katyn.

And when things once again grew hot
      From Western war-psychosis,
I damned the "cosmopolitan" lot
      Because of their hook noses.
The Doctors should be shot, I cursed,
      As filthy spy-recruiters.
But Stalin chanced to kick off first
      – So I cursed their persecutors.

Malenkov, now our Party's head,
      Tried out a tack quite new, Sir,
Saying what had never been said
      – And so I said it too, Sir:
I boldly cried that clobber and scoff
      Should go to the consumer.
– But his overthrow soon tipped me off
      This was a Right-wing bloomer.

When Khrushchev next came boldly on
      Denouncing Stalin's terror,
I saw that what we'd so far done
      Had mostly been an error.
My rivals all lay falsely framed
      Under the Russian humus
And their innocence I now proclaimed
      – Because it was posthumous.

But Khrushchev guessed his chances wrong
      And the present lot took over.
And I saw that though we'd suffered long
      At last we were in clover,
Now Stalin's name I freely blessed,
      A bonny, bonny fighter.
– And I told the intellectual West.
      When it's right to jug a writer.

Now the Collective Leadership
      Of Brezhnev and Kosygin
I'll back until some rivals slip

By intricate intrigue in;
And, if the worst comes to the worst
    And they're scragged in the Lubyanka,
I'll see they get as foully cursed
    As any Wall Street banker.

      And on this rule I will insist
      Because I have the knack, Sir!
      Whichever way its line may twist
      I'll be a Party hack, Sir!

EPILOGUE: A SONG FOR GORBACHEV, 1991

(On the 60th Birthday of Mikhail Gorbachev)

Well, those were boozy, lazy days
    Till Brezhnev chanced to pop off,
Then hard and sober toil I'd praise
    As ordered by Andropov;
And I told every journalist
    From Melbourne to Milwaukee
How I'd heard Sakharov insist
    He loved to live in Gorki.

But Gorbachev soon took the lead
    And *glasnost* ruled the nation.
When good old Sakharov was freed
    I chaired the celebration.
My speeches sneered at Uncle Joe
    And had some juicy bits in
From *Gulag Archipelago*
    By Alex Solzhenitsyn.

On Lenin's work I came down hard
    We'd wasted all that time at
And would have scrapped my Party card
    – But sniffed a change of climate:
So Marxism's now my middle name
    Our bureaucrats are brainy 'uns;
On liberals now I put the blame
    – And also Lithuanians.

Of course I'd feel completely free
    To damn this stuff as drivel;
But Yeltsin, Army, KGB
    – I don't know where to swivel.
Retirement, then, would suit me fine,
    And such was my intention,
But since the rouble's lost its shine
    I can't live on my pension.

When I sold my products (later pulped)
    Through the old-time Politburo
With my Stolichnaya I gulped
    Beluga's epicure-roe.
But now I'll blast the USA,
    Its violences and squalors
Only for publishers who'll pay
    My royalties in dollars.

There's threats against our way of life
    And cats that need a beller.
But when it comes to civil strife
    You'll find me in the cellar:
Whence I'll emerge with praise all pat
    Whether for saint or sinner
For despot or for democrat
    – So long as he's the winner.

        And on this rule I will insist
        Because I have the knack, Sir!
        Whichever way its line may twist
        I'll be a Party hack, Sir!

A TRIFLE FOR TRAFALGAR DAY

(with acknowledgements to G.K.C.)

"Drake ... Cabot ... challenge ... opportunity ... courage ..."
– The Prime Minister.

Who's the Dover-based day tripper
    Heir to, Heath?

– The captain of the close-rigged clipper?
        Is he, Heath?
(While for plump young brokers preening
        On the day that Britain joins
"Rigging" has another meaning
        And a "clipper" is for coins …)
Was the cry of Drake and Raleigh,
        Tacked into the tempest's teeth,
"Ah, thank God, at last – there's Calais!"
        Was it, Heath?

Belgian bureaucrats in boardrooms
        Differ, Heath,
From midshipmites in Nelson's wardrooms,
        Don't they, Heath?
Would the *Victory* quite suit your
        Grand adventures where they range,
When the Wave is of the Future
        And the Winds are those of Change?
Though Industry is advantageous
        Ask Sir Alec, ask Sir Keith,
Are its Captains so Courageous?
        Are they, Heath?

You'll be needing loyal comrades,
        Won't you, Heath?
– It's years since Germans came on bomb-raids,
        Ain't it, Heath ?
The red fool-fury of the Seine now
        Has not raged since Sixty-eight.
In Rome for one whole British reign now
        Mere millions cheer the Total State
While in the countries of our cousins,
        Bowed our lousy laws beneath,
Revolutions come in dozens,
        Don't they, Heath?

Nowadays what does "The Horn"
        Conjure, Heath?
Lorry-loads of Danish porn,
        Trader Heath?
Economic blizzards raving

Where the frozen assets clot
Are conditions you'll be braving
          Just like Frobisher or Scott …?
No, talk of profit and debenture
          Fix Liege with loans from Leith,
But the Spirit of Adventure …
          Chuck it, Heath!

A TALE OF ACADEME

(On the sixteen-hundredth anniversary of the war of 367–8)

The Sophist Sphincterides
Is at his usual pitch:
A stone bench in a beech grove
Beyond the Caelian Ditch,
His plump young students round him,
The children of Rome's rich.

"Young friends! We've lost half Britain.
What are we fighting for?
Moral philosophy demands
That we should stop the war
But Aulus looks unhappy? …"
The sleek young students roar.

"My brother Marcus writes, Sir,
– Who serves in Stanwix fort –
The Attecotti kill and eat
The young girls that they've caught.
The Province hates and fears them …"
"Well, what a vague report!

And when it comes to slaughter
We're worse, you understand?
Look at the cruel ballistas
By vicious Romans manned."
"The Picts use javelins too, Sir,"
"That's different, thrown by hand …"

"Philosophers and students,
All we whose thought is deep,
Can read Rome's moral sentence,
That what we sowed, we reap."
The battered Petriana
Hold out in Stanwix Keep.

"Besides, whose island *is* it?
One understands their wrath.
With what a fine ideal
Their spearmen sally forth:
– Destroy the Wall's false boundary,
Unite the South and North!"

Chained peasants, hobbled cattle
Driven from Fenland folds
Lie with the loot of Isca
Crammed in the raider's holds.
Blood stains the Severn lowlands,
Flame sweeps the Yorkshire Wolds.

"Count Theodosius marches
To escalate the war.
For civilisation? Come, sir!
The endless wealth we pour
On legionaries would buy us
A thousand sophists more!"

A draft for the Sixth Victrix
Falls in, three hundred men.
The Tribune checks their weapons,
He mounts his horse, and then
He looks at the plump students,
And looks away again.

"The Province! They lack fighters,
Which proves they must be wrong.
The fate of Isca's burghers
Need not detain us long:
Rome's friends are the fat merchants,
Pro-Pictish moods are strong."

Beside their burnt-out homesteads
The cheering farmers greet
The Palatine detachments
That fight up Ermine Street.
The raiders, fleeing seawards
Fall to the Sambric Fleet.

"You'd think those peasant state men
(Whom we've the nerve to call
'Barbarians') were aggressors
Out to enslave us all.
You'd think, to hear our generals,
That Rome itself might fall!"

*

Forty years on. Here's Alaric.
The streets of Rome run red.
The aged Sphincterides
Pleads as he's never pled.
But one Goth tears his scrolls up
And one cuts off his head.[1]

[1] For the specialized cannibalism of the Attecotti, see St. Jerome. The Ala Petriana (Augusta, Gallorum, bis torquata, Civium Romanorum), crack cavalry regiment of the command of the hard-pressed Duke of the Britains, was stationed at Stanwix, on the Wall. Legio VI Victrix, at York, was his main striking force. The *barbarica conspiratio* seems to have been especially destructive in East Yorkshire and south of the Bristol Channel.

A GROUCHY GOOD NIGHT TO THE ACADEMIC YEAR

(with acknowledgements to William Mackworth Praed)

Good night to the year Academic,
It finally crept to a close:
Dry fact about physic and chemic,
Wet drip about people and prose.
Emotion was down to a snivel
And reason was pulped to a pap,
Sociologists droning out drivel
And critics all croaking out crap.
For any such doctrine is preachable

In our tolerant Temple of Thought
Where lads that are largely unteachable
Learn subjects that cannot to be taught.

Good night to the Session – portentous
Inside the Vice-Chancellor's gown,
The personage who'll represent us
To Public and Party and Crown.
By enthusing for nitwitted novelty
He wheedles the moment'ry Great,
And at influence-dinner or grovel-tea
Further worsens the whims of the State.
So it is that, however much we rage,
The glibber of heart and of tongue
Build ladders to reach a life-peerage
From the buzz-sawed-up brains of the young.

Good night to the Session – the Chaplain,
Progressive and Ritualist too,
Who refers to the role of the apple in
Eden as "under review".
When the whole situation has ripened
Of his temporal hopes these are chief:
A notable increase in stipend,
And the right to abandon belief.
Meanwhile, his sermons: "The Wafer –
Is it really the Presence of God?"
"Is the Pill or the French Letter Safer?"
And, "Does the Biretta look Mod?"

Good night to the Session – what Art meant,
Or Science, no longer seemed plain,
But our new Education Department
Confuses confusion again.
"Those teach who can't do" runs the dictum,
But for some even that's out of reach:
They can't even teach – so they've picked 'em
To teach other people to teach.
Then alas for the next generation,
For the pots fairly crackle with thorn.
Where psychology meets education
A terrible bullshit is born.

343

Good night to the Session – the students
So eager to put us all right,
Whose conceit might have taken a few dents
But that ploughing's no longer polite;
So the essays drop round us in torrents
Of jargon a mouldering mound,
All worrying weakly at Lawrence,
All drearily pounding at Pound;
And their knowledge would get them through no test
On Ghana or Greece or Vietnam,
 But they've mugged up enough for a Protest
– An easyish form of exam.

Good night to the Session – so solemn,
"Truth" and "Freedom" their crusader crests,
One hardly knows quite what to call 'em
These children with beards or with breasts.
When from State or parental Golcondas
Treasure trickles to such little boys
They spend it on reefers and Hondas
– That is, upon sweeties and toys;
While girls of delicious proportions
Are thronging the Clinic's front stair,
Some of them seeking abortions
And some a psychiatrist's care.

Good night to the Session – the politics,
So noisy, and nagging, and null.
You can tell how the time-bomb of Folly ticks
By applying your ear to their skull;
Of course, that is only a metaphor,
But they have their metaphors too,
 Such as "Fascist" , that's hardly the better for
Being used of a liberal and Jew
– The Prof. of Applied Aeronautics,
For failing such students as try,
With LSD lapping their cortex,
To fub up a fresh way to fly.

Good night to the Session – the Union:
The speeches with epigram packed,
So high upon phatic communion,

So low upon logic and fact.
(Those epigrams? – Oh well, at any rate
By now we're all quite reconciled.
To a version that's vastly degenerate
From the Greek, via Voltaire and Wilde.)
Then the bold resolutions devoted
To the praise of a party or state
In *this* context most obviously noted
For its zeal in destroying debate.

Good night to the Session – the sculpture:
A jelly containing a clock;
Where they say, "From the way that you gulped you're
Therapeutically thrilled by the shock!"
– It's the Shock of, alas, Recognition
At what's yearly presented as new
Since first seen at Duchamp's exhibition
"Des Maudits", in Nineteen-O-Two.
But let's go along to the Happening,
Where an artist can really unwind,
Stuff like "Rapists should not take the rap" penning
In gamboge on a model's behind.

Good night to the Session – a later
Will come – and the freshmen we'll get!
Their pretensions will be even greater,
Their qualifications worse yet.
– But don't be too deeply depressible
At obtuseness aflame for applause;
The louts that are loudest in decibel
Melt away in post-graduate thaws.
Don't succumb to an anger unreasoned!
Most students are charming, and bright;
And even some dons are quite decent …
But good night to the Session, good night!

LETTER TO THE EDITOR

Sir,
    Yes, I wrote, no more from me,
Nor, I assure you, will there be
    Upon the major issue.
But that was not (as they suppose)
To grant impunity to those
    Who loose off with a tissue

Of petty personalities:
Your correspondent, Mr B's
    Extravagant emission
Does not seem, on the other hand
To merit anything so grand
    As a formal demolition.

The pomps of prose, the reasoning pen
Well suited the great themes and men
    With which we have been dealing.
For petty sneer and fancy fib
The rougher justice of a squib
    Marks well the change of feeling.

(May I, perhaps, suggest that you
Should use a different heading too.
    The splendid name that's been up
Needs moving over, none too soon,
From contact with this picayune
    Though necessary clean-up.)

Though, since your correspondent seeks
The right to nominate each week's
    Main subject of discussion,
Perhaps by now he's shifted to,
For "central" theme, my point of view,
    To void his gravid gush on.

Poor stuff, his argument *ad hominem.*
But, like those parcels with a bomb in 'em
    That morons send, or madmen,
It still needs dunking or disarming,

Its very bang might make it charming
    To agit-prop – or ad men.

It's all right when we do it. He
May criticise the KGB
    Or say a word for freedom.
When I (or Mr R) express
The same ides, no more, no less,
    Let lefty rage strike *me* dumb!

Queen Pasiphae – remember how
She got into a brazen cow
    To let the great bull mount her;
And brazen bullshitters since then
Have quite outbred the race of men
    – And now attack *Encounter,*

Which honest critics all concede
(Though not of course the other breed)
    Has won outstanding credit
Against oppressors left and right
– Your stuff might answer (well it *might*)
    With those who've never read it.

"Cold War" I've proved an Eastern ploy
To silence those who may annoy
    By voicing Western viewpoints.
While, as for "Ideology":
Because they have one, so must we?
    – Oh, mark him down a few points.

As for the Indochina War
(I've said this many times before.
    What? Need I use a Tannoy?)
No, I'm AGAINST it – rather more
Than many who proclaim I'm FOR
    – But lay the blame on Hanoi.

"As is well known" is *Pravda's* cry
To mark a newly minted lie
    (While "It's not accidental"
Suggests the deep-laid plot together

Of those who've had not contact, whether
    Physical or mental.)

Even with those who raged sulphuric
By now that propaganda's uric
    Salt has lost its savour.
Don't think (one of his worst mistakes)
That still the mere word "Vietnam" wakes
    The old Pavlovian slaver.

But even those who think one sins
To spurn the terror-mandarins
    Would scarcely quite believe an
Effort, apparently, to show
Disliking the odd Le or Ho
    Means loathing every Ivan.

– And so it goes. One works at this
Hoping to wholly stanch the piss
    That's daily drained, but duly
Bursts forth upon the following day,
Then we'd debate. But either way
    It won't disturb yours truly.

LIMERICKS

for Martin Amis and Christopher Hitchens

"Scorn not the sonnet, critic ..."

Then scorn not the limerick, either,
Though, as Tennyson said, who knows why the
    Fuck such a rhyme
    Makes the grim reaper Time
Such a markedly blither old scyther.

Seven Ages: first puking and mewling;
Then very pissed off with one's schooling;
    Then fucks; and then fights;
    Then judging chaps' rights;
Then sitting in slippers; then drooling.

There was a great Marxist called Lenin,
Who did two or three million men in;
    That's a lot to have done in
    But where he did one in
That grand Marxist Stalin did ten in.

My demands upon life are quite modest:
They're just to be properly goddessed.
    Astarte or Isis
    Would do in a crisis,
But the best's Aphrodite, unbodiced.

Charlotte Brontë said, "Wow, sister! What a man!
He laid me face down on the ottoman.
    Now don't you and Emily
    Go telling the family –
But he smacked me upon my bare bottom, Anne!"

Said Tennyson, "Yes, Locksley Hall's
A story that always enthralls,
    For it comes down to this:
    She gave me a kiss
And then a good kick in the balls."

There was a young fellow called Shit,
A name he disliked quite a bit;
    So he changed it to Shite,
    A step in the right
Direction, one has to admit.

Said a gloomy young fellow called Fart,
"The name's bad enough for a start,
       But my snob of a dad
       Makes it all twice as bad
With his ruddy Sir Mart ffart-ffart, Bart."

Said the famous philosopher Russell,
"One can come without moving a muscle.
       When sufficiently blotto
       Just watch Lady Otto
line's bum as it bursts from her bustle."

Said Arnold to Arthur Hugh Clough
"Why I don't instantly stuff
       Your *Amours de Voyage*
       Up my arse is – it's large,
But I don't think it's quite large *enough*."

Would you like a love-life like Dante's?
Consider the prose and the antis:
       He exalted his love
       To the heavens above
But he never could pull off her panties.

As I whizzed 'round my 35th lap,
I got quite bollocksed up on life's map,
       And the wood was damn'd dark –
       Fuck that for a lark –
Well, there I was deep in the crap!

Said a stammering wit out at Woking,
"Though I like d-d-drinking and smoking,
       One thing I suppose
       I like better than those
Is p-p-p practical joking."

Said Pedro, "I went out with Hester,
And I wish that I hadn't undressed her.
    Like a good macho Latin
    I go for black satin,
But her panties were pink polyester."

Oedipus said to the Sphinx,
My name's been perverted by shrinks.
    Who'd think that Jocasta'd
    Call me a bastard?
– I say that psychology stinks.

There was a young fellow called Bernard
Whose prick fairly flashed like a gurnard,
    And don't we all wish
    We had pricks like a fish,
Its colours all Titianed and Turnered?

We're very refined down in Georgia:
We never say "shit"; we say "ordure".
    And in speaking of piss
    Our usage is this ...
– I'm sorry. I see that I've bored ya.

I was thrilled when I went to the Zoo:
They allowed me to roger the gnu;
    And a young FZS
    Remarked to me, "Yes,
It's a privilege granted to few."

There was plenty of good-natured chaff
When I went back to screw the giraffe,
    And the old PZS
    Could hardly suppress
A dry, professorial laugh.

When I plunged in a little bit deeper
And attempted to fuck the Head Keeper,
    The old PZS
    (From his Hampstead address)
Was summoned at once on his beeper.

My prick's a deep heliotrope;
That's why they elected me Pope.
    "The others," they said,
    "Are just cardinal red,
But yours really goes with that cope."

One morning old Wilfrid Scawen Blunt
Went down to the Thames for a punt;
    But the puntmen had struck,
    So he shouted, "Good luck!
Your wage is a social affront!"

In palazzos along the old Appi-
an Way I make Contessas happy.
    But I first dip my penis
    In a brace of martinis
To make sure it doesn't get clappy.

A rebuke by the Bishop of London
To his randy young Dean, Dr John Donne:
    "In the Name of God, peace!
    If you won't wear a codpiece
Don't preach with your flybuttons undone."

I write about feudal times, Yes, Sir!
I'm a modern-type Pol Sci Professor.
    I don't go for crap-history
    Like that old Bayeux tapestry
Or Edward the fucking Confessor.

A taxi-cab whore out at Iver
Would do the round-trip for a fiver.
    – Quite reasonable, too,
    For a sightsee, a screw,
And a ten-shilling tip to the driver.

Shit. Yes, I've just found a morsel in
This ewer of finest Ming porcelain.
    Our Director again!
    Won't someone explain
It's not there for washing his orcelain?

Transcendentalists back in old Boston
Never tossed off. No, they tossed on,
    What the phrase may convey
    Is forgotten today
For it seems that the art is a lost one.

There was a young man called Debrett
Who treated his tool like a pet,
    But he didn't half holler
    When they clapped on a collar
And dragged it around to the vet.

"When I'm bored," said the learned Descartes,
"I turn to philosophy's art
    Till reality seems
    But the stuff of wet dreams
Or some far, faintly audible fart ..."

"Our brains," said the great Thomas Hobbes,
"Aren't up to philosophy's jobs:
    The pursuit of the True
    And the Beautiful too
Is far better left to our knobs."

The enormous great tool of John Locke,
Stuck up in a huge writer's block.
    Don't fall into Locke's trap
    But use a good jockstrap
Or your work will be chock full of cock.

An example of Kant's sterling wit,
Was his theory that farts could be lit;
    And it's said that at night
    By their flickering light
He composed his *Critique of Pure Shit.*

Said Edna St. Vincent Millay,
"At the poetry reading today
    They dragged Robert Frost off
    But not till he'd tossed off,
And that was as good as a play."

When Gauguin was visiting Fiji,
He said, "Things are different here; e. g.,
    While Tahitian skin
    Calls for tan, brushed on thin,
You must slosh it on here with a squeegee."

There was a young fellow called Crouch
Who was courting a girl on a couch.
    She said, "Why not a sofa?
    And he replied "Oh for
Christ's sake shut your trap while I...Ouch!"

When our Dean took a pious young spinster
On his cultural tour of the Minster,
    What they did in the clerestory
    Is rather a queer story;
But nobody holds it against her.

When Keats was at work on Endymion
He suddenly shouted, "Oh, gimme an
    Unashamed naked Nereid
    From the Ancient Greek period
– Not just Fanny Brawne with her shimmy on."

Said a dressy old beau up at Barnet,
"Me knob fairly gleams like a garnet;
    With some buffin' and wipin'
    It would do as a tiepin,
But I can't get it high enough, darn it."

We're all of us very much struck
By the way our new dean bellows "Fuck!"
    It's his yelling it when
    We're expecting "amen"
That singles him out from the ruck.

From the latest book on Miles Standish it
Appears that he was a randy shit.
    To impress a young chick
    With the power of his prick
He wouldn't just wave it, he'd brandish it.

It was sad for our bishop, who spent
Palm Sunday at Burton-on-Trent;
    There was bass and roast duck
    And a barmaid to fuck
But he'd given them all up for Lent.

There was a young girl of Mauritius
Who said, "No, I'm not really vicious;
    I get no sexual kick
    Out of sucking this prick;
It's just that it tastes so delicious."

Young Coleridge won, while at Ottery
St. Mary, his father's church lottery.
    What they gave him was this:
    A gallon of piss
In a suitable item of pottery.

"While confessing a lad," said Gerard
Manley Hopkins, "My prick may get hard,
    But celestial joys
    Are better than boys
For a bird bollocked, bum baffled bard."

When Eliot was in Tibet he
Remarked to a pretty young yeti,
    "You're not so abominable.
    Come on, give old Tom a nibble,
And them snowflakes will do for confetti."

A young engine-driver called Hunt
When out with his engine to shunt
    Saw a runaway truck
    And by shouting out "Duck!"
Saved the life of the fellow in front.

A usage that's seldom got right
Is when to say "shit" and when "shite"
    And many a chap
    When in doubt uses "crap",
Which is vulgar, evasive, and trite.

Said the learned philosopher Hume,
"I think we may safely presume
    That the truths we're imparting
    Aren't affected by farting,
And so I conclude with VAROOM!"

Dr. Spooner taught literature too.
"*The Shaming*," he said, "*of the True*
    Sounds fine. But the same's
    Not true of H. James
With his dreadful *The Stern of the Crew.*"

There was a young fellow called Peter
Who used to drink piss by the litre;
    The reason for this
    Was he liked to drink piss
– Straight piss, or a piss margarita.

There was a young man of Bermuda
With a prick like a swift barracuda,
    And a girl who went bathing
    Would not feel a thing
As it flashed through the shallows and screwed her.

Meanwhile back at the ranch
I was fucking a cowgirl called Blanche.
    She said, "It's a change
    From riding the range,
But I still prefer bourbon and branch."

When a man's too old to toss off, he
Can sometimes be consoled by philosophy.
    One frequently shows a
    Strong taste for Spinoza.
When one's balls are beginning to ossify.

Said a famous old writer called Spender,
"You may think my conscience is tender;
    You may think my heart
    Is my sensitive part
But you should see my poor old pudenda."

The first man to fuck little Sophie
Was awarded the Krafft-Ebbing Trophy
    Plus ten thousand quid,
    Which, for what the chap did,
Will be widely denounced as a low fee.

To prove that I'm not just a hack,
Have your secretary lie on her back
    And watch what I do:
    I can type while I screw.
(I admit that it's only a knack.)

"Fucking? Though I used to love it,"
Said Augustine, "I've risen above it.
    But I hadn't quite planned
    On my obstinate stand
Still seeking some place I can shove it."

Leigh Hunt once, when talking to Landor,
Remarked with considerable candour,
    "Though my rhyme has pleased many
    The fact is with Jenny
I can't get a stand, and can't stand her."

Said a sexy young lady called Sands,
"You may have the finest of stands.
    But you've done up your flies
    So it does not arise;
And the matter is out of my hands."

"Though I bullshit in Greek," said old Browning,
"Hoti-ing here and there oun-ing,
    It's my wife's Portuguese
    That's producing these seas
Of bullpiss in which we're all drowning."

An old East End worker called Jock
Lived a life full of danger and shock.
    Even now, if one calls,
    He will tell of his falls
In the Royal Victoria Dock.

To this snooty girl I tried to pick up
I said laughingly, "This is a stick-up."
    But she was so stuck up
    She managed to fuck up
My efforts to get my old prick up.

As Byron remarked about Shelley,
"We all of us know very well he
    Will make spousal scenes
    With a girl in her teens,
But stay with her? Not on your Nellie."

While visiting Arundel Castle
I sent my sick uncle a parcel.
    The contents of it
    Was the local grey grit
To rub on his sore metatarsal.

Said Gauguin, "I think that Tahiti's
Main fault is the girls are all sweeties,
    But if you're off screwing
    There's fuck all else doing
But going round getting the DTs."

With Jane Austen one's interest does quicken
As the plot is beginning to thicken,
    And one hangs on a cliff
    To know when, where, and if
Captain Wentworth will get his great prick in.

"Writing verse is a matter of luck,"
Said Blake, "and I often get stuck
    When I think of the times
    I've been held up for rhymes
To 'castle' and 'rowlock' and 'duck'."

"Your rhymes are all typed. Will you áffix
Your signature? I'll do the graphics.
    There's your wife's call from Lesbos.
    Shall I do what she says, boss?"
"No. Limericks come before Sapphics."

Biology II on our campus,
"Fucking sloths in the Argentine pampas",
    Is less hard, you'll agree,
    Than Biology III,
"How to roger a fully grown grampus."

Said Pound, "If one's writing a Canto
It should be a sort of portmanteau
    Full of any old crap
    That occurs to a chap
With patches of pig esperanto."

Said a humble young wooer of Tring,
"I've seen a remarkable thing:
    In response to my pleas
    She showed me her knees!
Who knows what tomorrow may bring?"

There are critics (said Crabbe) who pooh pooh
My poems as too pure to be true.
    I suppose if I wrote 'em
    An Ode to the Scrotum
They'd take a more tolerant view.

One midnight old Dante Rosetti,
Remarked to Miss Sidall, "Oh Betty,
 I wish that you'd stop
 Shouting 'Fuck me, you wop!'
It turna da tool to spaghetti."

It's sad about old Dylan Thomas,
Yes, alcohol's taken him from us,
 We all thought that screwing
 Would be his undoing,
But he didn't live up to his promise.

It wouldn't be easy to check a
Pilgrimage honouring Decca;
 It's no longer fair
 To say Oakland's not there,
She's made it a regular Mecca.

When verse seemed in need of improvement
We sat down and started a Movement:
 We foregathered in Hull
 Working hard to be dull
For we sure knew what being in the groove meant.

When Philip gets pissed off with death
He turns all prophetic and saith,
 "Fuck death and fuck dying
 The cosmos ain't trying
– And Christ all this gin on my breath!"

I'm glad that my monicker's "Bum".
It may sound unharmonious to some
 But it comes from my throat
 Like a great organ note
Or the sonorous roll of a drum.

What would old Philip have said?
The lesson being read by old Ted
    While the Dean tells the flock …
    He'd have thought it all cock:
"Ain't it grand to be blooming well dead!"

Your Committee reports with regret
There's no Press sex-equality yet,
    When this editress banned
    Kingsley Amis's stand,
He simply restored it with "stet".

So romantic, the cistern's soft hiss,
And the delicate odour of piss.
    – Oh, the spunk on my shoe
    Still reminds me of you –
Pricks aimed at the back often miss.

Hello! – Yes, it's me, Tony Benn.
I'm certain I'll reach Number 10.
    'Cos objections to rule
    By a fucking great fool
Come only from Yesterday's Men.

Tom, much maligned as "that pisser", peered
Till Lady Godiva had disappeared;
    What he gazed at, of course,
    Was her well-turned out horse:
Laurel-maned, ivy-tailed, and hyssop-eared.

As he sneaked off from Greenwich, once Halley
Made perhaps his wittiest sally:
    Though you may think my comet
    Absorbs me, far from it –
Fucking is more up my alley.

Said a bisexual bridegroom called Ern,
"Though it's better to marry than burn,
    I'd so much rather wed
    My best man, old Fred,
That I hardly know which way to turn."

There was a young fellow of Dorset
Who peddled a Little French Whore set,
    And – a wee whirling spray,
    A dildo (*trés gai*),
And a minuscule tight leather corset.

There was a young curate who shat
In the Bishop of Chichester's hat.
    "That will save you," he cried,
    "From spiritual pride,
And I cannot say fairer than that."

Whenever our bishop unfrocks
Those priests who've contracted the pox,
    He can tell every one
    Who's been fucking a nun
By the stigmata left on their cocks.

Unpleasant, that worship of Moloch's.
They cut off the acolyte's bollocks.
    But that's better, I find,
    Than to cut off his mind
As is done by the Roman Cathollocks.

There was an old copper called Brock
Who ceased to put people in dock,
    What led him, it's said,
    To write sonnets instead,
Was some trouble concerning his cock.

There was a young man with an Id
Which he used to keep carefully hid,
    He said to it "leggo
    Of my Super Ego"
Which, crying out "Bollocks", it did.

There was an old man of Lugano
Who constructed a bog from Meccano
    Which sharpened his wits
    And aided his shits:
Mens sana in corpore sano.

It's a pity that Casabianca
Was using his tool as an anchor;
    If he'd had it up higher
    He'd have put out the fire
—You never did see such a wanker!

The Postmaster-General cried: "Arsehole!
A pair of bull's balls in a parcel!
    Stamped 'IRA',
    With ninepence to pay,
And addressed to The King, Windsor Castle."

Said a bashful young hillbilly, "Shucks!
Me, go to the city for fucks?
    When here on the farm
    There's my sister and marm
And the cows and the sheep and the ducks."

In a gym with a girl at one's exercises
These days if one manually checks her sizes
    Of breast or behind
    One will bloody soon find
One's standing in dock at the Sex Assizes.

Fucking, some hedonists find,
Is just a monotonous grind;
    But after a brandy,
    If still a bit randy,
It's something to do when you've dined.

One cannot, when dealing with Toynbee,
Simply pay him back in his own coin be-
    Cause talking such piss
    Would seem rather amiss;
So how would a kick in the groin be?

There was an old poet named Betjeman,
And he was a bit of a lecher, man,
    – And with huge-bosomed chicks
    Of at least six foot six –
Conditions that certainly stretch a man.

A young girl of El Paso del Norte
Is almost incredibly sporty;
    To compare Messalina
    To her would demean her –
Where that empress fucked four she fucked forty.

My stands, when I go to the cinema
Are nowadays down to their minima,
    What with girls like Miss Farrow
    With bodies as narrow
As if stomach-pumped after an enema.

A recent pronouncement of Anne's:
"I see I must now be a man's.
    I'd rather of course
    Be wed to a horse,
But 'twould look so odd on the banns."

Till lately the Three Musketeers
Were seldom believed to be queers
    The chaps who worked them in are
    Our Sodomy Seminar
Seeking fine academic careers.

Old Landor rushed out and said this:
"Ballocks and arseholes and piss!
    – I thought it was best
    To get that off my chest
For Jenny just gave me a kiss!"

In the Nineties, that curious camp-age,
Oscar yelled, in the Ritz on a rampage:
    "Blasted Boots, bloody waiter
    I'll bugger them later –
Now fucking well send up that damn page!"

The writings of Barbara Pym
Make no reference to cock or to quim.
    When they said "Stage a screw
    As old Lawrence would do,"
She just sniffed and murmured "Oh, him …"

Now that I've joined the ranks
Of the Blessed, I'd like to give thanks
    For the time since my birth
    That I spent on the Earth –
All the fucks, gamarooshes and wanks.

Our existence would be that much grimmer ex-
cept for the solace of limericks.
    – A fact that's unknown
    To two lots alone
– The drearier dons and the dimmer hicks.

POEMS PUBLISHED ONLY IN JOURNALS AND ANTHOLOGIES

SONG

Yes, each was old enough to know
In theory, that the dark would pass
And through the years they would recover:
That in the accidents of time
They both would by another's image
Replace the only, perfect lover.

Yet they were young enough to feel
Unstartled when they never found
The consolation Time contrives:
And knew that in their hearts and knowledge
They still were happier than many,
And only wept for half their lives.

                                    1952

AT GODSTOW

An inn below an open weir. One swan
Floats by the wall, out of the foam-creamed rush.
We sip a vernal champagne, yellow and
Sparkling as this April light. Beyond
The bridge a peacock walks behind a bush
Of yew. The poetess by my side looks on.
She has, I remember, a poem about landscape
Which needs none of these pleasant properties
Or wine-mixed light to give a mood such shape.
Her relaxation charms now. But her art
Chastens the whole intelligence of sight.
Such colours fuse into one fire of white
When focussed through a clear strong crystal mind
To the centre, not the surface, of the heart.

                                    1957

EVENING IN THE CAMBRIDGESHIRE FENS

The emotions are truly there
But immobile, as it were.

No real tensions remain
From deeper thought or from pain.

So I take my pen and write
To focus on its fading light

And the energies disperse
Through the loose dykes of a verse.

FIRST FROST

*(On the first anniversary of his death,
a translation of a poem by Boris Pasternak)*

Cold morning; the sun blurs,
Pillar of smoky fire.
And I'm indistinct too
Like a smudgy snapshot.

Till it gets through the murk,
Shines on the grassy pond,
The trees see me poorly
Across of the far bank.

Passer-by, recognised
Late, as he's plunged in haze.
Frost wraps gooseflesh, air
Is false as thickest rouge.

You go by paths with rime
Like matting. The earth breathes
Potato-stalks, and grows
Cold, unbearably cold.

1961

APPENDIX I
JUVENILIA

PERSEUS

Polydectes, Perseus' guardian vile,
Tried all his wit, and also tried his guile
To kill young Perseus, yea, to cause his death
To make the hero draw his last deep breath.
And Lo, because he wished the hero dead,
He sent him out to get the Gorgon's head;
For well he knew that whosoe'er did see
The Gorgon's head soon solid stone would be.
But Perseus went to Hermes, the great god,
And with his winged sandals his feet shod;
A sickle too he got, and by my word,
This sickle was more useful than a sword.
A helmet too, which hid him from the sight
Of human eyes; a mirror from the bright
And glorious Pallas; and thus arm'd he went
With every nerve upon his object bent.
He found Medusa sleeping; her he saw
Within the mirror that like a shield he bore.
He seized her locks, her serpent-turning hair:
Once it was folded on her head so fair.
That was before the gods a monster made
Of the once fair damsel, once fair maid.
He cut her neck right through with his sickle bright,
And hid her head in goatskins, out of sight.
Returning home a damsel fair he saw
Tied to a rock; a monster on her bore.
With winged sandals he dropp'd down below,
And killed the monster foul with one stout blow.
Andromeda, the damsel he did wed,
And she remained his wife till she was dead.
He came back to his home and he saw there
His guardian holding feast day, without care.
Then from the goatskin bag he drew the head,
And Polydectes, turned to stone, was dead.

(verses written in a scholarship exam, May 1931)

CREATION

Dawn spouted in the desert and the sea
Drew tight its heart, its tentacles of light.
Blood sweated coldly from the glassy stars.

The hissing air shook as the fingers sprouted
To push a froth upon the breathing water.

The abrupt ice stirred; the shifting rocks
Strained with the bursting starlight in their bellies
To tear the sky, and there a tense aurora
Took the message, spat light around the earth.

The grim mouths of the granite broke with laughter
Lips foaming, a green spate of lunatic life.

Now was the scream, and drowned sea's churning chuckle.
A feverish power that set the sky a-quivering.
The huge and hairless world slid to its birth.

                                        1935

APPENDIX II
from
OXFORD
NOTEBOOKS
[1937–1939]

SUMMER LIGHTNING

Slow through the months the buds have ripened,
And now all root and grain is opened,
Earth nestles in the sun.
Now in the corn of our delight
We lie and watch the ears splash white
Their guileless sense of fun.

Swallows are happy in the eaves,
Upon the trees move smiles like leaves,
Bees buzz in comfort by;
For here is nothing bad or frightening
And friendlily the summer lightning
Drones round the evening sky.

And, magic to your little finger,
You lie by me and would malinger
From every witches' sabbath.
All through us penetrates content,
For who went deeper than we went
Along the forest path?

But, just the same, each night there seems
Some small addition to our dreams,
A small voice in our head;
And soaked in happiness too much
Becomes too sensitive to touch,
Grows in on us instead.

PERFECT GENTLEMAN

I made the gestures of my transience,
I drove the spiny angels from our towns;
Devoted cliffs sprouted with martyrs.
The loud white sea threw up its icy column;
Out of our kiss there limped the bitter lame
Crookedly laughing, talking of other matters.

And so I rise out of the breathing snow,
And ask you what to do and where to go

Among the dazed inevitable
Worlds of stone. Poised, erect,
Always the perfect gentleman, I select
The courtly lily-country of the fable.

And there gallant among the dark-eyed damsels
I'll track the ogre to his dreadful castle
With light bravado laughter.
You'll be my cool idyllic summer bride
In the heavily over-blossomed countryside.
And we'll live in idiot happiness ever after.

SONNET 1

Struck timeless by a magic edge of horror,
Dismembered by those pities in the omen,
He strains through sufferings of dread and woman
To break the dangerous endless inward mirror.
Yet no tradition warns him of tomorrow
To screw a homage out of the inhuman:
This drowning in the ritual cannot summon
A storm of flesh to persecute his sorrow.

A mask of parable could save his honour,
A bitter lameness limping from his kisses,
His brainflesh knuckled to a pure belief.
But better, lashed by his heroic anger,
The sympathy can crawl from the abysses
And grow athletic from its grip on grief.

SONNET 2

The murmur of the mummer, the green slick
Bark of the overbearer, the song of the strumpet,
These whistle in my ear-bones and are gone.
But, like the sweet startling cry of the sick,
Like moon's miracle of mirage, the dead comfort
Outside us, I see your eyes, feel you like a song.

Oh my fresh, dainty with death, lovely on the planet
Plunging through its destined darkness, Oh the doom
Which lies in your sweet commanding eyes!
And out of the welcome bitter kiss, this minute
It raises large as a mountain its murderous dome
Its planned distracting laughter, its pitiful certain cries.

So I greet the necessary hatred, the human terror that rips
Through the insolent rhythms of your body, the blood on your lips.

LILIES

Thank God that lilies fester.
I wish they'd do it faster.
Thank God I'm not a prep-school master.

Glastonbury, 1939

LEAVES AND ROOTS

in memory of L. N. Tolstoy

They bore him to his entombment.
They bore him to his enthronement.

Greyer than a monument's
Granite, a roan tint
Like its bronze, who had been
A locomotive in
Full steam,
                                unkempt
Found the spade more divine
Than any votive lamp.

Thirst parched his lilac …
Like a starstream
                        sweat
Steamed off his back,
An oven full of bread.

His house gaped, empty from
Cellar to roof, the whole;
No one in the drawing room.
In Russia – not a soul.

As in church, without hats,
The artists depart for
Echoing estates,
The oak-tree and the shore.

Vanishing, they vanquish.
Exiled, to exult,
Through the plains and planets
From deceitful gilt.

Above, the forests loose
Their leaves, but out of sight
Still the fivefold roots
Are twisting, tough and tight.

Appendix III
from
WAR NOTEBOOKS
[1940–1945]

Sanguinoso esce della trista selva. (*Purgatorio*, XIV, 64)

FOUR POEMS FOR MARGARET FREELING

1

TRAINING UNIT: WINTER

Intense clouds ache above the estuary,
Angles of bitter reflected light,
A knife of liquid lightning lies on the sea,
Cold acids etch the air and burn the sight.

Ice clamps the soil solider on its rocks,
In seven planes the vista recedes,
With mineral violence reaches away, strikes
Surfaces off the eye: the brain bleeds.

Set for whose plan or pleasure, scenery
Of the heart's year-long desert? But
Of what cold hatred this machinery
Of vision gripped like a vice at the throat?

Granite and water are tons in the heart
And the war is heavy and the winter's unfree
Fists of will. With numbing hurt
Hypnotic gales freeze the mind's sea,

Where the joy is long since lost, swept on that tide
Down years of time and half a world of space ...
Yet waking in the morning, by my side
I almost see her face.

2

AT THE TIME

Two years ago the permanent life of dew
In gardens in early morning, a cool delight
Translucent timeless pleasure
On the island of continuous love.

Sweet isolation in a double tremor
When the outer peace too trembled on an island,

Then lack of trust in
Both chanceries and kisses.

Today I only want to remember the kisses,
Alone with the poisons of winter and Europe
Remember the inextinguishable stars
And the comforting flowers.

The flesh a fountain of transparent flame,
A revelation and an absolute:
O dark hair and soft mouth
Remain with me forever.

But they did not remain. The whole dream seized up solid.
The lines of perspective became parallel.
Everything went away
And the pain stayed.

Yet today I only want to remember the time
When Time existed under all the surfaces
Before truth became memory:
The flower that really shone.

How she came closer, completely nearer
Than anyone, ever, visible in darkness,
In some absolute centre
Of complete illumined joy …

Meanwhile I wish her everything and only keep her
Sweet and soft in her blinding lightning
As the image in my heart
That lets life loose.

For I do not know how I can pierce without her
The absolute iron of this war, our frightful years.
So ask that image now to be
Always, always, by my side.

3

THAT GIRL, THAT WAR

Si Tacet Hane Loquitur (Martial)

Her image easily absorbs the music.
The poems circle it like angry wasps
And in the heart the shaping echo gasps
And stumbles in those labyrinths of magic,

Where it can never find the way
To sing into the centre of the pleasure,
Distorted wholly by the fearful pressure
That brings her image sweetly into play.

He sings. A voice that only speaks
The wars and angers as a clear distortion
Of where the presence and the image part.

She is the pleasure that the poetry seeks,
And in the War, sung through a thrice-torn heart,
She features as the pain and the exhaustion.

4

FIRST LOVE

Years pass, and now his heart leaks like a sieve,
Yet holds how absolutely he would know her
Before he set his aspirations lower,
Demanding more than life is used to give.

Demanding, yet receiving more as well,
Unorchestrated by extraneous thought
– Mutual advantage, marriage or support –
Across that windless valley, one clear bell.

The loss too was most absolute, unripest
– Pardon his early poems that could confound a
Boy's heartbreak with the images of war.
Well, some would say the wider love is sounder;

Yet those rare dreams that shape her still strike deepest.
– The rock breaks and gives up its glittering ore.

THE CORFU CHANNEL

(On a totalitarian frontier)

A heavy noon of silence: water and trees
Shiver, once only, as their warmth lies spread
Under the cold touch of an instant's breeze.
The distant, polished sky seems hanging dead:
A concave mirror focused on my head,

Composing all its weight of rays into
A cold persistent image signifying
– Against the illusory sweetness of the view
And unadapted to poetic lying –
The world's indifference to human dying.

To illuminate the whole with helpless beauty
May seem the poet's only purpose
There firmly close around his heart and body
– Picked out at random from the struggling mass –
The iron muscles of the foul morass.

He knows that death will yet absorb the mystic,
Refine his speech entirely of sense,
That luck moves awkwardly, a pure statistic,
To drop him with a simple change of tense,
Filed among the columns of odd pence.

For now he lives, among the death of millions,
A falling life against the falling time,
The heart laid bare beneath a horror brilliance
Cannot contain the roar of torturing crime
In the calm maxims of a formal rhyme.

Life chokes behind this calm and mine-sown sea.
Yet, past such sensuous green, such black discreteness,
On what free shore, what grand morality

Can verse throw up from tides of lustral sweetness
Small, short, but death-excluding, some completeness?

EVENING IN APULIA

Hours have passed. The sea glow
Warms and deepens into dusk. Swallows
Flicker and dip over the harbour. And the sun,
A ripe bursting slower, low on the Apennines,
Sheds on the paper an apocalyptic light.
But I look back upon lines awkwardly stating
The elements of a problem.

The train at half-past nine
Pulls north into another life. I am not ready
For the waiting questions. For five years, or ten,
Let me read, hunger and enjoy,
Live the poem's life
In the interstices of politics and horror:
The human sanity on its sandbank standing
In the rough rising ride.

And perhaps then
Through all the conscious disciplines,
Proud, sensuous and sceptical
A poem like a passionate sun might rise
From this small life to light an iron age,
Giving its independent ethic out against
Improbable messianic consolations,
The beast-cry and the sirening future.

And if not, still such failure
Is better than all the other loud successes,
And to have left inside the failure
If not the poet, the free human,
If not the colossal poem for which an age labours,
At least a few refreshing moments, the last sip of a flask
Supporting life for someone somewhere
Until the sweet oasis. I will try.

Yes, the chances are against it: and the method may be wrong,
For the art's rules are uncertain. —Perhaps already
By a damp northern hill now some neurotic
Works on, works on into that brilliant future
Burning his lonely anger to a poem.

BASE HOSPITAL: MENTAL CASE

"Yes, I was compelled to watch the spectacle,
The indescribable filth of terror that afternoon.
At intervals since then the memory has exploded
     In fits of vomiting."

Skies have closed in since then, and muscles,
His eyes blaze occasionally into unbearable whiteness,
The torsion on his organs straining till, incompatible,
     The world rejects them.

"Possibly I alone now am apart from history,
From poles of absolute cold can watch with purer
Affection the horrifyingly bestial manoeuvres
     For human advance.

Maturity cannot occur along those lines.
Only from my timeless planet can the cool observer
Examine, unbiased by his fearful privacy,
     Time's other logic.

And flung into forever by a whisper,
With gun for warmth and wound for sex, suddenly
The scalding ocean rolling over me
     Becomes articulate.

And in my blindest moments, posed between two fevers,
Through my own damp hands and through the clouds of blood
In the sky, I alone can see already writhing
     The unbearable future."

DRINKING SONG FOR SOME INTELLECTUALS, 1940

for John Willett

Come boy, and pour the wine's last drops (Hafez)

"Sing holiday! Board the gleaming bus!
It's the anarchist's heyday, the exodus.
From the howling machines in the horrible clouds
Lascivious destruction is singing aloud.

> Chorus:
> Then death to the dying, death to the West
> Distorting the nightmare on England's chest
> Rollicking death and mafficking rage
> To the delicate balance and Golden Age.

Deep in the sun glows his heart of blood,
His moss is soft in the evergreen wood,
His beer is brave and his tastes are grand
And the furrows of flesh get sown with sand.

> Chorus:
> Then death to the crucible, death to the witness
> The methodical one with the illegal illness,
> Death to the mystic social code,
> Death like a charabanc comes down the road.

For death is our friend, though some hate the sight
Of his gnarled left hand and his manicured right
He glows from the roses, his sunshine is lavish
He stiffens the virgins we're wanting to ravish.

> Chorus:
> Then death like kisses or death like knives
> To the symbolically faithful wives,
> Death like a surgical operation
> To the heart's horny root of insistent deception.

The fever is warm, though some wish it wasn't,
The pulse is articulate, the loins are complacent,

For death is casting a fishing line and
Catches his hook in the eye's gristle diamond.
.

> Chorus:
> Then death like a scientist or death like a mystic,
> To the careful collector of the erotic statistic.
> Death to the oracle's insidious flattery,
> A beautiful fountain that spouts from the artery.

Inside our big chests burn our hearts like red coals,
We don't want our England, we don't want our souls,
Death can pile them up with his loot
But leave us the muscle, the rose, and the root.

> Chorus:
> Then death like fire or death like a raid
> To the orgiast's sentimental blockade,
> Death to the costly and cultured whore
> Death like a river or death like a sore.

The energies share us under the stars
The forces balance and nothing stirs
But wait till the strain once starts to tell
And the bird in the air will burst like a shell.

> Chorus:
> Then death like a vision or, perhaps, a formality
> To the nightmen's emergency war-mortality;
> Death like pity or death like sex
> To the brains and the breasts and the buttocks and backs.

Death is virtuoso in saving from danger,
He will take off our faces, our hopes and our anger,
And we'll live in a beautiful country of dreams
Where the agonized soldiers adore the regime.

> Chorus:
> Then death like a tendril or death like a trumpet,
> To blow down the questions and alter the comfort,
> Death in our flesh, delightful and warm,
> The saviour from thought, from the spiritual storm.

Then Ho for the bombers! Let holocaust come!
Let the critical voice be entirely dumb:
And at last we can feel at one with blood
As we splash round like kids in the fiery flood.

> Chorus:
> Death rollicking, bollocking round at the party,
> So sexy and drunk, so witty and hearty,
> Death in our beds, such a very good friend
> For ever and ever, world without end."

Appendix IV

from

THE DEATH OF DIMITROV

LET ME REMEMBER

Let me remember, let me hope for
Rila that hung its snows across
My childhood; the tough peasantry,
Drinking slivova, talking politics,
Sweating the harvest out on the cramped slopes;
The cafés, the Sobranie, the little capital,
Violent like a family, vicious with intrigues
That yet held something of ourselves alone;
The Valley of Roses in its March fantasy;
The great grey Danube; those ancient towns
Perched high among the twists of mountain rivers:
Tirnovo, Sliven; the golden coast
With its island cities left us by the Greeks …
And mountains, mountain air, a mountain people.

What has happened is over. Nothing can be recalled.

I fortify these moments with a hope
I will not have the time, or perhaps the heart,
To make clear even to myself:
Hope for those green ….

Appendix V

MISCELLANEOUS UNPUBLISHED POEMS

NIGHT IN ROMAGNA

O let the honey's odours overflow
Upon the gentle slopes of sleep,
And let the soft snow
Pile dreamily around, drift deep.

And the ice-flame, the pure destructive flower,
Push up through the soft clay
As the sky's blue fires unceasingly shower
A shadowless hypnosis, more searching than day.

Distant, a liquid silver, the eyes stare.
A spreading circle troubles the quiet stream.
Till dawn swells the cloud sails, and the salt air
Cuts into the dream.

HOMAGE

When summer was the season
And soft the Shropshire sun
I loved a girl past reason
At Shagford-under-Clun.

Till autumn strewed the Wrekin
With linden leaves and she
Said "Aren't you a bit weak in
The head – not 'Clun' – it's 'Clee'."

So off I pushed to Hughley
Amidst December's gloom
A good place for yours truly
To find himself a tomb.

À LA MODE

He works all day at electronics
I think it's called – or ultrasonics.
The hours before my lunchtime pass
Then I'm off to my sculpture class

I want to commune, but the jerk
Will sometimes talk about his work
When I have better things to say
Of what I do with bronze and clay.

It's me my duty's to, not him!
But no one wants my stuff. Life's grim
—He's no encouragement. My God,
How could I marry such a clod?

I never realise, you see,
My full potential-ity.
Creative me's ground to a halt.
– It's all my fucking husband's fault!

FRED FEELS

Some girls call Fred insensitive:
    The opposite is true.
Though he can hardly aim to give
    The woman's point of view.

He knows they're hurt: but simple maths
    Will give you heavy odds
Mostly by psychic psychopaths
    – More briefly, rotten sods.

He finds it harder to get right
    – It's so hard to believe –
That modest chaps of his sort might
    Still make a woman grieve.

And while Fred feels they'll have to find
    Their own spokesperson, he's
Tried to bear their woes in mind
    – Though it's a tightish squeeze.

FRED'S FIRST

There's not much a young man can do
    To fill the voids of harm
When his first love has fallen through.
    Some find a certain balm

In verses running through their head
    Or cool concerto's sound.
The Fire Sermon was what Fred
    Wrote down and carried round.

"All things, *bhikkhus,* are on fire."
    And with what fires they burn!
The passions, most of all desire,
    Sear each of them in turn:

The eye, the seen, the contact with,
    Feeling and knowledge of
What's seen, in flamed delusion writhe.
    The wise man writes them off.

But why thoughts so profound and trite
    Could cheer a chap at all
– Back then Fred must have got it right
    But now it's past recall.

FRED IN A DIFFERENT KEY

Chaps whinge about a wife.
    Fred just intones
"Face facts"; "grow up"; "that's life".
    The bloke then moans

"She's sweet as she used to be
    To porters, guests.
She's horrible just to me."
    Fred suggests,

"They all claw power. If you
    Don't like a fight

There's countermeasure in view:
    Move out tonight."

"But ..." "So you've left it too late"
    Their instincts tell plain
When chaps can't contemplate
    Such effort again.

FRED'S FRIEND'S FATE

Fred cites a chap he knew who wed
    One richer than himself
And later ruefully told Fred
    That you'd expect the pelf

To help, in fact (as with an oath
    He often would aver)
While now his cash belonged to her
    Hers still belonged to her.

And when they bust up in due course
    Her lawyers ground him down
Through such incendiary divorce
    As left the chap done brown.

Her family too, like all the rich
    Thought any cash around
Was theirs by right, and grudged terms which
    Still left him the odd pound.

She took flat, plates, sheets, furniture;
    But still she left him stacks
Of what she felt was not for her:
    The sf paperbacks.

He built his savings back (it did
    Take lots of toil and time)
And then he married a sweet kid
    Who hadn't got a dime.

What of those tales of women who
　　Support a ne'er-do-well
Or "struggling writer", ever true
　　Although he gives them hell?

Perhaps such exist. Fred can't judge by
　　Chaps that he doesn't know.
And so he keeps a wary eye
　　On girls who roll in dough.

A FAILURE OF FRED'S

Fred isn't sexually inept
　　As far as we can trace.
But won't discuss technique, except
　　In one instructive case.

One girl, who never said so, yearned
　　To be on top, but that
Excited Fred until he turned
　　Over and she lay flat.

Sensible girls pipe up and say
　　Why not give that a try?"
She just performed her supine task
　　And took him with a sigh.

After some time she made an end;
　　And why, Fred only knew
When told it by a woman friend
　　That she'd confided to.

And maybe if she'd only said …
　　But then, with such a vast
Lack of communication, Fred
　　Sees that it couldn't last.

FRED ON FREEDOM

Possessive? Women get that way
    (Fred notes) when they deny
A chap his roll in the home hay
    And think that he might try

The other stacks, gold in the sun,
    In which the fields are strewn,
Not seeing what they might have done
    To keep him in his own.

And older chaps pre-emptively
    Are dragged across the coals
By wives who hope they'll take their spree
    With crosswords, or play bowls.

And if they manage to impose
    Their orders? Fred will talk
About an oldish chap he knows
    His wife watched like a hawk:

For all her vigilance and care
    The lad contrived to pop
With only half an hour to spare
    Into a knocking shop.

His smile as he remembered this
    Was warm and full of life
And got him, later, quite a kiss
    From his unwitting wife.

Good for morale, yet miniscule
    The leeway that he'd won
Exceptions merely proved her rule
    On how his life was run.

FRED NOTES FAULTS

What if the lady snarl and spit
    Like some ill-natured cat?
Just now and then, Fred must admit,
    They mostly get like that.

A few are always meek and sweet.
    That's dull, some chaps allege.
Fred's qualm is – since one can't compete –
    It keeps one so on edge.

More often, though, if they don't scream
    And never act perverse
A sullen silent head of steam
    Builds up, which Fred finds worse.

Each week of razor-tongue, fiend-frown
    Some half an hour he'll take
– She'd form, did he not then crack down,
    A habit hard to break.

Of course the crackdown mayn't come off
    In that case Fred reserves
His options on the balance of
    Cacophony and curves.

FRED DISAGREES

"In proportion as girls cease
    To be pretty
They tend to become increas–
    ingly shitty.

You'd think they'd compensate for
    Lessening charms
By providing more and more
    Solace and balm."

But Fred says, "Chaps don't really try:
Grown soft and slack,

They ask for all the aggro by
Not fighting back."

FRED OBSERVES

Nature doles its trouble out
    With an uneven hand,
Chaps get from women just about
    As much as they can stand.

Fred thinks girls like the tit-for-tat
    Resilience may bring,
As boxers prefer punching bags that
    Have quite a bit of spring.

FRED'S BALANCED VIEW

Fred came across a chap he knew
    In tears and nearly blind
Drunk, who groaned to him, "Don't you
    Despair of womankind?"

But Fred's experience is, since he
    Keeps expectation low,
He's often now agreeably
    Surprised; and answered, "No".

BALLAD OF THE BROTHERS-IN-LAW

Croak and screech and chatter and drone,
It's a woman's voice on the telephone;
I'd rather live in a cave alone
Than to live with a woman with a telephone.

She calls her sisters night and day
To see if they're hanging their curtains right,
And you should see my telephone bill:
Sixty-nine minutes to Chapel Hill!

She hasn't got time to make me a meal,
She opens a can and says "no big deal";
Then back she goes to the telephone
To cackle and shout and mutter and moan.

I'd love to be on an island fair,
'cause there ain't no telephones way out there,
And no wife's voice saying "if I were you,
I wouldn't paint my kitchen blue".

My head starts to ache and my ears start to pop,
And I'd do anything to make her stop;
A friend of mine's in San Quentin jail
'cause he just had to stop that frightful wail.

IN ANTICIPATION OF HIS SEVENTIETH BIRTHDAY

At the stroke of Big Ben
I'll be three score and ten,
When some get a yen
For things beyond our ken,
But I'm one of those men
Who don't care for Zen,
So pour me a Glen-
livit and then
Set a popsie on my knee
And call me again
At ten score and three.

EPITHALAMION

for Megan Taylor

Which is the greater likelihood,
She's doing good? Or she's looking good?
Here you're just showing your ignorance,
Megan can do them both at once.
Still, there's no real cause for alarm,
Just a slight excess of sweetness and charm.

409

Well, we've avoided Drake's sad fate
Who sailed past, missing the Golden Gate;
We're here now – but golden in this case seems
No more than a verbalisation of gleams,
For true, natural colours pervade the scene,
Trees, grasses, give selections of green,
And, rolling in from Ocean to Bay
Comes a varying blue flecked white with spray.

So, once more avoiding Drake's inadequate chart
We go back to her beauties of mind and heart.
Her work too – the figures she teaches kids,
Her figure like a slim Caryatid's,
With cool enjoyment of colourful thought
The sort of treasure that can't be bought.

Her smile's a harmony, sweet and strong,
It gives life a lyric transcending song.
With the scenery, "Golden" has little to do,
But somehow a "Golden Girl" rings true,
– Especially now that our time appears
To be one to remember as "Golden" years.
Yet still more gold are the years ahead
As both look back on the day they wed.

(You see we've observed the old convention
And given the husband a passing mention.)

INDEX OF TITLES

414

422

INDEX OF FIRST LINES

426

430

431

433

435

A NOTE ABOUT THE AUTHOR

Robert Conquest was born in Malvern, Worcestershire, in 1917, to an American father and his English wife. Educated at Winchester College, the University of Grenoble, and Magdalen College, Oxford, he took his B.A. and (later) M.A. degrees in politics, philosophy, and economics, and his D. Litt. in Soviet history.

In Lisbon on an American passport at the outbreak of the Second World War, he returned to England to serve in the Oxfordshire and Buckinghamshire Light Infantry, and in 1944 was sent behind enemy lines as liaison officer to the Bulgarian forces fighting under Soviet command attached to the Third Ukrainian Front, and later the Allied Control Commission. From 1946 to 1956, he worked in the British Foreign Service – first in Sofia, then in London, and briefly as First Secretary to the U.K. Delegation to the United Nations – after which he varied periods of freelance writing with academic appointments.

Conquest's poems were published in various periodicals from 1938. In 1945 the PEN Brazil Prize (for the best long poem of the war) was awarded to his "For the Death of a Poet" – about an army friend, the poet Drummond Allison, killed in Italy – and in 1951 he received a Festival of Britain verse prize. In the ensuing years he published nine volumes of poetry and one of literary criticism, *The Abomination of Moab*, 1979); a verse translation of Aleksandr Solzhenitsyn's epic, *Prussian Nights* (1977); and two novels, *A World of Difference* (1955), and (with Kingsley Amis) *The Egyptologists* (1965). In 1956 and 1963 Conquest edited the influential *New Lines* anthologies, and in 1962–1963 he was literary editor of the *Spectator*.

He was the author of twenty-one books on Soviet history, political philosophy, and international affairs. His classic, *The Great Terror* – which has since become the conventional term for the purges of the 1930s – has appeared in most European languages, as well as in Japanese, Arabic, Hebrew and Turkish.

In 1959–60 he was Visiting Poet and Lecturer in English at the University of Buffalo, and held research appointments at the London School of Economics, the Columbia University Russian Institute, the Woodrow Wilson International Center for Scholars, the Heritage Foundation, Harvard University's Ukrainian Research Institute, and Stanford University's Hoover Institution.

In 1990 he presented Granada Television's *Red Empire*, a seven-part documentary on the Soviet Union which was broadcast in the UK, the USA, and various other countries, including Australia and Russia.

Conquest was a Fellow of the British Academy, the American Academy of Arts and Sciences, the Royal Society of Literature, and the British Interplanetary Society; he was also a member of the Literary Society, and the Society for the Promotion of Roman Studies (contributing to *Britannia* an article on the Roman Place Names of Scotland).

His honours and awards included Companion of the Order of St. Michael and St. George; the Presidential Medal of Freedom; the Order of the British Empire; the Commander Cross of the Order of Merit of the Republic of Poland; the Ukrainian Order of Yaroslav Mudryi; the Estonian Cross of Terra Mariana Order of Merit; the Jefferson Lectureship; the Dan David Prize; the American Academy of Arts and Letters' Michael Braude Award for Light Verse; the Richard Weaver Award for Scholarly Letters; the Fondazione Liberal Career Award, and the Alexis de Tocqueville Award.

He died in 2015.

A NOTE ABOUT THE EDITOR

Elizabeth Conquest is the author of *The Colour of Doubt* – a study of "Movement" poetry. She received her PhD from the University of Southern California and taught English literature at the University of Texas at El Paso before marrying Robert Conquest in 1979. A member of the International Advisory Board of the Fabergé Arts Foundation from 1993 to 2005, she has lectured on the works of Carl Fabergé in the United States and abroad.

OTHER BOOKS FROM WAYWISER

POETRY

Austin Allen, *Pleasures of the Game*
Al Alvarez, *New & Selected Poems*
Chris Andrews, *Lime Green Chair*
Audrey Bohanan, *Any Keep or Contour*
George Bradley, *A Few of Her Secrets*
Geoffrey Brock, *Voices Bright Flags*
Christopher Cessac, *The Youngest Ocean*
Robert Conquest, *Blokelore & Blokesongs*
Robert Conquest, *Collected Poems*
Robert Conquest, *Penultimata*
Morri Creech, *Blue Rooms*
Morri Creech, *Field Knowledge*
Morri Creech, *The Sleep of Reason*
Peter Dale, *One Another*
Erica Dawson, *Big-Eyed Afraid*
B. H. Fairchild, *The Art of the Lathe*
David Ferry, *On This Side of the River: Selected Poems*
Daniel Groves & Greg Williamson, eds., *Jiggery-Pokery Semicentennial*
Jeffrey Harrison, *The Names of Things: New & Selected Poems*
Joseph Harrison, *Identity Theft*
Joseph Harrison, *Shakespeare's Horse*
Joseph Harrison, *Someone Else's Name*
Joseph Harrison, *Sometimes I Dream that I am Not Walt Whitman*
Joseph Harrison, ed., *The Hecht Prize Anthology, 2005-2009*
Anthony Hecht, *Collected Later Poems*
Anthony Hecht, *The Darkness and the Light*
Jaimee Hills, *How to Avoid Speaking*
Katherine Hollander, *My German Dictionary*
Hilary S. Jacqmin, *Missing Persons*
Carrie Jerrell, *After the Revival*
Stephen Kampa, *Articulate as Rain*
Stephen Kampa, *Bachelor Pad*
Rose Kelleher, *Bundle o' Tinder*
Mark Kraushaar, *The Uncertainty Principle*
Matthew Ladd, *The Book of Emblems*
J. D. McClatchy, *Plundered Hearts: New and Selected Poems*
Dora Malech, *Shore Ordered Ocean*
Jérôme Luc Martin, *The Gardening Fires: Sonnets and Fragments*
Eric McHenry, *Odd Evening*
Eric McHenry, *Potscrubber Lullabies*
Eric McHenry and Nicholas Garland, *Mommy Daddy Evan Sage*
Timothy Murphy, *Very Far North*
Ian Parks, *Shell Island*
V. Penelope Pelizzon, *Whose Flesh is Flame, Whose Bone is Time*
Chris Preddle, *Cattle Console Him*

* Co-published with Picador